# The Last Murder

# The Last Murder

## The Investigation, Prosecution, and Execution of Ted Bundy

George R. Dekle, Sr.

 PRAEGER

AN IMPRINT OF ABC-CLIO, LLC
Santa Barbara, California • Denver, Colorado • Oxford, England

**Library of Congress Cataloging-in-Publication Data**

Dekle, George R., 1948–
    The last murder: the investigation, prosecution, and execution of Ted Bundy / George R. Dekle, Sr.
        p. cm.
    Includes bibliographical references and index.
    ISBN 978-0-313-39743-1 (hard copy : alk. paper) —
ISBN 978-0-313-39744-8 (ebook)   1. Bundy, Ted.   2. Criminals—United States.   3. Trials (Murder)—United States.   I. Title.
    HV6789.D395   2011
    364.152'32—dc22        2011004637

ISBN: 978-0-313-39743-1
EISBN: 978-0-313-39744-8

15   14   13   12   11     1   2   3   4   5

This book is also available on the World Wide Web as an eBook.
Visit www.abc-clio.com for details.

Praeger
An Imprint of ABC-CLIO, LLC

ABC-CLIO, LLC
130 Cremona Drive, P.O. Box 1911
Santa Barbara, California 93116–1911

This book is printed on acid-free paper ∞

Manufactured in the United States of America

**Copyright Acknowledgment**

The author and publisher gratefully acknowledge permission for use of the following material: Portions of "A Juror Reviews the Bundy Case" by Patrick Wolski, February 17, 1980, used by permission of the *Orlando Sentinel*, copyright © 1980.

*To the memory of Kimberly Diane Leach*

# Contents

# Illustrations

# Acknowledgments

When I undertook to write this book, I soon discovered that my memories of significant events were sometimes faulty. Usually, I correctly remembered the gist of the events, but the details were obscured by the passage of three decades. Wanting to give an accurate account, I sought help from many sources. Invaluable help came from my wife, Lane; my mother, Anne Dekle; and my mother-in-law, Laverne Dicks, each of whom had kept extensive scrapbooks of newspaper clippings about the case. They made sure that the clippings were well annotated as to the dates of publication and the paper from which the articles came, but because they had no idea they were providing me with research materials for a book, they did not record page numbers. Despite the lack of page numbers, these clippings proved an invaluable aid to memory and an excellent resource for learning new facts about the case.

Dewitt Cason, the Columbia County clerk of courts, gave me full access to the court file, and Third Circuit state attorney Skip Jarvis allowed me to read his office's copy of the trial transcript. Discussions with Kenneth Boatright and Talmadge Pace, retired highway patrol officers, and with Don Kennedy, administrative director for the Third Circuit Public Defender, supplemented my memory and corrected many errors. Three men involved in the prosecution—Jerry Blair, Len Register, and Larry Simpson—read portions of the manuscript and corrected me on a number of points. Dr. Robert Keppel, of the Henry C. Lee College of Criminal Justice in West Haven, Connecticut, provided me with otherwise unavailable documents and critiqued a portion of the manuscript. Todd Wilson, publisher of the _Lake City Reporter_, allowed me access to the _Reporter_'s archives. My wife, Lane, performed the onerous task of proofreading the manuscript; and my son, John, gave the manuscript a thorough critique.

I am grateful to each person I have named for helping to make this a better, more accurate narrative. Any mistakes or errors that remain are the sole responsibility of the author.

# Prologue

When UPS delivered the package containing Robert K. Ressler's book, *Whoever Fights Monsters: My Twenty Years Tracking Serial Killers for the FBI,* I wasted no time opening it. Before reading any nonfiction book, I like to examine the table of contents and, if there is one, the index. I could tell from the table of contents that it would have been nice to have been able to read this book at the beginning of my career as a prosecutor, rather than three years after it had ended. Turning to the index, I found the names of several killers whom I knew slightly: Ottis Toole, who had tried to confess to a murder in our jurisdiction (the Third Judicial Circuit of Florida) but couldn't wheedle enough information out of us to concoct a convincing story; Henry Lee Lucas, Toole's cohort in crime; Ailene Wuornos, who killed one of her victims in our jurisdiction, and who looked nothing like Charlize Theron; and Danny Rolling, the Gainesville Student Murders killer.

Ressler mentioned one serial killer whom I knew as intimately as any prosecutor can know a murder defendant—Theodore Robert Bundy. Naturally, I wanted to see what Ressler had to say about my old acquaintance. As I flipped back and forth from the index to the pages speaking of Bundy, I agreed with most of Ressler's descriptions. Ressler described Bundy's narcissism and manipulativeness, his claims to have been abused as a child, his attempt to stave off the death penalty by giving 11th-hour confessions to 30 murders, and his final, bizarre interview with Dr. James Dobson. Ressler also wrote about Bundy's suave demeanor, articulate speech, handsome features, and well-concealed depravity. One thing seemed wrong.

Ressler said that Bundy had killed his last victim, Kimberly Diane Leach, by shoving her face into the mud and suffocating her while he sexually assaulted her.[1] I had trouble believing it. Ressler didn't give a source for his information, but it appeared that he got it through a personal interview with Bundy. If so, I concluded that Bundy had lied. Wanting to see if my reasoning was correct, I e-mailed Ressler at Forensic Behavioral Services International, telling him I thought Bundy was the source of his information concerning Kimberly Leach's death and I believed Bundy had lied. I also told him I believed I knew why Bundy lied.

The reply did not come from Ressler, but from an associate, Mark Safarik, who had served for 12 years as a senior profiler in the Behavioral Analysis Unit of the FBI. Safarik wrote:

> I spoke with Bob yesterday about your question. He indicated to me that Bundy told this to him personally during one of his interviews with him.
>
> With her degree of decomposition it seems that it would have been difficult to determine the exact location of the homicide. Perhaps Bundy tried to use this as a way to obfuscate the truth. Telling such a lie doesn't seem to provide any gain for him except perhaps to confuse law enforcement, a small consolation considering his predicament. Although you did not elaborate on it, you seem to have a hypothesis for why you believe that Bundy lied. We would be interested in your take on this.[2]

Ressler and Safarik were completely justified in doubting me. Had the shoe been on the other foot, I would doubt someone who told me Bundy was lying. Bundy had confessed to committing a horrific murder in a brutal, disgusting fashion. Why would he give such awful details unless they were true? I thought I knew. I wrote back giving my reasons for believing Bundy lied, and explaining why I thought he had lied. They responded, adjudging my reasoning to be sound and concurring with my belief about Bundy's motive for lying.

From what I have said, you might ask two questions: (1) What facts and inferences told me Bundy lied? (2) Why did he lie? This book presents "fair play" mystery, providing sufficient information to resolve both questions, but requiring you to piece the clues together for yourself as you read it. The first question should be the easier of the two; and when you solve the first question, you should have enough information to work out the answer to the second. The solution won't be as difficult as the mysteries Agatha Christie gives you in the Hercule Poirot stories, or even the simpler but more elegant mysteries that Rex Stout poses in his Nero Wolfe novels. It will, however, have this advantage over Christie and Stout—it will be a real-life solution to a real-life puzzle.

# Abbreviations

| | |
|---|---|
| ABA | American Bar Association |
| AP | Associated Press |
| APA | American Psychiatric Association |
| DOT | Department of Transportation |
| EMT | Emergency Medical Technician |
| FBI | Federal Bureau of Investigation |
| FDLE | Florida Department of Law Enforcement |
| FHP | Florida Highway Patrol |
| Fla.R.Crim.P. | Florida Rules of Criminal Procedure |
| Fla.Stat. | Florida Statutes |
| FSU | Florida State University |
| UPI | United Press International |
| U.S.C.A. | United States Code Annotated |

# 1

# The Cold and Rainy Day

On February 8, 1978, Lake City, Florida, was Smalltown, Deepsouth, USA. It wasn't Mayberry, but the residents felt safe and secure. Crime occurred on the other side of town. Murders were easily solved. Simply arrest the person holding the smoking gun. On February 9, 1978, everything changed. The sun rose that morning on a cold, rain-soaked town, but the weather couldn't dampen the spirits of Kimberly Diane Leach, a pretty 12-year-old student at Lake City Junior High. Her classmates had just elected her to the Valentine Queen's court, and her mother, Freda Leach, had promised she would take Kim that afternoon to buy a formal gown for the Valentine Ball. Kim's morning began normally. She dressed in a royal blue football jersey and blue jeans. The jersey bore the number 83 and had Kim's name on the back. Because of the cold, Kim wore a white long-sleeve turtleneck sweater under her jersey. She also wore a tan jacket with a fur collar. Freda Leach drove Kim and her brother to the junior high, dropped them off, and waited as they crossed the street under the watchful eye of Clinch Edenfield, the elderly crossing guard. Normally, Mrs. Leach would have gone to her beauty shop just a short distance from the school, but she felt ill and went home to lie down. Her husband, Tom Leach, had already left for his job as a truck driver at North Florida Concrete.[1]

Upon crossing the street, Kim met her friend Elaine Hendricks. They bought some donuts and went into the auditorium to get out of the weather. They talked about the kind of things girls that age discuss— the Valentine Ball, Kim's plans to buy a gown, Kim's recent breakup with her boyfriend. When the bell rang, Kim went to her homeroom in John Bishop's class, located in the Central Elementary Building, a

Aerial Photograph of Lake City Junior High Viewed from the North.
(Courtesy of the State Attorney's Office of the Third Judicial Circuit,
Florida)

horseshoe-shaped building at the rear of the junior high campus. Hendricks went to another homeroom, but she expected to see Kim at least twice more—once during class change before second period, and again in sixth-period Social Studies. Kim had a first-period class in the auditorium and Hendricks had second-period PE.[2] Since it was raining, PE would be held in the auditorium, and Hendricks would see Kim there. When Kim arrived in Bishop's homeroom, she bought a ticket to the Valentine Ball and talked with her friend Lisa Little.[3] The bell rang for first period and Kim left for the auditorium carrying her books cradled in her arms. After she left, Bishop noticed that she had forgotten her purse.

Tandy Bonner, another of Kim's friends, had first-period math with Bishop in the Central Elementary Building. When she arrived in class that morning, Bishop asked her to take a note to Juanita Caldwell, the PE instructor, in the auditorium. The note asked Caldwell to have Kim return to get her pocketbook. Bonner took the note and walked out the south door of the Central Elementary Building. She then walked across the campus toward the door to the auditorium. As she walked across the campus, she noticed a man standing on the other side of the street. He was slim, looked to be 35, and had brown hair. Bonner went into the auditorium, handed the note to Caldwell, and Caldwell sent Kim back to Bishop's class. The girls retraced Bonner's steps back to the Central Elementary Building, and when they arrived in Bishop's class, he pointed out Kim's purse. Kim got it and left the classroom heading back across campus to the auditorium. She never made it. When Kim didn't return, Caldwell assumed that Kim had simply gone on to second-period class.[4]

When Hendricks arrived in the auditorium for second-period PE, she didn't see Kim, but she did see Kim's books. Hendricks took charge of the books and got permission to take them to Kim's second-period class. Kim wasn't there. Hendricks went back to the auditorium and gave the books to Lisa Little to put in Kim's locker. Kim wasn't in sixth-period class, either. Hendricks never saw Kim again.[5]

During sixth period, Bishop got a call from the attendance officer wanting to know if Kim had been in his class. He learned that Kim had disappeared after leaving his classroom. Bishop felt bad about Kim's disappearance, and that evening he conducted his own personal search for Kim in the woods behind the school. Bishop then went back to the school building and telephoned all his homeroom students hoping one of them might know Kim's whereabouts. On the way home, he stopped at the Greyhound Bus station to see if any young girls had taken a bus that day.[6] For years afterward, Kim's disappearance haunted him.

Clinch Edenfield was something of an institution at Lake City Junior High. Although elderly, he was fit as a fiddle and had been the crossing guard in front of the junior high for many years. As was his custom, he began his morning tour of duty at 7:30 A.M. on February 9. It wasn't long before he noticed a white van driving slowly east on Duval Street with the driver staring hard at the school campus. By 8:00 A.M., the van came back westbound, and the driver again stared hard at the school. The driver looked to be 30 to 35 years old and had a medium build. He had no passengers. Around 8:15 A.M., the van came back, going eastbound. Again it drove slowly. Again the driver looked hard at the school.[7]

Lieutenant Andy Anderson, an EMT with the Lake City Fire Department, worked irregular hours and long, hectic shifts. The firehouse

stood on First Street, just north of Duval Street, and only a few blocks
from the junior high. February 8 was Anderson's day off, but the rescue service was busy that day, and Anderson got several callbacks. He
finally telephoned his wife and told her he would not be able to take
their daughter to the movie that night, and that he might as well spend
the night at the firehouse. By the time Anderson's regular shift began
at 8:00 A.M. on the morning of February 9, he felt grimy. He received
permission to go home to shower and change clothes. Getting into his
car, he drove west on Duval Street toward home. When he arrived at
the junior high, he saw something unusual. A white van was stopped
in the middle of the westbound lane blocking traffic. Two other automobiles were stopped behind the van. Anderson then saw a man leading a girl across campus toward the van. The man looked clean-shaven,
approximately five feet seven to five feet ten, with medium brown,
wavy hair. Anderson decided the man looked like Tom Brown, a local
attorney who had offices near the junior high. The girl looked to be 12
to 13 with dark hair parted in the middle. She wore blue pants and a
football jersey bearing the number 63 or 83. The girl had a pocketbook
in one arm, and she didn't look happy. She was pulling back a little bit
but wasn't offering much resistance. The two stopped at the edge of the
street to allow a car to pass, and then the man led her to the passenger
side of the van, put her in, and jogged around the front of the van to
the driver's side. He got in, and the van drove off. Anderson, who had
worked three consecutive shifts without rest, thought he was looking
at a father picking his daughter up from school. Judging from the girl's
tearful expression, he thought she must have gotten into some trouble.
Anderson followed the van down Duval before turning off to his home.
As he followed the van, he saw the driver scolding the girl. Anderson
got home, showered, changed clothes, and went back to work. Within
24 hours he heard of Kim's disappearance. He began to wonder whether
Kim might be the girl he had seen, but he shared his suspicions with no
one until months later.[8]

A little later that morning, Jackie Moore was driving east on US 90
between Live Oak and Lake City. She saw a white van coming west on
US 90. It was driving erratically. As the van approached, she saw that it
contained a white male driver. The driver did not look happy. He had a
scowl on his face and appeared to be looking down into the passenger
side floorboard. The van passed Moore and went on westward. When
she heard of Kim's disappearance, she wondered if the van might be

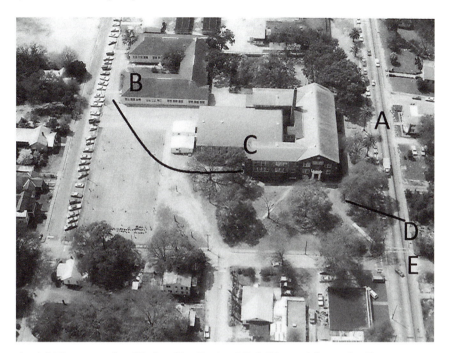

Aerial Photograph of Lake City Junior High Viewed from the East.
(Courtesy of the State Attorney's Office of the Third Judicial Circuit,
Florida)
*Legend:* A: Clinch Edenfield's Post; B: Kim's Homeroom with John
Bishop; C: Kim's PE Class in Auditorium; D: Location of Bundy's
van; E: Location of Andy Anderson; Curved Line B–C: Path taken
by Tandy Bonner as she went to summon Kim back to Homeroom;
Straight Line D: Path taken by Bundy as he led Kim to the Media
Center van.

involved. Then she saw Ted Bundy on television. He looked like the
man driving the van. She came forward and told what she had seen,
and the investigating officer wrote a one-sentence report. The report
got buried in an avalanche of paperwork, and nobody followed up on
it for more than a year.

Around 2:30 P.M., Freda Leach got up and began to dress to go to
school and pick up her children. As she prepared to leave, she got a call
from the school. The caller told her that Kim had not attended all her
classes and asked if she might be skipping school. Kim never skipped

school. Tom and Freda Leach both drove to the school and picked up their son Michael. They met with Assistant Principal Morris Williams, and together the three searched the grounds of the school. Kim could not be found. The Leaches returned home and waited, hoping against hope that Kim would return. By 5:00 P.M. she had not gotten back. They called the police.[9]

# 2

# On the Road with Ted Bundy

During the early morning hours of December 31, 1977, Theodore Robert Bundy, a man with at least 27 murders to his credit, escaped from the Garfield County Jail in Glenwood Springs, Colorado, where he sat awaiting trial for the 1975 murder of Caryn Campbell. Why he escaped is a puzzle. The case against Bundy, weak from the outset, had recently become much weaker. The prosecution hoped to connect Bundy to Campbell's murder with evidence suggesting that he had assaulted and killed three Utah women—Laura Aime and Melissa Smith, of Midvale; and Debbie Kent, of Bountiful—but Judge George H. Lohr had dealt the prosecution case a near fatal one-two punch. First he held evidence of the Kent and Aime murders inadmissible,[1] and then he refused to allow evidence of the Smith murder.[2] Lohr did, however, hold out the possibility of allowing the prosecution to present evidence of Bundy's attempted kidnapping of Carol DaRonch in Salt Lake City. Bundy's motivation to escape possibly came not from his impending murder trial, but the 1- to 15-year sentence that a Utah judge had given him for the attempted kidnapping of DaRonch.

Bundy worked a light fixture out of the ceiling of his jail cell and climbed into the crawl space between the ceiling and the roof. Jail inmates complained to a guard that someone was moving about over their heads in the crawl space, but the guard ignored them. Bundy kicked in a closet ceiling, stole two shirts, and walked out the door of the jail. He wanted to go south, and he decided upon Tallahassee, Florida, where he felt he could blend in with the student population at Florida State University.[3]

Bundy arrived in Tallahassee on January 7, 1978, and met with Larry James Wingfield, the assistant manager of the Oak Apartments, located near the FSU campus. Wingfield told Bundy the rent would be $100.00 per month. Although Bundy could only afford the $80.00 security deposit, Wingfield allowed him to sign a lease for Apartment #12 and move in on a promise to pay the rent as soon as possible.[4] Bundy began to support himself by stealing, but he never got around to paying any rent.

On January 12, Bundy stole a set of van keys from a keyboard at the FSU Media Center. When Media Center personnel couldn't find the keys, they decided to take precautionary measures. For the next several days, whenever they parked the van for the evening, they blocked it in by parking other vans around it.[5]

On January 13, as Randal Ragans waited for his brother to pick him up at his 1002 West St. Augustine Street address, he noticed that his orange van was missing its tag, 13d-11300. Ragans notified the tag office of his loss and received another tag.[6]

During the early morning hours of January 15, Bundy went to the Chi Omega Sorority House on 661 West Jefferson. Picking up a piece of firewood from the stack at the back of the house, he entered through a door that should have been locked. He went to the sleeping quarters and into the bedrooms of several sorority sisters. Using the piece of wood, he bludgeoned four women. When he left, Lisa Levy and Margaret Bowman lay dead or dying, Karyn Chandler and Kathy Kleiner were grievously injured, and he was not through. Nita Neary, another sorority sister, entered the Chi Omega house about the time Bundy left. She saw him leaving but thought he might be Ronnie Eng, a houseboy who worked at the sorority. Bundy went to the apartment of Cheryl Thomas a few blocks away on Dunwoody Street. As his crime was being discovered at the Chi Omega house and police were rushing to the scene, Bundy was beating Cheryl Thomas within an inch of her life. The noise of the beating wakened Thomas's neighbors, Debbie Ciccarelli and Nancy Young. They considered going next door to see what was happening, but the noise frightened them. They decided to call Thomas on the telephone instead. This decision probably saved Thomas's life. When the phone rang, Bundy fled.[7]

On January 21, Bundy stole Francis Labadie's wallet at the Publix Supermarket in Tallahassee. He immediately went on a spending spree with Labadie's credit card. Between January 21 and February 3, Bundy used the card no fewer than 15 times, mostly for food and clothing.[8] On February 3, Kathleen Evans visited the FSU Media Center. During her visit, Bundy got into her pocketbook and removed credit cards belonging to her father, William Evans.[9] Later that evening, at the Silver Dollar Bar, Bundy stole Martha Miller's wallet, which contained a Visa card in the name of Martha's father, Ralph Miller.[10] Bundy also stole the wallet of Thomas Evans, a guest at the Hilton Hotel in Tallahassee.[11] He immediately began using the cards.

During the first week of February, Robert Fulford, the manager of the Oak Apartments, confronted Bundy about his failure to pay rent. Bundy said he could get the money from his mother in Michigan and even borrowed Fulford's telephone to supposedly call his mother to wire the money to him. By February 11, Bundy was gone from the Oak Apartments.[12]

Bundy really wanted that Media Center van, but the Media Center personnel had frustrated his efforts to steal it. If he could just trick them into unblocking the van at night. He went to a hardware store, had copies made of the van keys, and returned the keys to the dashboard of the van. When the Media Center personnel found the keys, they stopped blocking the van in, and on February 5, between the hours of 2:00 P.M. and 6:00 A.M., Bundy stole the van,[13] replacing its tag with Ragans's tag, 13d-11300.[14] Bundy had wheels, he had supplies, and he still had a need to satisfy. With the extensive media coverage of the Chi Omega murders and the massive law enforcement response, Tallahassee was not the place to satisfy that need. He drove east toward Jacksonville, Florida.

On February 7, between 11:00 A.M. and 11:30 A.M., Bundy pulled the Media Center van into the Gulf Oil service station at the intersection of I-10 and US 441 North in Lake City, Florida. He got out, filled the tank, went into the station, and gave William Evans's card to the attendant, Martha Jean Stephens. She asked for his tag number, and he said, "I don't know it. You'll have to get it yourself." Stephens went outside and copied down the tag number, 13d-11300.[15]

By mid-afternoon, Bundy needed more gasoline. He stopped at the Gulf station on the corner of Roosevelt Boulevard and St. Johns Avenue in Jacksonville, where he bought 8.4 gallons of gasoline for $5.12. Milton Johnson waited on him. Johnson couldn't identify Bundy, but he did remember that Bundy wore a coat with a name tag on it. The name tag bore the name of some celebrity. Johnson could not remember the name of the celebrity but could remember that Bundy's name tag did not match the name on the credit card—Thomas Evans.[16]

The FSU Media Center Van. (Courtesy of the State Attorney's Office of the Third Judicial Circuit, Florida)

Bundy headed south on Roosevelt Boulevard to the Holiday Inn at I-295, where he used William Evans's card to purchase a meal. He prowled around Jacksonville until after midnight and finally checked into the Holiday Inn at 555 Stockton Street, again using William Evans's card. Early the next morning he went on the prowl again. He drove north to the Gulf station on the corner and used Labadie's credit card to purchase gasoline and a map.[17]

By noontime, Bundy had found his way to Green Acres Sporting Goods at 8774 Normandy Boulevard. John Farhat, the proprietor, waited on Bundy. He noticed that Bundy was unkempt and unshaven but polite. Bundy looked at several knives before settling on a Buck General, a huge hunting knife configured like the legendary Bowie knife. Bundy paid the $26.00 price for the knife and returned to the van, where he removed the red price tag and let it flutter to the floorboard.[18] The price tag was still there when the authorities processed the van for evidence. Seven miles and 12 minutes away, Leslie Ann Parmenter, a pretty 14-year-old girl, neared the end of her school day at Jeb Stuart Middle

School. Because of the inclement weather her brother Danny, a construction worker, had arranged to pick her up from school. Danny arrived on time to pick Leslie up, but when Leslie saw him she remembered that she needed to go to her locker. She went back into the school to her locker without telling Danny what she was up to. Danny became irritated and drove to their home, a short distance away. When Leslie got back out front, she found Danny gone. She called home and spoke to him. Danny told Leslie to start walking toward the house and he would pick her up on the way.[19]

As Leslie left the school and walked across the neighboring K-Mart parking lot, Bundy pulled the van up to her, stopped, and jumped out in front of her. Leslie stopped. She noticed that he was unkempt and unshaven and wearing a blue coat. On the coat was a printed name tag that said "Richard Burton, Fire Department." Bundy appeared fidgety and dug his hand into his coat pocket as he tried to engage her in conversation. Bundy asked her if she was going to K-Mart and if she went to Jeb Stuart. He told her that someone had pointed her out to him. Leslie became fearful and stood stock still, saying nothing. Before Bundy could say much more, Danny arrived in his pickup truck. Danny did not like what he saw. He pulled his truck as close to the two as possible. Leslie saw him and called out "Danny, come here!"[20]

Bundy turned to leave as Danny got out of the truck and walked over to him. Danny Parmenter was a prototypical mesomorph. He had very little body fat, thick muscles stretched over huge bones, massive calloused hands, and a frown on his face. It was Ted Bundy's turn to be afraid.

As he stood towering over Bundy, he asked, "Can I help you?" Bundy got into the white van without saying a word. "Leslie, get in the truck," Danny said. He then walked up to the driver's side door and asked Bundy again, "Can I help you?" Bundy replied, "No." "What do you want?" Danny asked. Bundy answered, "Nothing. I thought she was somebody else. Somebody pointed her out to me. Never mind." Bundy drove off. The celebrated serial killer posed no threat to anyone who could threaten back. Danny got in the truck and gave chase, but he lost Bundy in traffic. He did manage to get Bundy's tag number—13d-11300.[21] Two years later, while preparing Danny to testify at the trial, I asked him why he followed Bundy. He said was trying to catch Bundy. "And what were you going to do when you caught him?" I wanted to know. I saw a hard look come into Danny's eyes—probably the same look that frightened Bundy. He didn't explain, and I didn't press him.

After his near miss with Danny Parmenter, Bundy headed west. When he got back to Lake City, Bundy did a little exploring. About 21 miles north of Lake City on US 441, there was an agricultural inspection station on the east side of the road. Another station sat on US 41 north of Lake City, and three others were located along the Suwannee River on US 90, Interstate 10, and Interstate 75. Back in 1978, Inspector Austin Gay manned the station on US 441. Bundy pulled his van into the inspection station, asking directions. He said he was from Tallahassee, and he wanted to know where to find a campground. Gay directed him to a campground just to the south of the inspection station. Gay shined his flashlight into the rear of the van and found it completely empty. Bundy became agitated and asked what Gay was doing. Gay told him he was looking for agricultural products. He informed Bundy that all trucks, including vans, had to stop for inspection at agricultural inspection stations. Bundy thanked Gay, got back into the van, made a U-turn, and headed south toward Lake City. As Bundy pulled off, Gay noticed that the van had a tag bearing the number 13 with four additional digits.[22] Inspector Gay was later killed in the line of duty and did not testify at the trial.

Dale Sconyers worked as a desk clerk at the Lake City Holiday Inn located at the intersection of I-75 and US 90. On February 8, he worked the night shift from 3:00 P.M. to 11:00 P.M. Sometime after 7:00 P.M., Bundy came in and registered under the name of Ralph Miller. Sconyers asked for Bundy's license number, but Bundy just mumbled something. Because the desk was busy at that hour, Sconyers told Bundy to phone the number back to the front desk when he got into his room.[23] Bundy ate supper in the Holiday Inn restaurant, paying for the meal with the William Evans card.[24] He next stopped at the Holiday Inn Disco Lounge and ran up a bar tab under Evans's name. When it came time to pay up, he told the bartender, Sharon Colquitt, to charge the tab to Room #443, which he had rented under the name of Ralph Miller. Bundy showed her the key to Room #443, and Colquitt crossed out the name of Evans and wrote Miller on the tab.[25]

On February 9, Bundy got up, left Room #443 at the Holiday Inn, and his paper trail goes cold for the remainder of the day until shortly after 6:30 P.M. Around that time, Rainey Vivier opened her restaurant, the Chez Pierre, an upscale French restaurant in downtown Tallahassee. Shortly after opening, she received a telephone call from Bundy. He told her he was across the street at Clyde's Restaurant drinking and that he wanted a table for four at 8:15 P.M. Vivier noticed two things about Bundy when he arrived—he was inebriated, and he was alone. He behaved himself, though, and ate a quiet meal, paying for it with William Evans's card.[26]

Bundy decided to get rid of the Media Center van and find another ride. On February 10, he stole another tag from the Ragan-Roberts service station on West Tennessee Street.[27] He also stole a green Toyota. Douglas Jacobson, the owner, had left it for repairs at the Firestone Tire Company on West Tennessee.[28] Bundy now had two vehicles and some extra tags. Needing to move his paraphernalia from the van to the Toyota, he parked the two cars together on the corner of Jefferson and Boulevard and waited for nightfall, when he would make the transfer and say goodbye to Tallahassee. He did have one matter he could attend to in the meantime. He asked Frances Messier for a date.

Bundy had gotten close to only one person while in Tallahassee— Messier. She had moved into the Oak Apartments on January 17 and befriended the reclusive Bundy, whom she knew as Chris Hagen. On the evening of February 10, Bundy and Messier walked together from the Oak Apartments to the Chez Pierre, where they talked over a meal of steak and champagne.[29] He paid the tab, again with William Evans's card, and the evening ended—but not for Bundy. He had preparations to make for a trip to the Florida Panhandle.

After leaving Messier, he began his transfers. He removed the 13d-11300 tag from the Media Center van and put it on the floorboard of the Toyota. He placed a new tag on the van—the one he stole from the Ragans-Roberts service station. While making the transfers, he met Keith Daws, a Leon County Deputy Sheriff.[30]

Daws was on patrol at approximately 1:44 A.M., when he saw Bundy fiddling with the door of Jacobson's green Toyota. Daws noticed that it was parked near the Media Center van but didn't make a connection between the two automobiles. He stopped to see what was going on. When he got out of his patrol car, he saw that Bundy had a key to the Toyota. He asked Bundy, "What are you doing?" Bundy replied that he had come to get his book. Daws said, "Well, I must be stupid or something, but you just locked your door and you don't have a book." Bundy said the book was on the other side of the car. Daws looked and saw a book on the passenger side dashboard. Daws asked Bundy where he lived. "College Avenue," Bundy replied.[31]

Daws shined his flashlight into the car and saw a tag on the floorboard. Daws asked, "Well, whose tag is that?" Bundy asked, "What tag?" He then walked around to the back of the Toyota, opened it, and began fumbling around on the floorboard near the tag. Bundy's hand brushed the tag as he repeated "What tag?" Daws said, "That tag you just hit with your hand." Bundy handed the tag to Daws; it bore the number 13d-11300. Daws wanted to know where Bundy got the tag. "I found it on the street." Daws asked, "Don't you think somebody would want it?" Bundy said he had never found a tag before and didn't know what to do. Daws stepped to his patrol car to radio for a check on the tag and registration. As he did so, Bundy ran. Daws couldn't catch Bundy, but he did determine that the green Toyota was stolen. He called the Tallahassee Police Department and turned the stolen items over to them. Daws determined that the 13d-11300 tag belonged to Randal Ragans and decided to see if it was Ragans whom he had just confronted. He drove to Ragans's house, which happened to be just a block from Cheryl Thomas's Dunwoody apartment and woke Ragans up. Ragans told Daws he had lost the tag a few days earlier and had gotten a replacement from the tag office.[32]

The Tallahassee Police Department confiscated the green Toyota and eventually returned it to Jacobson, but they did not disturb the white van. After the officers cleared the scene, Bundy returned and got the van again. That evening he ate a final meal at Chez Pierre.[33] The next day he would make a diligent search for another ride, but his luck would not be good.

On the morning of February 12, Bundy walked across campus toward Doak Campbell Stadium looking for a car. He found an old Mazda at 312 Stadium Drive. The owner, Myrline Allen Reeves, had left her keys in the ashtray. Bundy took it, but the front end shimmied at speeds more than 45 miles per hour. He drove north on Stadium Drive to High Road, and from High Road to Old Bainbridge Highway, where he parked the Mazda at an apartment complex and walked across the street to a church parking lot.[34] In the church parking lot, Bundy found another set of keys in another ashtray and stole the 1969 Volkswagen belonging to Theresa Connie Shriver.[35] Shriver's car wasn't satisfactory, either. He began looking for another ride.

Bundy's search proved fruitless until around 10:15 P.M., when he parked Shriver's Volkswagen at 414 East Carolina Street and began prowling the area looking for another car. A little more than 350 yards away, at 515 East Georgia Street, Ricky Garzaniti was parking his orange Volkswagen at his babysitter's house. When Garzaniti and his wife went inside to get their child, he left the keys in the ignition. The Garzanitis stayed inside the babysitter's approximately 45 minutes and came out to find their car gone. Bundy had encountered so much trouble finding a good car that by the time he stole Garzaniti's car, he neglected to change the tag.[36] This would prove to be a mistake.

Bundy now got rid of the van. First, he took a soft drink, probably Coca Cola, and placed it on a rag. With the rag, he thoroughly wiped down the van before abandoning it. He also wiped down Apartment #12 at the Oak from ceiling to floor. He left no fingerprints in either location. During the early morning hours of February 13, Bundy parked the Media Center van in front of Beatrice Hampton's house at 806 West Georgia Street.[37] By 11:00 A.M. that day, he was eating a meal at the Holiday Inn in Crestview, Florida, 129 miles to the west of Tallahassee.[38] Bundy had made it out of town just ahead of the posse. That very morning Chris Cochran, an employee of the FSU Media Center, spotted the van.[39] Cochran notified the police, who immediately believed they had made a significant find. They handled the van with kid gloves trying to make sure they could wring every last molecule of evidence from it.[40]

During the early morning hours of February 15, Patrolman David Lee of the Pensacola Police Department was on routine patrol on Cervantes Street. As he neared V Street, he saw Garzaniti's Volkswagen pulling out from behind Oscar Warner's Restaurant. Lee knew all the employees at Oscar Warner's, and this car did not look like any of their cars. There was no through street behind Oscar Warner's, and Lee could not imagine any legitimate reason for a car to be behind the restaurant at that hour. He decided to investigate. As he followed the Volkswagen north on W Street, he called in Garzaniti's tag number to have it checked with the National Crime Information Center. Bundy headed out of the city limits, but Lee, who was also sworn as an Escambia County Deputy, stayed with him. Lee put his blue light on, but the Volkswagen continued north on W Street. About six blocks outside the city limits, Lee heard back from his dispatcher—the Volkswagen was stolen. Lee finally got the car stopped just north of Croft Street.[41]

Lee pulled his car up behind the Volkswagen and approached the driver's side door. He found Bundy sitting behind the wheel. Bundy asked, "What's wrong, officer?" Lee drew his service revolver, telling Bundy to get out of the car and put his hands where they could be seen. Lee had to repeat his instruction several times before Bundy finally complied.[42]

Lee directed Bundy to the front of the car where Lee told him to lie face down on the pavement in the glare of the headlights. Because Lee noticed sleeping bags, suitcases, and other paraphernalia in the car, he thought someone else might still be in the front passenger seat. Lee called out to anyone who might be in the car but got no response. He asked Bundy if there was anyone else in the car but got no answer.[43]

Lee attempted to handcuff Bundy but divided his attention between Bundy and the passenger compartment of the car. As he got the cuff on Bundy's left wrist, Bundy rolled over, kicking Lee's feet out from under him. As Lee hit the ground, Bundy got up and moved toward Lee as if to attack him. Lee fired his revolver. At the report of the revolver, Bundy changed directions and ran south on W Street. Lee gave chase, yelling for Bundy to halt. Bundy turned left and ran east down a side street into a residential area.

Lee followed about a half block behind, calling on Bundy to stop. Bundy spun around and raised his hand. Lee could see something flash in Bundy's hand.[44] Thinking it was a weapon, Lee fired a second shot. Bundy went down. Although Lee thought he had hit Bundy, he approached the prone man carefully. Finding Bundy face down, he rolled Bundy over to see how badly Bundy was hurt. When he did this, Bundy attacked, trying to take Lee's revolver. With Bundy in one hand and a pistol in the other, Lee could either shoot Bundy or pistol-whip him. Lee chose to pistol-whip him. Bundy began to call for help, and the noise attracted the attention of some of the residents of the neighborhood. A few came to watch, but no one offered Lee any assistance. Someone berated him for police brutality. Lee finally beat Bundy into submission. He finished handcuffing the man and marched him back to the patrol car. By this time reinforcements had arrived in the persons of three other patrolmen. Bundy refused to get into the patrol cruiser, but with the other patrolmen's assistance, Lee forced him into the car.[45]

On the way to the jail, Bundy told Lee, "I wish you had killed me." Lee wasn't in the mood for light conversation. Bundy asked Lee, "Would you kill me if I tried to run?" Lee continued to drive. Bundy made one more comment before he fell silent: "You'll make sergeant for this arrest." When he was booked into the jail, Bundy gave the name of Kenneth Misner.[46] His criminal Odyssey had ended; his legal one was just beginning.

# 3

# A Tale of Two Cities,
# Part I: Tallahassee

The Chi Omega murders fell under the jurisdiction of three agencies—the Leon County Sheriff's Office, the Tallahassee Police Department, and the FSU Police Department. All three agencies responded to the scene. Don Patchen of the Tallahassee Police Department was one of the first investigators to arrive. He secured the scene as best he could and began his investigation. It was not long, however, before other agencies arrived and things became muddled. Sheriff Ken Katsaris, a newly elected former college professor, assumed command of the investigation. In the days immediately following the murders, two law enforcement spokespersons emerged—Katsaris and Sergeant Jim Sewell of the FSU Police Department. The first news broke on radio and television, with WCTV in Tallahassee running two stories on February 15.[1] The next morning it hit the papers. The United Press International story began "Two pretty Florida State University coeds were strangled in their sorority house beds . . ." and went on to quote Katsaris as saying that the assailant was "depraved." Katsaris told the press that the assailant entered the sorority house through an unlocked door and went to the second-floor living quarters looking for rooms occupied by only one girl. Katsaris said the girls didn't know what hit them; the assailant rendered them unconscious by bludgeoning their heads and then strangled them. Katsaris named strangulation as the cause of death, but he said the blows to the head would have been sufficient to kill. He said that one, and possibly more, of the girls had been raped. Then Katsaris said, "his lust perhaps not satisfied," the assailant went to Dunwoody, where he broke into Cheryl Thomas's apartment and bludgeoned her.[2] In high-profile investigations, there are many reasons why intimate details of the crime should be withheld as much as possible. First, media attention will be intense enough without disclosure of lurid details. Second, the revelation of lurid, intimate details will render it difficult to select an untainted jury. Third, mentally unbalanced people will seek attention by giving false confessions; and the more details there are in the public domain, the more difficult it becomes to invalidate the false confessions. Fourth, initial impressions can prove wrong, and early dissemination of inaccurate details can come back to haunt you.

On January 16, Katsaris gave an interview to Pete Spivey of the *Orlando Sentinel.* He told Spivey that he had no suspects and did not have enough information to make a composite drawing of the assailant.[3] Don Patchen, working with Officer Linda Presnell of the FSU Police Department, had been able to interview witnesses on the scene and get a composite drawn of the intruder. Presnell's artistic ability was vindicated when Bundy was finally arrested. The composite bore a striking resemblance to Bundy and became a key piece of evidence in the Chi Omega trial.[4]

Katsaris announced the opening of a special command post to coordinate the investigation. He also said he had called in the FBI and Florida Department of Law Enforcement (FDLE) to help analyze evidence and compile a psychological profile of the murderer. That same day, Sewell told Spivey that "everything is going absolutely yah yah around here" with people trying to get information on the killing and asking for advice on how to improve their personal safety.[5]

The next day Katsaris told Spivey that they had painfully few clues but were devoting all the manpower and technological advances possible to solving the case. Katsaris said they had received more than 300 telephone tips from concerned citizens, and they were running each of them down as quickly as possible. He discussed the possibility of offering a reward for information leading to the capture of the killer. He also named Nita Neary as an eyewitness who saw the murderer leaving the sorority. Katsaris went on to say that he had put a 24-hour guard on her even though she wouldn't be able to identify the intruder if she saw him again.[6] Despite Katsaris's prediction, when the case came to trial in Miami, Neary took the witness stand and positively identified Bundy as the man she saw leaving the Chi Omega house.

Sewell told Spivey that the FSU Police Department had received 58 calls for escorts on the previous night, far in excess of the usual five requests per night. Sewell also reported that the FSU Police Department was conducting a security check of all sororities. Although he would not detail any of their findings, he did admit that they had "some room for suggestions" for improving campus security.[7]

On January 18, the Florida Highway Patrol (FHP) sent 60 troopers and recruits to help search a 12-block area around the FSU Campus. They searched trash bins, garbage cans, gutters, sewers, underbrush, and backyards between the Chi Omega house and Thomas's apartment. A reporter inquired as to what they were looking for. "Anything with blood on it," replied one anonymous trooper. At the conclusion of the search, Captain Jack Poitinger of the Leon County Sheriff's Office said Katsaris had ordered the search to make sure nothing had been missed on the night of the crime, but they had found nothing. The reward fund climbed to $15,000.00, and Katsaris was campaigning to have it increased. He guaranteed police protection and anonymity to anyone coming forward with clues.[8]

The investigation briefly focused on Arthur Burns, an escapee from the state mental hospital at Chattahoochee, but by January 19, Sewell told the press that Burns was eliminated as a suspect.[9] Katsaris, who by this time had a crew of 20 detectives working full-time on the case, said he still had no suspect and no accurate description of the killer. On January 21, the United Press International ran a story in which Katsaris announced plans to hypnotize Nita Neary and the two surviving Chi Omega victims to see if their minds might be blocking out a description of the attacker. Katsaris also speculated that there might possibly be a link between the Chi Omega murders and an attack that had been made seven months previously on a Chi Omega pledge. The pledge had been beaten so severely that she had no memory of the incident, and Katsaris held out the possibility of hypnotizing her also. He said there were several possible links between the attack on the pledge and the Chi Omega murders. Katsaris also revealed that 18 suspects had been questioned and all but a few of them had been eliminated. He said the killer appeared to be familiar with the FSU community, but it was unknown whether he was a student. "It's still a jigsaw puzzle. We feel we have most of the pieces, but either for lack of a clue, they do not fit together, or we are missing that one big piece that would make it all come out."[10]

On January 25, the *Orlando Sentinel* ran an article detailing an interview with Sergeant Wayne Smith of the Leon County Sheriff's Office. Smith said they were investigating between 40 and 50 possible suspects. Smith said that Neary, Kathy Kleiner, Karen Chandler, and the pledge had been hypnotized by a professional hypnotist named Julian Arroyo, but the sessions failed to produce any evidence. Cheryl Thomas was not hypnotized because she was still in the hospital, recovering from her injuries. Katsaris said that Thomas probably wouldn't be hypnotized,[11] but Arroyo hypnotized Thomas on February 2, with no success. On January 27, the United Press International ran an interview with Alexander Bassin, a professor of criminology. Bassin said his analysis was highly speculative, but he thought that the killer was a shy, introverted man who felt rejected by everyone around him and fed emotionally off the intense news coverage. Bassin said that the killer was likely to kill again.[12] On February 11, authorities released a profile done by Howard Teten, from the FBI's famed Behavioral Sciences Unit. According to Teten, the killer was a semiskilled laborer with a mental problem who lived alone and frequented bars.[13]

In mid-February, a story ran under the headline "Impostor quizzed in coed killings." Describing the impostor as an articulate, young mystery man, the paper said he had masqueraded as an FSU track star by the name of Kenneth Misner.[14] When the news first broke that Misner had been arrested in Pensacola and was suspected in the Chi Omega killings, the real Kenneth Misner immediately notified the police and the press that he was not the man in Pensacola. Misner said he had lost his ID card a couple of months previously, and that just recently someone identifying himself as an FSU employee had called him asking for personal information. The fake employee had claimed that the university had lost his information and needed to complete its records. Misner became a victim of phishing and identity theft long before the Internet.

Because "Misner" looked good as a possible suspect in the Chi Omega murders, Don Patchen of the police department and Steve Bodiford of the sheriff's office drove to Pensacola to interview him. Arriving at 4:30 P.M. on February 15, they learned about the real Kenneth Misner's call, and the bogus Misner started looking even better as a suspect. That first evening they did a little verbal sparring with "Misner" but accomplished little. With the help of Norman Chapman of the Pensacola Police Department, they resumed the interrogation on the following day at 7:00 A.M. The suspect was now known as John Doe. Doe gave a tape-recorded statement admitting to stealing the credit cards, stealing Garzaniti's Volkswagen, stealing Jacobson's Toyota, and running from Deputy Daws. He just wouldn't admit his name. Finally, around 7:30 P.M. on February 16, he agreed to reveal his name if they would allow him to telephone a lawyer in Georgia named Millard Farmer. They provided Doe with a phone; he made the call, and then told them, "I'm Ted Bundy."[15] Norman Chapman asked, "How do you spell that?" Bundy was taken aback. He had been so famous in the Far West he assumed that everyone knew his name.

While Patchen, Bodiford, and Chapman were busily trying to figure out Bundy's true identity, there was a minor media flurry over whether Katsaris had identified the mystery man as a suspect in the Chi Omega case. The *Pensacola News* quoted Katsaris as saying that he was a "serious suspect," but Katsaris denied saying that he was any more serious a suspect than any of the others. John Hanchette, Tallahassee bureau chief for the Gannett News Service, stood by the quote, saying that Katsaris had said it in a telephone interview.[16] By February 17, the headlines were saying "Mystery man tagged as No. 1 mass killer." When the mystery man was finally identified as Ted Bundy, the press quoted Jack Egnor, a Utah FBI agent, as saying that Bundy was suspected in three dozen killings in California, the Pacific Northwest, Utah, and Colorado.[17] With this turn of events, the authorities became less reticent to call him a suspect. Wayne Smith, a spokesperson for Katsaris, said "certainly he is a serious suspect" because the Chi Omega murders were similar to the western cases.[18] In assessing the evidence for the *Orlando Sentinel*, Katsaris said, "It looks real good, although we haven't any physical evidence tying him to [the Chi Omega case]. He was in Tallahassee and there is a similar modus operandi to the other murders. The chance of having two people with the same m.o. in the same community at the same time is pretty remote."[19]

Bundy's neighbors at the Oak Apartments could hardly believe that he was the Chi Omega murderer. Tina Louise Hopkins, who lived two doors down from Bundy, said, "He looked like a student. He blended in. He wasn't ugly and gross and slimy."[20] Others said that "Chris" was a "really nice guy," although he was somewhat aloof. Hopkins did remember, however, that "When police said the sorority girls were probably beaten with an oak club, it seemed funny to us and we joked about it coming from here. Bundy, or Chris as we knew him, seemed kind of bitter and didn't want to talk about it."[21]

When Bundy made his first court appearance in Pensacola before Judge Jack Greenhut, the papers said he wore a blue blazer, a partially open blue shirt, rumpled blue bell-bottom jeans, and the beginnings of a Fu Manchu moustache.[22] That blue blazer would assume great significance in the coming months.

Bundy's notoriety in the Far West did not extend to the Southeast, but by February 18, the papers were beginning to introduce their readers to him. They reported that Bundy was a former Boy Scout who had worked as a bellboy, busboy, cook's helper, dishwasher, janitor, office worker, social worker, salesman, and security guard. He was into physical fitness and could fake a perfect British accent. He had a bachelor's degree in psychology and served on the staff of a crisis clinic in Seattle. Larry Anderson, a Mormon missionary who baptized Bundy in 1975, said, "I wouldn't hesitate to line him up with my sister." Bundy's first appearance in the news came in 1972 in connection with his work as a volunteer for Republican Dan Evans's gubernatorial campaign committee. He attended political events put on by the opposition, posing as a political science student, and got accused of spying for Evans. After that he moved to Salt Lake City and entered law school. He had his first brush with the law in 1975 during a routine traffic stop. When the officer discovered that Bundy had handcuffs, a pantyhose mask, and an ice pick in his car, he carried the law student to jail. It wasn't long before police in five states had zeroed in on Bundy as a suspect in a string of unsolved murders.[23]

Bundy's arrest caused the Chi Omega murders to draw national attention.[24] Media coverage, which had been intense, became overwhelming as reporters from the four corners of the country flocked to Tallahassee. Katsaris announced that Bundy was being transferred from Pensacola to Tallahassee. "I say it reluctantly, because we're a little bit security conscious at this point." Katsaris said that Bundy would be charged with a string of burglaries, thefts, and fraudulent uses of credit cards, but not murder. He expressed optimism about the possibility of eventually charging Bundy with the murders. Katsaris said Bundy had been extensively interviewed but that they would probably wait until they got back lab results from the FDLE Crime Lab before attempting further questioning. He confirmed reports that bite marks were found on one of the FSU victims, and that they had contacted a Miami doctor about analyzing the marks. "I don't think we're going to be able to do anything with that, though," he opined. "That would be a very, very weak point of evidence because the marks were not real distinct."[25] Testimony concerning the bite marks would later prove a cornerstone of the State's case against Bundy for the Chi Omega murders.

Sometimes, when the media coverage is intense and the reporters don't think they're getting enough action from the story itself, they begin to interview each other. On February 19, the *Orlando Sentinel* ran an interview with Richard Larsen, a reporter from Seattle, Washington. Larsen defended Bundy against the accusation of political espionage, "It wasn't dirty tricks. They had him doing what any smart campaign has someone doing: scout the enemy, find out what they're saying and be able to lay it to them later." Larsen talked about Bundy's legal problems out west, describing Bundy as "very attorney-like." Larsen said that he and Bundy had half-seriously talked about writing Bundy's biography together.[26] Larsen later went on to write such a book without Bundy's help.[27]

On February 19 and 20, Katsaris was back in the news describing the three-day interrogation of Bundy and discussing his strategy for further questioning. "He's smart, very smart. Right now we're probably playing by his rules and that's what I need to reassess with the investigators." Katsaris added that Bundy knew a lot about the law and justice, and that "So far, he is just rambling—talking about everything but the FSU murders." Katsaris said, "[Bundy]'s going to be hard to get anything from," but he did point out that Bundy "lived four blocks from the murder scene and has a modus operandi similar to the Chi Omega killer." Katsaris said that he was going to let Bundy sit in his cell and think for a while, but he predicted that when the interrogation resumed, it would be under new rules. "We've played his game until now. He's decided when he'll talk." Katsaris said, "We'll establish when we'll talk to him and under what conditions."[28] The American Bar Association's Criminal Justice Standards discourage the making of news releases concerning the substance of statements made by suspects, or even reporting whether they have made a statement.[29] The wisdom of this standard was demonstrated the following year when the Chi Omega trial judge ruled all of Bundy's recorded statements inadmissible.

On February 17, the investigation of Bundy took a new turn when Investigator Tom Trammel of the Leon County State Attorney's Office went to Lake City tracking down Bundy's use of the stolen credit cards. FHP trooper Harold E. Scott assisted Trammel, and they soon discovered that Bundy had spent the night in Lake City the evening before Kim's disappearance.[30] With this discovery, the story of the Chi Omega investigation became inextricably intertwined with the story of Kim Leach.

# 4

# A Tale of Two Cities,
# Part II: Lake City

The day after Kim's disappearance, the first ripples of the publicity tsunami rolled into Lake City with a headline reading "Girl reported missing" above the *Lake City Reporter*'s daily police blotter.[1] The *Reporter* told the story of Kim's disappearance in 13 lines. February 10 was also the day that Ted Bundy made the pantheon of public enemies—the FBI added his name to its 10 most wanted list. On February 12, Sheriff Glenn Bailey told the local paper, "We literally have had dozens of calls [on the disappearance], but nothing concrete." Bailey said she may have run away, but "It could be more. It is a little strange that if she ran away she would not have called her friends or parents."[2]

Nobody outside Lake City cared about Kim's disappearance, but the citizens of Lake City took it very seriously. The *Lake City Reporter* ran a story on February 14 detailing efforts to find her. Police Chief Paul Philpot told the paper that authorities were "working around the clock following leads," but had found little to go on. Philpot said that the police had not discounted the possibility that she ran away. "We have to look at it from all directions," he said. Philpot said that the police had searched all over the junior high campus and on top of the school buildings, the woods to the south and west of the school, and the lake behind the campus. "We are doing everything in the world possible." He went on to tell the paper that Kim was an A student who was loved by everyone who knew her.[3]

By February 15, Bailey announced a $500 reward for information on Kim. Philpot said that they were still diligently searching for Kim.

"By no means have we quit. We'll just continue to spread out our search."[4] Students began reporting that they had seen Kim get into one car or another, and the police ran down each description. Philpot said of the leads that "all of them have been futile." Philpot said he had assigned a six-man team to the investigation, and they had combed the vicinity of the school for a third time that week.[5]

By February 17, a 30-man team was still searching, but Bailey told the *Reporter,* "I think we have done whatever we could. After the party concludes its search Friday, we'll have to wait for a lead. Honestly, we don't know where to look." Upon publication of Bailey's statement, numerous people called the sheriff's office and police department offering to aid in the search. A private citizen named Charles Clark called the *Reporter* and all local radio stations urging them to put pressure on Bailey to continue the search. Clark went on to say, "With as many Columbia Countians that own trucks, jeeps, and CB radios, we could have the county covered thoroughly in two days. I know Columbia County will band together to work to find this girl if only they are given the opportunity." When asked why he didn't organize a search party of civilians, Bailey replied, "We hope everybody keeps their eyes open, but I don't think a search will be beneficial at this time."[6]

On February 18, something happened that never made the papers, but it changed the course of the investigation and made an enormous contribution to the final solution of the case. Tom Leach went to the Florida Highway Patrol. He met with Captain Jimmy Love, the local troop commander, and asked that the patrol become involved in the search for Kim. The highway patrol is tasked with enforcing traffic laws, not searching for missing persons. It had no jurisdiction in the matter at all unless, as had happened earlier in the Chi Omega case, a local law enforcement agency asked it to assist. Love called the director of the patrol, Colonel Eldridge Beach. Despite his lack of formal authority to do so, Beach ordered Love commence a search for Kim. Had he not done so, we might still be looking for her.

The *Lake City Reporter* dutifully followed the Bundy story, but by February 20, had made no link between Bundy and Kim. That would change the next day when the Associated Press reported a statement by Philpot that Bundy had stayed in a Lake City motel the night before Kim disappeared. Investigator Larry Daugherty of the Lake City Police Department refused to say whether Bundy had been identified by anyone at the motel and refused even to name the motel, giving as his reason, "An investigation is under way and I would hate to jeopardize the outcome."[7] February 21 was a busy day for news about Bundy. The *Jacksonville Journal* broke the story of the attempted abduction of Leslie Parmenter. The *Journal* flanked the article with two pictures—on the right was a picture of a disheveled Bundy, on the left was a composite made by the Parmenters after hypnosis.[8] The resemblance was striking.

That same day, the *Lake City Reporter* ran an interview with Philpot. He said that a credit card found in Bundy's possession had been used to check into a Lake City motel and buy a meal. The man checked out of the motel the morning that Kim went missing. When asked if he had plans to send an interview team to Tallahassee to speak to Bundy, Philpot said, "Yes sir, we will. We feel that we have sufficient evidence to talk to him about it." Bailey called Bundy "our first lead," but cautioned, "How far it will go we don't know." Both Bailey and Philpot said there were really no strong suspects because so far they didn't know if a crime had been committed. At this point, they said, they had not discounted any theory, including the theory that she had simply run away.[9]

Love told the *Reporter* that FHP trooper Harold Scott discovered the evidence of Bundy's presence in Lake City while assisting local law enforcement in canvassing motels in the area. He also advised that special units of the FHP were continuing to assist in the search for Kim. An anonymous caller told the Tallahassee television station, WCTV, that he had been drinking with a man resembling Bundy in Lake City the night before the disappearance. Daugherty told the *Lake City Reporter* that they had reason to believe the phone call was not a prank but refused to give details. Daugherty also told the *Reporter* that a "massive air and land search" by the FHP was under way, and that they were being assisted by the Florida Division of Forestry. Although all efforts had been "fruitless" up to this time, Daugherty said, "We have done everything humanly possible and will continue to do so." This included enlisting the aid of citizens to help with search parties on foot, motorcycles, ATVs, and on horseback, and searching every one of the 1,250 square miles of Columbia County. Daugherty told the *Orlando Sentinel*, "We don't have anything definitely linking [Bundy] to the little girl's disappearance. The only thing we know is he was in town the night before she vanished. We cannot place him anywhere near the school." Daugherty also said that they were turning everything over to the Leon County Sheriff's Office for its investigation. "What we have is too minor in view of the other charges against him."[10]

Katsaris told the media that as far as he knew, there was no connection between Bundy and Kim's disappearance, except that one of the credit cards Bundy had stolen was used in Lake City. "I cannot say that Bundy was the only one who used the credit card in Lake City, but it appears that he is." Katsaris also said that although his agency was not investigating the Leach disappearance, he would "work it out" if Columbia County authorities wanted to interrogate Bundy.[11] Katsaris's spokesman, Wayne Smith, told the press that Katsaris had met with members of the FDLE to talk about the lab tests being run on the evidence seized from Bundy. Smith said that the meeting went well, but that they still hadn't found that single piece of evidence that would allow them to charge Bundy.[12]

On February 22, Jim Leusner of the *Florida Times Union* wrote an in-depth article on Bundy. Leusner said Bundy had a law enforcement background. He quoted King County Detective Robert Keppel as saying, "It was sort of a part-time thing. He worked for the Seattle Crime Commission and the King County Law and Justice Commission. But as far as what type of work he did, I'd rather not say." Leusner said Bundy's work involved researching jurisdictional problems between law enforcement agencies and working at a crisis center. He also revealed that Bundy worked for a time as a night watchman in a girl's dormitory.[13]

Leusner also interviewed Salt Lake City detective Jerry Thompson, who had investigated the kidnapping of Carol DaRonch. Leusner quoted Thompson as saying, "I have worked on him for three years and he seems to attack the same type of girls. They are always attractive with long hair parted in the middle and between the ages of 17 and 23. The killer strangles and beats all of his victims. Then he just throws them in the woods along the road. He doesn't hide them at all. In Bundy's trial in Salt Lake City, he never admitted anything and always said he was being railroaded. But he then apologized to me because he was making me work so hard. He was a very intriguing individual."[14]

That same day the Associated Press ran a story connecting Bundy to the Media Center van and connecting both of them to Lake City. The article cited unnamed "authorities" who said Bundy was driving a white van that may have been stolen in Tallahassee. The article went on to say that Larry Daugherty refused to confirm reports that the van had been spotted near the junior high on the day of Kim's abduction. According to the story, Bundy (or someone else) attempted to kidnap

Leslie Parmenter in Jacksonville on February 8 and later checked into a Lake City motel just a mile and a half from the junior high. It also quoted Investigator Johnny Walker of the sheriff's office as saying, "We have motel workers who think they saw Bundy drive away in a white van."[15] No motel workers ever testified to seeing any such thing at Bundy's trial.

The *Lake City Reporter* ran the headline "Bundy link here result of 'one plus one'—FHP." In the article it quoted Love as saying, "We knew he had reportedly been involved in an assault attempt in Jacksonville. We also knew he had been living in Tallahassee. It was a natural addition of the two which led us to make a check of the area motels when we decided to assist in our own investigation of the Kimberly Leach matter." Love went on to identify the hotel as the Holiday Inn at the intersection of Interstate 75 and US 90. He said, "We later turned our information over to the city police and they subsequently reaffirmed what we had discovered." Love said he was "positive the man staying at the Holiday Inn was Bundy." Love also said that the FHP would continue its search for Kim to the west of Lake City. "We are going to increase our manpower and our air surveillance. We are doing everything we can to find clues." He said that any clues they uncovered would be turned over to the Lake City Police Department. Love described the search as "systematically looking over areas" beginning in Lake City and moving outward from there in a westward direction toward Tallahassee. The *Reporter* also said that Philpot was still talking about interviewing Bundy. When asked about a timetable for the interview, Philpot said, "We will go when we get our chance." Philpot went on to say that only two or three people in Lake City had reported seeing a man fitting Bundy's description. He identified two of those witnesses as "a couple of girls" at the Holiday Inn. Philpot went on to say that all attempts to identify the man who had called WCTV had failed. "We don't know where he called from, and he hasn't been heard from since." Philpot described the investigative effort by saying, "We are running around going in all directions."[16]

The next day, the headlines read "Local search effort is intensified— FHP mounts wide search for missing girl." The article said that the search team numbered approximately 150 mounted and foot searchers. The team consisted of FHP troopers, Division of Forestry personnel, Public Service Commission officers, and private citizens.[17]

In another story, Love told the paper, "We have marked our search into sections, and we're working the hottest area first, and then we move on." Love went on to say that "several leads" had been developed and "we checked them out, but they did not yield anything. However, we think we are in the right general area." Love went on to say that "the best lead yet" had been turned up on Wednesday. Love wouldn't say what it was, but the *Reporter* speculated that it might be some hotel towels that had been found beside the road on US 90. Love went on to say, "We know that Bundy was in Lake City at about the time the girl was reported missing and we know he lived in Tallahassee. This [area where they were searching] is the most direct route from Lake City to Tallahassee." The article quoted an unnamed FHP official as saying, "If this follows known patterns, and if in fact what we are looking for is a victim, then the body is usually within a few miles of the abduction."[18]

Warren Goodwin, the chief assistant state attorney of the Tallahassee State Attorney's Office, announced that six arrest warrants had been served on Bundy, although formal charges were yet to be filed. Goodwin explained that Bundy would have a first appearance hearing before a judge and that the state attorney's office would then have 21 days to file formal charges. Wayne Smith said that Bundy was confused and nervous at the first appearance, which was held before Judge Haywood Atkinson in the Leon County Jail. "He seemed surprised. He did not seem to be expecting them." Bundy reportedly waived counsel and said he would represent himself. The charges were three counts of burglary of motor vehicles and three counts of grand theft.[19]

The *Florida Times Union* reported an announcement by Katsaris that he had talked telephonically with both Philpot and Bailey and had agreed to provide a helicopter to the Lake City authorities to assist in a treetop search. Katsaris said they agreed that any evidence found would be turned over to his crime scene technicians to maintain continuity of the evidence.[20]

On February 24, the Associated Press reported that the FDLE Crime Lab in Tallahassee had become "the inconspicuous center" of the Bundy investigation. Crime lab personnel were tight-lipped about what they were doing, but they did say that they were being buried under an avalanche of clues. One anonymous official told the Associated Press, "This is a major project." Randy Desilet, a supervisor in the lab, said, "It's a routine case in the sense that we have an awful lot of evidence to go through. It's hard to establish where we are. The evidence keeps coming in." Although the crime lab workers were reticent to share the details of what they were doing, others were happy to tell the press what was being submitted to them. The *Jacksonville Journal* reported that blood and hair had been found in the Media Center van, and that a comb and brush belonging to Kim had been submitted to the lab to compare with the hair found in the van.[21]

The media spent the next couple of days rehashing what had already been revealed. Pete Spivey of the *Orlando Sentinel* wrote a summary of the investigation under the caption "One thing baffles police on Bundy—no evidence." He quoted an unnamed "key figure" in the investigation as saying, "We have enough circumstances; enough known facts from his crimes in other states; enough police suspicion and reasoning to believe he is no doubt the only one who could have done it. What we don't have is any evidence." Spivey also quoted unnamed investigators as saying that because they had no hard evidence in the Chi Omega case, they felt they had a better chance with the Leach case. Spivey repeated the reports concerning the search of the Media Center van. In discussing those reports, he quoted Katsaris as saying, "There was something that looked like blood in the van when we recovered it, but I don't expect to hear from the lab for several days. But hair is one of those things found in abundance just about anywhere, so I'm not too excited about that yet." As things turned out, hair analysis played a key role in obtaining Bundy's conviction in the Chi Omega murder case, but not the Leach case. Spivey reported that a detective told him that Bundy was enjoying himself in the jail. "He's reading law books, eating, sleeping a lot and generally having a great time." The detective also told Spivey that Bundy was thrilled over "pulling a fast one" on Ken Katsaris by smuggling a letter out of the jail.[22]

The smuggled letter caused a media stir. Over the next few days the papers were peppered with quotes from that letter. Bundy told the media, "Outside of a few minor thefts, I have done no wrong. I have killed no one. What the media reports now is completely one-sided, nothing but accusations and insinuations . . . spoon-fed by the authorities." He went on to say, "Several additional locks have been welded to my cell door. They regard me with Houdini-like awe. They are scared to death I will escape from them. Imagine such an unjustified fear."[23]

Katsaris had been considering allowing the media access to Bundy, but after the letter's publication, he clamped down on Bundy's contact with the outside world. Katsaris told the press, "Nobody will be allowed to visit Ted Bundy at jail, with the exception of lawyers from Millard Farmer's office in Atlanta or the public defender's office in Tallahassee, regardless of whose name appears on his visitor guest list." Katsaris defended his action by saying, "If I let one person interview him, I'd have ten thousand others mad at me."[24] He also said that "only a court order" would make him change his mind.[25]

Two substantive events were reported. The first development involved the Florida Department of Transportation. The DOT had provided a plane to the search effort. Bailey explained to the press that "The DOT has an infrared camera that will hit hot spots up to six feet under the ground."[26] What he meant to say was that the infrared camera would detect the heat generated by decomposing bodies.

The second event occurred at the Suwannee County landfill. The local National Guard unit had been called out to assist the FHP in excavating the landfill looking for clues. Colonel Beach explained, "This is the most massive search the patrol has ever conducted, and this is the best lead we have had. I had two calls from two different responsible people in two different towns and they say they saw a van near a dumpster a few weeks ago. I hope we find some evidence."[27] An unnamed National Guardsman working at the landfill told a TV crew that they had uncovered a pair of blue jeans and a pocketbook that were positively identified as belonging to Kim.

On February 27, the media reported an event that brought order to the chaos of the Leach investigation. That event was the formation of a multiagency task force and the designation of a single press spokesperson—me. I explained to the media that the task force had been formed to coordinate search efforts and let "the right hand know what the left is doing." I said that the task force would work out of the recently vacated post office building and that information gathered by the task force would be strictly guarded. I went on to say, "Since I am an attorney, I have some expertise in what should and should not be disseminated. There is a fear that should a prosecution develop, pretrial publicity could have an adverse effect. Information of a wrong kind can damage a defendant's right to a fair trial." I added that there "was no central outfit for the collection and dissemination of information" and the task force would serve as that central coordinating agency. I described the first task force meeting as "very fruitful in getting things coordinated, getting a good flow of information and a little more direction." I said that investigators had nothing "really solid" yet, but "we have got leads which may develop into something."

I went on to say that many of the leads had nothing to do with Bundy. "No theory has been ruled out, even the possibility that she ran away." I concluded the interview by saying that there were no plans to question Bundy. "We feel that the questioning he is undergoing from Tallahassee would be more likely to turn up information relative to this case than any questioning we can do at this time."[28]

Because my job as an assistant state attorney gave me more than my share of information on criminal activity, I paid little attention to news stories about crime. Consequently, I knew very little about the Chi Omega murders. When I first heard of Kim's disappearance, I made no connection between it and Chi Omega. I simply thought, "Well, she's either run away and she'll turn up in a few days, or she's been snatched by one of those roam-around-the-country-kill-at-random mass murderers, and we'll never see her again."

I had no choice but to follow the progress of the Leach investigation. I heard about it every morning at breakfast. All small towns have at least one breakfast restaurant where men gather to drink coffee and gossip. The restaurant where I went to catch up on the gossip was not five blocks from the junior high. Located downtown on the corner of North Marion Street and US 90, it was called the Corner Kitchen. The hour you arrived at the Corner Kitchen dictated who you would find sitting at the round table near the front door. Because I varied my times of arrival and departure, I was plugged in to several different groups of men. A number of officers from different agencies frequented the restaurant, and they all wanted to talk to me about the Leach case.

It would be more accurate to say that they all wanted to complain to me about the officers from other agencies. From what I gathered, each agency thought the other was hogging the limelight and taking unjustified credit for progress in the investigation. The sheriff's office thought the police department had no business conducting investigations outside the city limits; the police department thought the sheriff's office was trying to usurp its jurisdiction by investigating a case inside the city limits; both agencies thought FHP had no jurisdiction at all in the matter, and FHP thought that neither the sheriff's office nor the police department was doing enough to find Kim. As I saw things, neither the sheriff's office nor the police department had the expertise or the manpower to properly investigate the case, and although FHP had the manpower, it had neither the jurisdiction nor the expertise. I don't say this as a criticism. No small-town sheriff's office or police department would have been equal to the task. I knew of only one state agency that could conduct a proper investigation. The Florida Department of Law Enforcement had the jurisdiction, the expertise, and the manpower. The ideal solution would be interagency cooperation among all four law enforcement bodies, with FDLE coordinating the effort. Getting FDLE involved in the investigation would be tricky, however. It had a strict policy of not getting involved in local matters unless requested to do so by a local law enforcement agency. It would be a hard sell to get the sheriff's office or the police department to request assistance from FDLE. I discussed my concerns with my boss, State Attorney Arthur Lawrence, and we decided to try to mediate a settlement. We spoke with both Bailey and Philpot, and they assured us that the investigation was proceeding well, everyone was getting along splendidly, and they'd let us know when they needed us.

Not long after that, Love telephoned Lawrence and asked that he call a meeting of all agencies involved in the Leach investigation. Love was concerned about friction and lack of progress in the investigation, and he wanted something done about it. Love also asked that a representative of FDLE attend the meeting. Both Love and Beach had already requested that FDLE take a hand in the investigation, but FDLE had declined, saying that it must be invited by an agency with primary jurisdiction for the investigation. Love said he had asked whether the state attorney's request would be sufficient, and FDLE told him yes. Neither Bailey nor Philpot would voluntarily invite FDLE into the investigation, so the ball was in Lawrence's court.

A little background is in order here. The Florida Department of Law Enforcement evolved from the Florida Sheriff's Bureau. The sheriff's bureau, located in Tallahassee, primarily did forensic analysis of evidence submitted to the bureau's crime lab. Sometime before I began to practice law, the legislature had decided that Florida needed a statewide police agency of original jurisdiction. The idea was coolly received by the 67 elected sheriffs in the state. The thesis of a state police met the antithesis of the sheriffs' opposition, and the synthesis was FDLE, a statewide law enforcement organization with limited investigative authority. FDLE sought to expand its jurisdiction and local law enforcement resisted. Eventually FDLE won a qualified victory and is now a full-fledged state police with broad jurisdiction in a number of areas. Even though it won, it is still very careful not to step on the local sheriffs' toes. Around 1978, FDLE was losing its fight for survival.

The catalyst for the decline of FDLE came from a rather unfortunate incident. Shortly after Governor Reuben Askew had appointed

William A. Troelstrup as commissioner of FDLE, the legislature dis-covered that FDLE was keeping files on a number of legislators. As I recall, the files were mainly collections of newspaper clippings. Harm-less as the files might appear, the legislature was not amused. If you are in state government, you don't want to anger the legislature. FDLE's budget was cut, and the legislature changed its name. FDLE became the Florida Department of Criminal Law Enforcement, FDCLE. The name change served to remind everyone that FDLE had no business keep-ing tabs on legislators. As a further reminder, the legislature launched an investigation of power abuse within the agency.[29] Although this had happened around 1974, the legislature was still giving FDLE a hard time in 1978. There was much behind-the-scenes talk about either abolishing FDLE altogether or putting it under the jurisdiction of the FHP. Abolition of FDLE would have been unfortunate. More than that, it would have been disastrous for the investigation and prosecution of the Leach case. Eventually, FDLE worked its way out of the legis-lature's doghouse and got the "criminal" dropped from its name. I be-lieve that the excellent work it did in the Leach case helped in that process.

Lawrence agreed with Love's request. He decided to call a meet-ing and invite FDLE to send a representative. We made a lot of mis-takes during the Bundy investigation, but calling in FDLE wasn't one of them. Although we could unilaterally call in FDLE despite the op-position of Bailey and Philpot, it was not a wise thing to do. We really needed the cooperation of the two agencies, and we decided to use di-plomacy to get it. We embarked on a series of meetings with the three agency heads—Bailey, Philpot, and Love. We met with each official in-dividually and got them to agree to a group meeting. The location of the meeting was something of a sticking point, with nobody wanting to go to anyone else's turf for a meeting. We finally got everyone to agree to meeting on a neutral site.

The meeting was set for February 26, 1978, in the city council meet-ing room in Lake City's City Hall. Representatives of all the agencies showed up, including Steve Bodiford of the Leon County Sheriff's Of-fice. Special Agent J. O. Jackson represented FDLE. Jackson was a well-respected officer who would become a near legend before he retired. He was highly intelligent and well able to organize and direct a mas-sive law enforcement investigation. He could assemble a vast body of seemingly unconnected information and distill it into a comprehen-sible, compelling case. I believe that this was the first case in which he fully displayed these abilities, but it wasn't the last. He later served as the case agent for the Austin Gay murder case, a case that resulted in the indictment and conviction of nearly a dozen current and former Chicago public servants, including police officers, paramedics, and building inspectors; and he also played an important role in the Gainesville Student Murders investigation (the Danny Rolling case).

We finally hammered out an arrangement. FHP would concentrate its efforts on the massive ongoing search for Kim's body. Bailey and Philpot would contribute two investigators each to running down leads in the criminal investigation. Two FHP troopers would help out in the criminal investigation. Jackson would serve as task force coordinator. He would receive and assign the leads and would collect and collate all reports by all agencies, incorporating them into an overall case file. I would serve as legal advisor, passing on the lawfulness of proposed investigative techniques. We needed a neutral site for task force headquarters. The post office, which stood across the street from the courthouse, had been recently vacated when the postal service moved to a newer building. It had sold the building to the county, and it was in the process of being renovated. There was a corner office in the building that could serve as our headquarters and "war room." Every morning we would gather in the "war room," go over the results of the previous day's investigation, and plan the current day's investigation. Press relations proved the thorniest problem. Who would be the spokesperson for the task force? I was for Jackson acting as press spokesperson, but nobody else seemed to think it was a good idea—especially Jackson. Someone nominated me. The motion carried unanimously. The meeting produced much good—the only mistake we made was the choice of a press spokesperson.

My first act as official task force spokesperson was to read the American Bar Association's standards for fair trial and free press in order to determine what I could and couldn't say to the press. I determined that I could say very little. Next I familiarized myself with the media coverage of the investigation. I decided that entirely too many people were saying entirely too much. I determined to work hard to correct that situation. My method would be simple. I would use as many words as possible to say as little as I could to the press, and I would say it as vaguely as possible. You might ask why I would take such an unfriendly attitude toward the press. Doesn't the public have a right to know? They certainly do. That's why trials are held in public rather than behind closed doors. On the other hand, nothing good—and much bad—can come from trying your case in the newsroom before you try it in the courtroom. Juries should decide the case based on the law and evidence they hear in the courtroom, not the gossip and speculation they learn from the media.

My first press release ran something like this: "Monday's ground search for Kimberly Leach failed to produce any finds currently thought to be of any significance. A television report aired Monday night to the effect that National Guardsmen participating in the search uncovered a pair of blue jeans and a pocketbook positively identified as belonging to Kimberly Diane Leach is erroneous. Numerous articles of clothing were found at the Suwannee County dump, but all have been eliminated as belonging to the Leach girl." It went on to request no inquiry should be made of anyone connected with the task force except the task force spokesperson. I gave out two telephone numbers. One number was the number for the press to call for information (the Lake City State Attorney's Office number). The second number was a tips hotline (task force headquarters). I requested that the press not call the tips hotline to keep it free for use by people having information helpful to the investigation. The tips hotline rang off the hook, but most of the callers were members of the press. It got so bad that we finally installed an unlisted number so that we could make and receive phone calls to and from officers working on the case.

I thought all I had to do was issue one press release each morning, the media could call our office and get the release, and all would be well. I soon learned how wrong I was. The press was not satisfied with the meager information in the press releases. The media wanted more information; in fact they demanded it. Everywhere I went, everything I did, I was dogged by reporters, cameramen, TV cameras, and questions. My home phone regularly rang until 2:00 A.M.

I did an abominable job as task force spokesperson. Although I was determined to keep as much information as possible out of the paper, my naivety made me a babe in the woods compared to the media sharks. I gave out far too much information. Time after time a reporter would tell me "We already know X has occurred. We simply want you to confirm it." I'd think, "Well, they've got me. No harm in confirming what they already know." The next day a story would run in the paper citing me as the sole source of a piece of information that should never have been released to the press. It took awhile for the light to come on, but I finally realized that the stories would never run if I didn't confirm them. I started telling reporters they'd have to seek elsewhere for their confirmation.

On March 2, I issued the mother of all press releases. The search crews were working north of town, and they found a pair of panties lying in the woods. It looked as though there might be bloodstains on the panties. We sent the panties to the lab and decided that, pending results, we would intensify the search in the area north of Lake City. I issued a press release saying that we had found something north of town, and we were going to intensify our search in that area the next day. "The nature [of the find] is too sensitive to go into at this time because it is quite possible that it has nothing to do with the case,"[30] I told the *Lake City Reporter*. "However we are encouraged to the extent that the search will be intensified in that area of town." I might as well have announced that Halley's Comet was going to crash to Earth at Memorial Park in front of the courthouse in Lake City. I only thought there was a media circus before. The media was relentless in their efforts to find out what had been discovered. All I would tell them was "There is a great possibility that this does not have anything to do with the case. We do not want to stir up a tempest in a teapot."[31] As a matter of fact, the "bloodstains" were tentatively identified as the juice from a can of baked beans. Since the stains weren't blood, no definitive analysis was done. I decided never to share that particular piece of information with the media. The media hurricane intensified to Category Five despite the fact that I kept saying over and over, "It's no big deal. It probably doesn't mean anything." Nothing worked. Then I had another revelation. If we completely stopped the flow of all information coming out of the task force, the media would go back to Tallahassee and bother the people working on the Chi Omega murders. The next day I issued what I believed to be my final press release. I said there weren't going to be any more press releases, and I meant it. And there weren't for a good long while.

# 5

# Much Ado about Something

ESPN periodically runs a show on "X-games," the implication being X-games are more extreme than regular sports. You could say that we conducted an X-investigation, because some of the measures we took were extreme by anyone's standards. We've already discussed one of the extreme measures: the excavation of the Suwannee County landfill. That operation was mild compared to some of our other efforts.

Massive search parties beat the bushes with instructions to pick up anything that looked in the least unusual. Everything they picked up went to the FDLE Crime Lab. The crime lab tried to do something with everything sent to them. Some items sent in bordered on the ridiculous—broken tree limbs, for instance. A broken tree branch had been found trapped in the door of the Media Center van. We believed that if we could find the tree that branch had come from, we could find Kim. Scores of broken limbs were sent to the lab for a possible fracture match to the van's broken branch. We never found the correct limb. The most ridiculous item collected may have been the dirty diaper that one diligent searcher found near the Suwannee River State Park. I thought it was funny, but the folks at the lab were not amused. We also collected large quantities of underwear and used condoms. Apparently North Floridians engaged in a lot of sexual activity in the woods.

We've already talked about the aerial reconnaissance flown by the Leon County Sheriff's chopper and the DOT photo planes, but we used other forms of aerial search. From February 25 through March 5, an FHP airplane with a pilot and a spotter assisted in the search. They used a unique reconnaissance method. Whenever the spotter found circling buzzards, the plane tried to follow the buzzards to wherever they congregated on the ground. When the spotter found where the buzzards were landing, he directed ground search crews to the location. Using this method the search crews found a half dozen rotting cows, two cow skeletons, a dead calf, a dead hog, a dead armadillo, a dead turkey, and a bucket of chicken bones. In addition to following buzzards, the air crew looked for blue objects on the ground, hoping to find Kim's jersey. They found a blue shirt, a pair of blue jeans, a blue-green plastic bag, and a scrap of blue cloth floating in a pond.[1]

Aerial reconnaissance didn't exhaust our use of buzzards. Someone reported that he had seen a buzzard with a blue cloth wrapped around its neck. If that buzzard's scrap of blue cloth came from Kim's jersey, it would narrow our search area. How much would it narrow the area? Someone called the University of Florida in search of a buzzard expert. The expert said that buzzards pretty much stayed within a few miles of their nest. Armed with that information, we reasoned that if we could find the buzzard, and if the blue cloth on the buzzard's neck came from Kim's jersey, we'd be within a few miles of her body. We needed to verify that the blue cloth was jersey material. We needed to capture that buzzard. Two troopers were detailed to capture the buzzard. Lieutenant Kenneth Boatright, who headed up the FHP search party, remembers that the troopers went up and down the Ichetucknee River in a canoe, hoping to find the buzzard and shoot it down. After several days of fruitless effort, we called off the buzzard hunt.

The DOT flights, the Leon County helicopter, and the FHP buzzard patrol were nothing compared to another aerial reconnaissance. We had been told that the military, during the Vietnam War, had recovered the bodies of U.S. soldiers using a highly classified aerial photographic process. Supposedly, decaying bodies emitted heat or gas that the photographic process could detect. There were supposed to be two airbases on the East Coast that had the equipment to take such pictures. When we discussed whether we might enlist their aid, we decided there was no harm in asking. Who should make the call? Everyone but me thought the press spokesperson ought to do it.

I called both bases. The first place gave me a flat "No." I made the second call and got through to someone who was either a general or a colonel (I'll call him the General). The General's first objection was the *posse comitatus* law, which states that the military cannot be used for domestic law enforcement.[2] I talked him around that objection by characterizing our effort as a search and rescue operation. When we disposed of that objection, he asked how large an area we wanted his unit to reconnoiter. I told him 2 miles on either side of US 90 from Jacksonville to Tallahassee. He asked me if I had any idea how much that would cost. I didn't have a clue. He told me. I don't recall the exact amount, but I do remember that it included six zeroes. I asked him when he could start. After some consideration, he decided he could justify the expense by characterizing the mission as a training operation. The third objection wasn't as important to the General. Much of the airspace was restricted to naval aviation out of Jacksonville. The General thought it would be fun to sneak his planes into and out of the restricted airspace undetected by the Navy. The final objection: The photographic process was classified, and they couldn't let us see the pictures. We got around that objection by agreeing that a military technician would study the pictures and then tell us where to search.

The General cautioned me that the entire operation had to be kept in the strictest confidence. The photographic technology was classified, the operation was a questionable evasion of military policy, and the photographic film was outrageously expensive. The pilots flying the missions would not even know what they were doing. They would be told that they were doing training exercises, and they would think they were shooting with dummy film. Only a photographic specialist and the representatives sent to the base from the task force would know what was going on. The jets would fly far out into the Atlantic and then sneak in under the Navy's radar near Jacksonville. They would then fly west along I-10 until they got to the area to be photographed. Then, flying at 400 mph, they would descend to a height of 100 feet and rattle the windows of houses in rural Columbia and Suwannee counties. They would fly back to the base, the film would be unloaded and processed, and then the military photographic specialist would call Boatright and tell him where to search. The search teams dispatched to those locations found all manner of dead and decaying animals, but no Kim. The flights did not cover as wide an area as I had asked. They ranged from Lake City to just east of Live Oak. If only they had gone a little bit farther.

Almost any highly publicized murder mystery attracts its share of psychics. It is a measure of our desperation for leads that we listened to every one of them. We even had a "psychic patrol" whose primary assignment was dealing with the messengers from the beyond. One psychic wanted to go into Kim's bedroom with a tape recorder. She sent everyone else out of the room, saying that she would turn on the tape recorder, go into a trance, and disclose Kim's whereabouts. We complied with her wishes, leaving her behind closed doors in Kim's room. After the passage of about a half an hour, she emerged from the room with the recording. When we played it, it was nothing but static.

One of Kim's girlfriends had a dream about where Kim's body was. On a Sunday afternoon I took a drive with her and her mother out into a pine forest west of Lake City. She had me stop at a clearing in the woods, and we spent about a half an hour stomping through the underbrush before we gave up. Although I spent a rather nonproductive couple of hours working with the girl, I felt that some good came from the effort. She was obviously traumatized by the loss of her friend, and she seemed to have achieved a degree of comfort from having done something to try to help find Kim.

We had another man attempt to divine Kim's whereabouts with playing cards. Larry Daugherty wrote a report on the attempt.

> On 032178 [a certain psychic] came to the Lake City Police Station and advised that he could locate the body of Kimberly Diane Leach, I was summonsed [*sic*] to the department to interview this subject. I did carry him at his request to an area off of Doublerun Road and he did attempt to locate the body with the use of playing cards with no success. I did introduce this person to Agent J. O. Jackson and after a brief display of his ability to answer questions by the use of his cards proved that he was inaccurate about 90% of the time, he was advised by me that we would contact him if we needed his assistance and that we did appreciate his concern.[3]

Daugherty gave a much more vivid oral account of the incident. According to Daugherty, the psychic began his performance by cutting his cards and studying them. He then told Daugherty to drive him in a certain direction. After driving in that direction for some distance, he cut his cards again, studied them, and directed Daugherty down a side road. After several twists and turns, they finally arrived at a field behind a farmhouse. The man got out and began running about the field. He would periodically stop, cut his cards, study them, and take off in another direction. When the farmer came out of his house to inquire what the heck was going on, Daugherty loaded the psychic back up in his patrol car and carried him to task force headquarters.

A female "psychic" took another officer into a secluded place in another pine forest and made a pass at him. He went back to the task force office and angrily resigned from the psychic patrol. Although he always wrote thorough reports, he never memorialized that incident with a written report. We had one other psychic report, but I'll save that story for a little later.

We also used hypnosis, although most of the hypnosis was done by the Lake City Police Department before the formation of the task force. One lady thought she saw Bundy walking down MacFarland Avenue not far from the junior high on the afternoon of the abduction. Under hypnosis she said the man definitely was not Bundy.[4] Tandy Bonner, the girl who escorted Kim back to Mr. Bishop's class, underwent hypnosis. The session caused Tandy to remember that while she was with Kim she saw a white female drive by the school in a silvery-blue pickup truck with burgundy stripes.[5] The use of hypnosis did nothing to help solve the case and actually proved counterproductive, as we shall see a little later.

My favorite extreme measure was the "body sniffer." J.O. Jackson told me that the FDLE Crime Lab had a piece of equipment that could "smell" buried bodies by detecting the methane gas emitted by decaying flesh. Jackson said that the "body sniffer" had been used on an old Civil War battlefield, and it had found a well-preserved Union officer buried in an unmarked grave. Jackson assured me that if we ever found a possible grave site, they would break out the "body sniffer" and it would tell us whether there was a body in the grave.

One rainy day we got a report that a fresh, unmarked grave had been found near the chain link fence at a small cemetery deep in the woods near Wellborn, Florida. We contacted the cemetery administrator and learned that there had been no recent burials at the cemetery. It was time to break out the "body sniffer." I drove to the scene to see the "body sniffer" in action. Jack Duncan, who had been with the lab for years, came to conduct the search. I stood in a drizzle of rain watching in rapt anticipation as Duncan, wearing a raincoat, stood over the grave site and studied it intently. After studying the grave site, he walked back to his vehicle, reached in it, and came out with a rod that was about four feet long. The rod had a T handle on one end and an auger on the other. It made me think of a giant corkscrew. Duncan walked over to the grave, straddled it, and stuck the auger into the ground. He began to twist the auger into the ground. In a moment he announced that he had hit something. He gave the rod a couple of hard twists and pulled it out of the ground. There was hair and skin stuck to the auger. Duncan held the auger to his nose, sniffing. After having thoroughly sniffed the end of the auger, Duncan announced that it was decayed flesh. I was standing about 20 yards away, and I could see that it was decayed flesh. Based upon this observation, Duncan voiced his expert opinion—there was a dead body buried in the fresh grave. I asked Jackson, "This is the body sniffer?" "No," he said, "It's too wet to break out the body sniffer, so Jack is doing it the low tech way." Duncan then began a careful forensic excavation of the grave. In short order he uncovered a cardboard box containing somebody's dead pet dog. I never saw the "body sniffer" during the investigation. I never again, during a 30-year career in prosecution, ever even heard anybody mention a "body sniffer."

An eclectic group of officers were assigned to the task force. You have already met J. O. Jackson, whose investigative skill was an essential ingredient in finally solving the case; Lieutenant Kenneth Boatwright, who oversaw the ground search for Kim; and Larry Daugherty, a plainclothes investigator for the Lake City Police Department. The police department also detailed Dale Parrish, another plainclothes investigator, to the task force; the sheriff's office assigned Johnny Walker; the FHP assigned Troopers Harold E. Scott and Leroy Tompkins to work with the task force as investigators; and the state attorney's office committed two men to the case—Investigator Al Williams, who later became sheriff of Suwannee County, and a young prosecutor whom you have already met.

After the organizational meeting at City Hall, we took up residence in the old post office building and held daily meetings. Each morning I would get up, go to the FHP station and attend the briefing of the search crew; then I would go to the post office and attend the task force strategy session. After that, I either went on to work at the state attorney's office or did whatever I could to assist the task force. As time dragged on, I spent less and less time working in the office and devoted more and more time to the task force effort. Eventually, the state attorney reassigned my caseload to someone else and I worked full-time on the task force.

We almost immediately concluded that someone had killed Kim and structured our effort upon that assumption. We did not overlook other possibilities, but the investigation quickly ruled out those theories. Because we were satisfied that Kim was dead, we made bringing her murderer to justice our ultimate objective. In order to do this, we set three preliminary objectives: (1) Determine who killed her; and (2) gather sufficient evidence to (a) file criminal charges, and (b) have a reasonable prospect of obtaining a conviction. It is sometimes possible to prove up a murder case without a body, but it wasn't going to happen in the Leach case. We needed the body because we believed the body would provide sufficient scientific evidence to give us a reasonable prospect of obtaining a conviction. This gave us our last preliminary objective: (3) Find Kim. Achieving this last objective was essential to achieving the first two.

Bodies are hard to find and easy to overlook. In my 30 years as a prosecutor and 2 as a defense attorney, I had lots of experience searching for bodies, and lots of experience with the discovery of bodies for which nobody was searching. Over the years, I came to understand that hidden body cases fall into three broad categories: (1) those where the suspect helps the search party find the body, (2) those where the killer does not transport the body far from the scene and makes little or no effort to hide it, and (3) those where the body is found by blind staggering luck. Category 3 falls into two subcategories: (a) those where we are diligently looking for the body and some citizen unconnected with the search stumbles over it, and (b) those where we have no clue that a murder has occurred and a citizen stumbles over the body. I only recall one case where a search party actually found a well-hidden murder victim without help from the defendant or a private citizen. Unfortunately, we had been looking for an elderly black male and found a young white female. We eventually convicted the girl's killer, but we never found the murder victim for whom we were searching. When I got assigned to the Bundy case, I was not as experienced with hidden body cases as I would later become, but I had enough experience to know that we had a monumental task ahead of us. Before Bundy became connected to Lake City, Sheriff Bailey had resisted attempts to organize large-scale search parties to find Kim. The paper summed up his comments as "Honestly, we don't know where to look."[6] And we didn't. With no direction to work toward, searching would be like buying a lottery ticket. The chances of hitting the jackpot are miniscule. You might waste a dollar on such a miniscule prospect of success, but do you really want to invest your life savings in it?

Connecting Bundy to Lake City changed the equation. It gave direction to the search, but not much. The first narrowing of the search came from the Media Center van's odometer reading. Captain C. S. Hooker of the FSU Police Department took the last mileage reading from the van's log (8,987.3 miles) and subtracted it from the reading on the odometer (9,776.4 miles) and determined that the van had been driven 789.1 miles while it was stolen.[7] From this number we subtracted the distance from Jacksonville to Tallahassee (157 miles), and divided the difference by two (316 miles). This gave us the farthest distance Bundy could have driven the van north or south of a straight line between Tallahassee and Jacksonville. Draw a line that distance north of I-10 and another that distance south of I-10. If Bundy killed Kim, her body had to be in an area bounded on the north and south by those two lines and on the east and west by Tallahassee and Jacksonville. Given the distance between Tallahassee and Jacksonville, that meant the possible area of search would cover some 99,240 square miles. Bailey believed it too much territory for there to be any sense in organizing a search party. Captain Love thought otherwise. The search seldom strayed more than 2 miles north or south of US 90 between Lake City and Tallahassee, which meant our area of search was a more realistic 420 square miles. Still, that was a lot of territory to cover. The search was guided by the assumption that Bundy had kidnapped Kim and that anything odd found in the 420 square miles between Tallahassee and Lake City ought to be sent to the lab to see if it could be tied to Bundy. If it could, we would know to come back to the location where the item was found and conduct a painstakingly thorough search. Before the formation of the task force, Sergeant Winston Barber of the FHP gave the press a memorable quote that later became our unofficial motto. He said, "We're kind of looking for the haystack that would have the needle in it, but we haven't even found the haystack yet."[8] Thus our motto became "If we can find the haystack, we'll find the needle." And that was the model that the search teams worked on. We were looking for Kim's body, but we were also looking for that one clue that would point us to the haystack that contained her body.

The task force began to winnow through all the various items of information gathered in Jacksonville, Lake City, Tallahassee, and Pensacola. The problem we confronted was one investigators often confront in whodunit murder investigations—too much information and too little evidence. We had lots of information, some good, some bad, some crucial, and we had no way of recognizing what was really relevant. Slowly, however, we separated the wheat from the chaff, and we were able to narrow down the search area to a more reasonable acreage.

Because Bundy had been driving the Media Center van when he was in Lake City, we assumed that he had snatched Kim and transported her in the van. If he did so, the huge bloodstain on the carpet remnant in the back of the van came from Kim. The bloodstain would become relevant when we found Kim's body and matched it to her blood type, but I saw little hope for it showing us where to look for her. Something else from the back of the van did help, however, and it wasn't broken branches.

Sand had been thrown onto the carpet in the back of the van. We reasoned that Bundy, after killing Kim, had tried to conceal the blood by covering it with sand. Although the soil didn't do a very good job of concealing the blood, we believed it might reveal Kim's whereabouts. Bundy would have wanted to conceal the blood as quickly as possible after he dumped Kim's body, which meant that the soil probably came from very near where Kim was hidden. Crime laboratory analyst Dale Nute determined the soil came from a river flood plain. His opinion helped only a little, because North Florida is full of rivers. The search parties began collecting soil samples to send to the crime lab. Nute examined all the samples, but none could be matched to the soil from the back of the van. He eventually testified for the defense at the trial. One crucial, critical, vitally important piece of evidence went completely overlooked. Two FHP troopers took a sample of the soil from the van and showed it to a soil expert who lived in Lake City. T. B. Houston, who worked for the Soil Conservation Service, knew the soils of the Suwannee Valley like he knew the back of his hand. He told them exactly where the soil came from. And exactly where the soil came from was less than a mile away from Kim's body. The next day the FHP search crew went to the area identified by Houston. A foot patrol searched one side of the highway, and a horse patrol worked the other side. The horsemen rode down a dirt road through a pasture to a tree line. Just past the tree line, they came to a fence running parallel to the road. Across the fence they saw a tumbledown shed. In the shed lay Kim's body. They rode on past the shed. It began to sprinkle, then it began to rain hard, then they called off the search. Before they quit, though, the foot patrol on the south of the highway found a pile of cigarette butts and a crinkled five-dollar bill lying on the ground. The cigarette butts were submitted to the FDLE Crime Lab, but it would be months before the lab analyzed them. That same day another search party working more than 20 miles away found the infamous panties stained with baked beans. The next day the search intensified in that area, and search parties didn't return to the location of Kim's body for weeks. Houston's pronouncement as to the origin of the soil was forgotten, and the jury that ultimately convicted Bundy never heard his vital evidence.

I did not learn about Houston's identification of the soil until almost 35 years after the fact. I was in a coffee shop reminiscing about old times with a retired trooper when he told me about taking the soil to Houston and the opinion Houston gave. I nearly fell out of my chair. I immediately asked him, "Did you write a report on that?" He looked a little nonplussed and said, "No. I guess I should have. But you know us old troopers. We never were much for writing reports." Almost every big case has at least one pertinent fact that the investigators fail to disclose to the prosecutors. Prosecutors should know and understand this and should take countermeasures. The best countermeasure is an insatiable curiosity about the case, an indomitable drive to find out everything there is to know about it, and meticulous attention to detail.

Sand on Carpet in the Media Center Van. (Courtesy of the State Attorney's Office of the Third Judicial Circuit, Florida)

One matter about which we had a lot of curiosity was what Bundy had told the investigators in Pensacola. Jackson undertook to find out. He described his efforts as follows:

On February 28, 1978 SA J.O. Jackson telephonically contacted Norman Chapman, Investigator, Pensacola Police Department. Chapman was contacted reference his rapport with THEODORE ROBERT BUNDY. Chapman had spent approximately 40 hours interviewing Bundy since he was arrested in Pensacola on 2/15/78. Tapes made of these interviewed [*sic*] had been turned over to the Leon County Sheriff's Office by Chap. Attempts by SA J.O. Jackson and other members of the Task Force to obtain access to these tapes had been unsuccessful. Therefore, Chapman was requested to travel to Lake City where he could be debriefed by the Task Force as to knowledge he had relative to the disappearance of KIMBERLY DIANE LEACH. On March 2, 1978 Chapman was interviewed at the Task Force Office in Lake City. The interview was conducted by SA J.O. Jackson, Larry Daugherty and Dale Parrish, Investigator, Lake City Police Department.

Chapman gave a general statement as to the information that Bundy had given him. Of particular interest to this investigation was Bundy's reply to specific questions concerning KIMBERLY DIANE LEACH. One of these replies was to a specific request to show Chapman where Leach's body was. Bundy replied that he couldn't because the scene was too bad for him (Chapman) to see. Bundy at one point said, Norman, you have got to remember that I'm a cold blooded son-of-a-bitch. Other information that Chapman gave will be of a circumstantial nature, but has some evidentiary value.[9]

Jackson's main objective was to build a case against Bundy, and he zeroed in on the two statements that would best serve to obtain a conviction. Before we could get a conviction, however, we had to have a case; and before we could have a case, we had to find Kim. Where would Bundy have hidden her? Jackson did not include it in his report, but Chapman did give us some information relevant to where and how Bundy would hide evidence of his wrongdoing.

Chapman's lengthy, rambling interview was tape recorded and transcribed. He began with some armchair psychoanalysis, saying that Bundy exhibited three distinct personalities. The first personality was

Normal Ted, who was a compassionate, caring person. "He made the statement one time that he was the type person that would give his life to save a baby or things like this." Chapman went on to say, "The second personality is a personality which he referred to himself as the Lawyer Ted." Chapman said that Lawyer Ted could become quite aggressive in legal situations. The final personality was Vampire Ted, who was anything but normal. Chapman elaborated: "At one time he referred to himself as a vampire-type personality because it came out at night and when he did things that he wasn't pleased with himself for doing." Chapman said Bundy blamed Vampire Ted for his legal problems. Vampire Ted "required certain physical conditions for it to come out, such as he needed to have a certain amount of alcohol in his system, he needed to use soft pornographic material such as *Playboy* or view books which contained cheerleaders, majorettes, things of that nature. And he also operated with a lot of fantasies. This is what he stated to us that he dealt in a fantasy world when he operated in this personality. . . . He said that he was able to operate on three hours sleep a night so he required very little sleep to operate. . . . During our questioning he reported to us that about 12 or 13-years old he got to where he liked to go around and peep in windows he became a voyeur and he maintained this all the way up to the present time. . . ." Chapman continued:

> When he was about 23 years old he had an affair with a young lady named [Paula Polite],[10] and there's been a lot of hypothesis about [Paula], the people that have been involved in his crimes resembling [Paula]. . . . [Bundy said] that [Paula] wanted to marry him very badly and he refused to marry her because she was wanting a life to be a professional individual and she had a lot of problems. I think she came from a family that was a well to do family and had a lot of political influence. [Dr. Carlisle of the Utah Department of Corrections] says it was the reverse, said he wanted to marry [Paula], but [Paula] flatly refused to marry him. And about this time that his [Bundy's] problems really came out. He started these violent crimes that he had been committing. This was about 1970, anywhere from 1969 to 70, somewhere along there. He talked about when he would do this riding. It was a fantasy for him. He dealt in fantasies, and he mentioned several times about pornographic material. About while it was one person's pleasure, another person's vice or whatever downfall. He

said pornographic material was one thing that caused him a lot of problems. And like I said before it wasn't harder pornographic material, it was soft type stuff. . . . We know he was into bondage to a certain extent, he had a girlfriend named [Valerie].[11] Her last, I don't what her last name is. He talked about her quite a bit, and in one of their episodes he tied her up with stockings to the bedpost. And she, it frightened her pretty bad so he never tried this anymore with her. . . .

He was stopped in Salt Lake City the first time, and he brought this up to me when I first started talking to him. He says when it all comes out you'll see the irony of being stopped by Officer Lee. Officer Lee was looking for a burglar. He said when I was in Salt Lake City, the first time I was stopped out there, they were looking for a burglar out there also. He was stopped early in the morning riding through a neighborhood and they searched his car, and in the car they found an ice pick, some cord, I believe there was a pair of pantyhose with eye holes cut in the seat, and he was arrested at this time. One thing that they discovered in following this, he was using his own credit cards at this time, and backtracking and getting background information on him, he would indeed drive many, many miles in a night's time. And he was putting a lot of miles on his car.

I questioned quite extensively one time, I'm not sure if it's on tape or not, about why he used Volkswagens, and he indicated that number one, he knew how to work on VW's. He was familiar with them, that he could—because of the economy of the VW gas mileage—he could live his fantasies and drive a great number of miles. Also with VW the way the seats were situated, that it was easy for him to take the back seat out. Take the passenger seat loose and slide it around behind the back seat. And at this time we were talking in generalities, and to get information about other things. And we used the word cargo and things like this to talk about his victims, and he indicated at that time that—I believe he said—it didn't matter whether the cargo was alive when he put it in the car or deceased when he put it in the car or whatever. You know, there, that there wasn't any pattern to how he carried out his fantasies. We could never pin him down to the tool he used to complete the fantasy with. He said there was no specific tool he used, but there have been a lot of indications that he liked to use short crowbars in assaulting his victims. Now the one individual who got away from him that was in the car was in Salt Lake City—and I've forgotten her name—but anyway, this case they tried him on and convicted him was in Salt Lake. And I asked him specifically. He kept saying that she was lucky. And I kept asking him why she was lucky, and he indicated the fact that she did get away, so that's how she was lucky, she got away.

What had happened from talking to other investigators that were familiar with the case was that he approached her, showed her a badge and indicated that he was a police officer. I believe he said that he told her her car had been burglarized, that he was going to take her back and fill out a report. When she got in the car he tried to handcuff her, and during the scuffle he put both cuffs on the same wrist and she escaped. So this was an unfortunate instance for him.

He kept himself in extremely good physical condition at all times even when he was in prison. He's the type of person that has great control over his body and can control his mind. He, even when he was in prison, he was planning his escape from Colorado by jumping out the second story court house window. He would run in his cell. He would get on the top bunk and practice jumping off the top bunk to the floor to be able to withstand the fall, get himself in condition to withstand that jarring.

There's significance in the two jail breaks and he related this information to me. He said that he has a degree in psychology and he has a year and a half law school. The significance of the two jail breaks are the first one, he planned to jump out of this courtroom window. And he planned it extensively, and he worked it out and he wore three sets of clothes that day. Okay, then they were in the court, he and his attorney were conversing with the judge, and they called a recess, and he went into the library I believe. And he caught the guard not looking, and he jumped a good two and a half stories down to the ground. He ran across the back of the courthouse. . . . He ran a couple blocks from the courthouse, took his clothes off. He had his first layer of clothes off. He had on a turtleneck sweater, turned that turtleneck sweater inside out, put that set of clothes in there, tied a knot in the arms hung it over his shoulder, tied a bandana around his head, and put a patch over his nose and walked down the street. And he said the police cars were screaming by him right and left and never noticed him. . . .

He was gone approximately six days when he was apprehended again.

The second time he planned his escape he was in a cell, and he looked up at the ceiling and he saw the ceiling light fixture had been welded, the one side was welded all the way down and the other side had two short arcs on it or strips. And he procured him some hack saw blades, and he cut through. And he lost 15 pounds to be able to fit-in this hole. He also, they wouldn't make visual checks on him every time they fed him, so he timed from the time he was fed that night to the next day at dinner time, and he set up a pattern to where he wouldn't eat breakfast. And they just come by and beat on the door, and if he didn't beat back they didn't give him breakfast. And he was in an iron box from the way he described it so they, weren't doing visual checks on him. So the last time he escaped and made his way to Florida he had cut a hole in that roof, he had wrote people he knew and told them that he was needing money for cigarettes and things like this, and they would send him 5, 10, 15 dollars at a time and he cubby holed this money. . . . He climbed up through the hole in the ceiling got out, and subsequently ended up in Florida. . . .

The second time he escaped he came to Florida. He indicated he had had problems with these fantasies that he had eliminated a few people. And he realized then that he would never be able to function in society again, as an individual, because he knew it was something he himself could not work out by himself. He would need professional help. And he was wanting to go back to Washington, to be sent back to Washington to stand trial for those persons who were missing out there at the time, but because of political implications he realized he couldn't get back out there. . . .

Of course his irony he said about the second time he was caught and Officer Lee caught him, the two times he's been caught was the fact that he had been in these areas riding around in a car late at night looking for victims. He made the statement that he had been on I-10 going to Mobile and he got the urge to come into Pensacola. He couldn't resist it, he came into Pensacola, started driving around, Officer Lee stopped him and subsequently arrested him.

One thing that came up that never came out again in our discussions was when I first interviewed him and thinking that he was

Kenneth Misner and I was questioning him to the fact that he had three complete sets of identification of female students from Florida State University. He said well, he hadn't had a chance to get rid of it. And I asked I said, well you know, I said you came two hundred miles, why didn't you just throw it out the window. . . . He said if I was going to get rid of them I either throw them in a stream or a river or someplace like this. He said I wouldn't throw them out of the highway where they could be easily found. This is the only time during the questioning that I can remember that he indicated he had gotten rid of some of the evidence, or some of the items in the commission of these crimes. As time come along he started to reverting back to the Ted the lawyer personality and it was getting more and more difficult to get information from him. . . .

One of the last things he said to me when I talked to him in Tallahassee was that they had put him in solitary confinement, said he could handle that, that solitary confinement didn't bother him, that he'd been there in solitary confinement two years. He said this other personality's coming back, said he could read his law books and sit down and work himself out a defense, that sitting there in that cell that he could convince himself that he was not guilty of anything, and that was the end of my conversations with him. . . .

Q:  *Did he ever make any reference to Kimberly Diane Leach in the Lake City area?*
A:  I'm trying to think and be specific because at one time he said he would not answer any questions concerning anything that happened in Lake City, and he denied even being over here at one time. I specifically asked him, of course this hadn't anything to do with this thing over here, I specifically asked him one day if we needed to look for anybody else in relation to these crimes that occurred in Tallahassee or relating areas and he said no, that he would not admit to committing the crimes but he said that we did not need to look for anybody else in relation to, commission of the crimes.

Q:  *Did you ever ask him about the location of the victims?*
A:  Yes, I asked him about the location and he would not give me a location. I told him that the parents of these kids needed to have some relief and I asked him about this girl in Lake City.

I said, Ted, I said her parents need to know where she's at regardless what condition she's in. And I said if you will tell me where she's at I will go get her, and he said I cannot do that because the scene or, I forgot the exact words he used, he said it's too bad for you to see, and I believe it was the same approximate area he said Norman, he said you got to realize I'm a cold-blooded son of a bitch.[12]

I was not present for Chapman's interview. I was in Tallahassee that day speaking with Katsaris about the Bundy interviews and the results of the scientific testing done in connection with the Chi Omega and Dunwoody cases. Katsaris summarized the significant information from the interviews, and it coincided with what Chapman was at the same time telling the task force in Lake City.

You may recall that before Bundy emerged as a suspect, the Tallahassee authorities had consulted the FBI to make up a psychological profile of the Chi Omega killer. We did a little amateur psychological profiling of our own. Most people who perform repetitive tasks find a system that works and stick with it. Serial murder is a repetitive task. If Bundy was a serial murderer as advertised, he would likely dispose of his bodies in similar fashion. We could look to the western murders in which Bundy was a suspect, plot out the sites where the bodies had been found, and see if we had a pattern that could guide our search in Florida. Jackson got a map of the western United States and pockmarked it with red dots representing each location where a body was recovered. A pattern emerged. Each body was located within a couple of miles of an interstate highway. When we read the map in light of what Bundy had said about "hauling cargo," we began to get an idea of where we should direct our search.

We didn't stop with that, however. We needed to know the terrain where the bodies were found. In an attempt to further refine the profile of the probable dump site, I had an off-the-record talk with Richard Larsen, Bundy's journalist friend from Seattle. What could he tell us about the western dump sites? Three things stood out. The bodies were usually found in wooded areas, near bodies of water, covered up by leaves or something else. A clearer picture of the probable dump site emerged. We needed just a few more items of information, and then we should have an accurate picture.

# 6

# The Searchers

On March 3, Austin Gay provided the last piece of the puzzle we needed to draw an accurate profile of Kim's location. He came to the FHP station where his wife worked and gave a statement about his meeting with Bundy at the agricultural inspection station.[1] At this point, if Nero Wolfe had been investigating Kim's disappearance, he would have sent Archie Goodwin and Saul Panzer to the general vicinity of Kim's body. They would have found the body in an hour or two, and the mystery would have been solved. Nero Wolfe actually solved two of his cases by fixing on a suspect, asking where the suspect would have hidden vital evidence, and then sending Archie Goodwin and Saul Panzer to the likely hiding places.[2] Unfortunately, Nero Wolfe is a fictional character and the task force had insufficient faith in the profile to do what I am about to ask you to do.

You now have more information than we did when we formulated our profile of the site where Kim should be located. You also do not suffer from the handicap of knowing hundreds of other pieces of data that later proved to be irrelevant. You should be able to formulate a profile of Kim's location for yourself. You might want to stop at this time and study a map of North Florida. Keeping in mind the information we had gathered, draw a circle around the most likely area where Kim was found. If you give the circle a five-mile radius, you should have no trouble circling the site. If we had studied the map, drawn the circle you just drew, and searched within it, we would have found Kim much sooner than we did.

Now that you've drawn your circle, we can reveal our profile of the probable dump site and describe how we produced it. We reasoned that because of his encounter with Gay, Bundy would not risk driving through an inspection station with Kim in the van. All inspection stations were west and north of Lake City. Adding in the other pieces of the puzzle gave us a clear picture. Kim's body should be east of the inspection stations on Interstate 10 and US 90 and south of the inspection stations on Interstate 75, US 41, and US 441. It should be within two miles of Interstate 10, under a makeshift cover, in a wooded area, on a river flood plain, and near a body of water. With that profile in mind, we should have gotten on US 90 and driven west from Lake City. When we arrived at the Suwannee River and saw the sign saying "Agricultural Inspection Station ahead: All trucks stop for inspection," we should have turned off on the first side road and started looking for bodies of water.

In addition to our lack of faith in the profile, we had missed two other golden opportunities to find Kim: T. B. Houston had pointed us directly to Kim's location, but we overlooked it. Early in the search, a mounted search party rode to within spitting distance of Kim's body, stopped because it was raining, and never went back to finish the search. Three strikes. We should have been out. The size of the search party dwindled steadily. The task force became increasingly disheartened. When the media asked me how long we intended to search, I answered, "As long as it takes,"[3] but I did not voice my growing fear that it was going to take forever. It seemed to me that the only sensible thing to do was call off the search, but Captain Love assured me that as long as Kim was missing, FHP would have at least one team in the field searching. The dreary repetitiveness of the futile search sapped everyone's morale. The attitude of the men who actually worked on the search party from day one through to the end is summed up in a report written by FHP trooper Ken Robinson:

> While on routine search for Kimberly Diane Leach on April 7, 1978, at approximately 12:36 p.m. I observed what appeared to be an old abandoned hog pen. The pen was constructed with tin over the top and around the sides. The tin top was so low to the ground that it was not possible to make a thorough observance without getting on my knees. I then leaned forward and on to my knees. After getting into a low position I observed a shoe which matched the description of the type of shoe which Kimberly Leach was allegedly wearing when last seen. I then called to Sergeant T. A. Pace and advised him I believed I had found a shoe

like we had been searching for. I then moved a little closer while still on my knees and observed another shoe, a brown fur-lined jacket and a blue shirt. I moved closer again and observed what appeared to be a human foot and leg bone. Sergeant Pace had then moved to my location and I showed him what I had found. I, along with Sergeant Pace, then moved back and Sergeant Pace called Lieutenant Ken Boatright by radio to our location.[4]

Trooper Robinson's characterization of his efforts as "routine search" says volumes about the dogged determination of the searchers. Robinson had been involved in the search from the very beginning. He had spent every day for three and one-half weeks walking the woods looking for Kim. He had walked US 90 through four North Florida counties. When the search teams began to be cut back, he returned to regular duty. When the search party was beefed up for the final day's search, he returned to the party but had little hope of finding anything. Robinson was later quoted as saying, "It's one of those deals like you

The Hog Shed Containing Kim's Body. (Courtesy of the State Attorney's Office of the Third Judicial Circuit, Florida)

think you are dreaming. After looking so long you wonder if you are seeing what you think you are."[5] But it wasn't just dogged determination that led to Kim's discovery. We hadn't just stumbled onto Kim's body by accident. The FDLE Crime Lab had given us a piece of evidence that pointed us almost directly to the location, and we didn't flub our fourth strike at finding Kim.

On April 6, 1978, FDLE Crime Lab fingerprint analyst Doug Barrow went to the mass of evidence submitted by the search teams and pulled out the cigarette butts and five-dollar bill that had been collected two months previously. Barrow can't be faulted for taking so long to get to the cigarette butts because of the flood of irrelevant items that had poured into the lab from the search parties. The lab staff had dutifully plowed through all the irrelevance, doing what they could with each submission, until Barrow finally opened the butts and the five-dollar bill and looked at them. He immediately made one vital observation. Because it had been raining, the items had been packaged wet, and they had mildewed. The mildew process had been sped along by the fact that the evidence had been packaged in plastic. The evidence should have been allowed to dry before being packaged in paper bags. Although you can't raise latent fingerprints from mildew, Barrow thought he could do something else. Remembering the cigarette butts removed from the Media Center van, Barrow retrieved those butts and laid them beside the mildewed butts.

He noticed similarities. The type of filters on the butts, the way the butts were bitten, the length to which they had been smoked, the way they had been crushed out—all these characteristics were very similar. Barrow concluded that the same person smoked both sets of butts. He telephoned his conclusions to Jackson and suggested that the search return to the Suwannee River State Park. "You should consider this merely an investigative lead," he cautioned, "this is not scientifically sound enough for me to testify about in court."

Jackson called Boatright and advised him of Barrow's findings. They agreed that the next day they would send a search party back to the area where the cigarette butts had been found.[6] We decided to reconnoiter the area before sending in the search party. As I recall, the scouting party consisted of Love, Boatright, Jackson, FHP trooper Leroy Tompkins, and me. We left Lake City and drove west toward the Suwannee River State Park. As we neared the park entrance on US 90, we noticed the sign calling upon all trucks to stop for agricultural in-

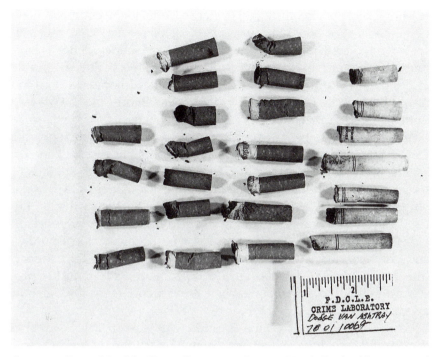

Cigarette Butts Used by Doug Barrow to Locate Kim's Body. (Courtesy of
the State Attorney's Office of the Third Judicial Circuit, Florida)

spection. Bundy would have driven up on that sign, seen it, and immediately begun looking for a place to dump Kim. The most natural thing
for him to do would have been to turn right and north toward the entrance to the park. The park looked like a promising area to search. It
lay on the Suwannee River flood plain; it was close to Interstate 10; it
was just to the east of an agricultural inspection station; and it was a
wooded area infested with water-filled sinkholes.

We decided to scout the east side of the river north of US 90. First,
however, we wanted to look at the place where the cigarette butts had
been found. It was to the south of US 90, and it was bone dry. We focused on the north side of US 90. We reconnoitered the same dirt road
searched on horseback two months earlier, and we found a promising
water-filled sinkhole near a dilapidated tin shed. The sinkhole fit our
profile perfectly. We decided to begin the search the next morning at
that sinkhole.

Three pieces of circumstantial evidence led us to the body, and none of them were presented in court. T. B. Houston's evidence wasn't presented because it was overlooked. Doug Barrow's evidence wasn't presented because its scientific foundation was too shaky. The profile of Bundy's western dump sites wasn't presented because it was too inflammatory, and the evidentiary tie between Bundy and the western dump sites was too tenuous.

Up to this point, the task force had taken a somewhat schizophrenic view of the case. We had not focused our criminal investigation on Bundy; we had run down all kinds of leads and refuted all kinds of theories as to what had happened to Kim. As a matter of fact, at the outset of the case, I had been highly skeptical of the theory that Bundy had been involved at all in killing Kim. To me, Bundy's presence on Lake City on the day Kim disappeared was just a coincidence unless and until somebody showed me convincing evidence to the contrary. But the search for Kim had always been bedrocked upon the presumption that Bundy had taken her. What accounts for the different approaches?

Early on I had discussed the question with Jackson, and he told me that the differing approaches were dictated by the very nature of sound investigation. As a good investigator, you examine the evidence and form theories to explain the evidence. You then go out and search for evidence to either confirm or disprove the theories. As the investigation continues, you begin to discard refuted theories and concentrate on those that the evidence supports. Eventually, you have eliminated all theories except the correct one. I didn't know it at the time, but the methodology described by Jackson was almost identical to the scientific method described by the philosopher of science, Karl Popper, in his book *Conjectures and Refutations: The Growth of Scientific Knowledge.*[7] On the question of who killed Kim, we had a number of available theories to test, and we tested them all. On the question of where to find Kim, we had only one rational theory that could give any direction to the search. Rather than thrashing around blindly, we worked on the only rational theory that could give our search direction—the theory that Bundy murdered Kim.

By the time we found Kim's body, the criminal investigation had exhausted all other theories except the theory that Bundy killed her, and I think that theory was strongly supported by the fact that we found Kim by answering the question, "Where would Bundy have put her?" This fact, of course, is another piece of evidence that the jury never heard. Figuring out "whodunit" is a step in the right direction, but knowing "whodunit" isn't enough. The next thing you have to do is figure out "how-prove-it." The investigation had entered another stage, and the task force would have difficulty successfully negotiating that stage.

If you read the previous two paragraphs carefully, you would have noticed that I characterized the Bundy-killed-Kim theory as the only *rational* theory we used to find the body. We did use an irrational theory to direct our search—the theory that a psychic could tell us where to find Kim. When previously discussing the "psychic patrol," I reserved telling about one psychic. I considered omitting the story from this narrative altogether because it is bound to cause confusion and draw attention away from the good police work that led to Kim's discovery. I have decided to tell it for three reasons: (1) A garbled version of the story is already in the public domain, where it has been embraced by the credulous and rejected by the skeptical. (2) If the credulous and the skeptical want to form opinions on the story, they should base their opinions on the actual facts of the story. (3) It is an interesting story that I have enjoyed telling over the years. Most of what I've written so far—and most of what I intend to write—can be substantiated by reference to contemporary news reports, the FDLE file, the court file, or the copy of the trial brief that I saved. Where I give an uncorroborated fact, I try to make it clear that I'm relying on memory. I know of no official record nor any contemporary news account that tells this story.

According to the garbled version of the story, the FBI consulted a psychic by the name of Anne Gehman, who lived in Orlando, and Gehman gave them a number of facts: She said the killer's first name was either Ed or Ted and that his last name sounded like Brady or Bradley, that the killer was driving a van and could be captured by investigating stolen credit cards he had used. She also identified the motel where Bundy was staying and, most important, told the FBI where to find Kim's body. I have compiled this story from the writings of Michael Mello,[8] Christine Wicker,[9] Cyndie Zahner,[10] and Walter F. Rowe.[11] Both Wicker and Rowe base their information on actual interviews of Gehman. Both Rowe and Mello undertake to refute Gehman's claims of psychic power.

My story is a little different. As I recall, the task force hotline got a telephone call one day from an Orlando area police officer. The officer recommended that we contact Gehman, saying she might be able to help us find Kim. He told us Gehman specialized in finding lost articles. She could draw a picture of the location of the lost article if she could touch something associated with it. The officer said that the picture sometimes helped in finding the lost article and sometimes didn't, but whenever the lost article was found, the location always resembled Gehman's picture. After much discussion, we decided we had nothing to lose except time running down false leads.

Captain Love, J.O. Jackson, and one other officer went to Orlando to see Gehman. Gehman told the officers that she knew nothing about the case because she didn't follow the news. Jackson later told me that he saw evidence in her office that led him to believe she subscribed to a news clipping service. After the preliminaries were concluded, Gehman handled whatever it was that they took for her to touch and drew a picture. She may have given them the information about the killer's name, what he was driving, and his use of stolen credit cards. If she did, it made so little impression on me that I can't remember it. All that information was readily available from the newspaper. Mello describes Gehman as doing the same thing in the murder case he handled. She told the authorities she didn't read the paper and then gave them information about the killing that was readily available from newspaper accounts. What wasn't readily available from news accounts was the map of Kim's location.

The original map is probably at the bottom of the Suwannee County landfill, but I vividly remember what it looked like. In the middle of the picture stood two bodies of water connected by a canal. To the south of the two bodies of water lay a highway and a railroad. To the north were horses. To the west were picnic tables and tents. On the east side of the two bodies of water was a burnt area. Between the two bodies of water near the canal Gehman had marked an X. We immediately set an airplane to looking for dumbbell-shaped bodies of water. The aerial search definitively established that the Suwannee Valley area was full of dumbbell-shaped bodies of water. Love went back to Gehman and said she was going to have to do a little better job of pinpointing the location. She passed her hand over a map of North Florida and then pointed to an area in Lafayette County, some 20 or more miles away from where Kim's body lay. After some more futile searching based on her drawing, we discounted her information and went back to our routine of searching along US 90 between Lake City and Tallahassee.

We forgot about her until the day we reconnoitered the Suwannee River State Park. As we drove down the dirt road toward the sinkhole, we found another dirt road branching off to the right. We took it and soon came to a burnt field. We turned around and went back. We saw the huge water-filled sinkhole in the woods to our right. Stopping the car, I got out and walked down the hill toward the sinkhole. Arriving at the bank, I walked around to the west of the sinkhole. As I rounded the sinkhole, I saw a canal going off from the sinkhole and connecting with another water-filled sinkhole. At that time I was less than 10 yards from Kim's body. I turned around, went back to the car to meet with the rest of the reconnaissance team, and reported what I had seen. We discussed Gehman's map. To the south we had US 90 running parallel to a railroad track. To the east we had a burnt field. To the west was the Suwannee River State Park. Although we didn't verify it, we decided that the park would naturally have picnic tables and campsites. I said the only thing missing was the horses to the north. Tompkins called a man's name and said the man lived to the north of the sinkhole and had horses on his farm. Someone suggested that we begin our search the next morning around the sinkhole that looked so much like Gehman's map. Everyone agreed.

The next morning I went out to the scene where the search crew was assembling. I listened to Sergeant Talmadge Pace debrief the searchers and watched him line them up to begin the search. I drove back to my office in Live Oak, leaving instructions to call me if they found anything. Around noon a call came—they had found Kim. Between the two sinkholes. Next to the canal. Almost exactly where Gehman had marked her X.

Assuming that the articles accurately quoted Gehman, was she telling the truth? Walter F. Rowe has already made a case for her story being untrue. Let's analyze his points. The first point he made looks pretty bad for Gehman. He argues: (1) She said she helped the FBI find Kim. (2) The FBI wasn't involved in finding Kim. Therefore (3) she did not help find Kim. The heart and soul of this argument is the *falsus in uno, falsus in omnibus* ("false about one thing, false about everything") fallacy. Gehman is incorrect when she says she helped the FBI, therefore, Gehman is incorrect when she says she helped find Kim. Just because Gehman is wrong about one detail doesn't mean she is automatically wrong about another. Just because she says she helped the FBI doesn't mean she's lying, either. I have interviewed lots of Floridians who confused the FDLE with the FBI. Normally the people who make this mistake are not among the smartest Floridians, but it does happen enough to give Gehman the benefit of the doubt. You would think, however, that a bona fide psychic should know who she was talking to. The second argument: (1) Anne Rule, who believes in ESP, said nothing about Gehman in her book *The Stranger beside Me,* although she did mention our use of the other psychics. (2) Stephen Michaud and Hugh Aynesworth said nothing about Gehman in their book *The Only Living Witness.* (3) If Gehman had helped, Rule, Michaud, and Aynesworth would have written something about it. Therefore (4) Gehman didn't help. The problem with this argument is that before Rule, Michaud, and Aynesworth could write about our use of Gehman, somebody had to tell them about Gehman. I didn't. We were overwhelmed by press coverage already. Telling the Gehman story could have turned a carnival into a three-ring circus. Rowe's final point is: (1) Either Kim was found through good police work or Gehman directed us to her body. (2) Kim was found through excellent police work (the analysis of the dirt in the van, and the finding of the cigarette butts). Therefore (3) Gehman's claim to have directed us to Kim is untrue. Rowe has set up a false dichotomy. It isn't an either/or proposition. We could have used, and did use, both sources of information.

Except for her claim that she never read the paper, I'm willing to say that Gehman could very well be recounting the incident exactly as she remembers it. J. O. Jackson's evidence of her clipping service explains

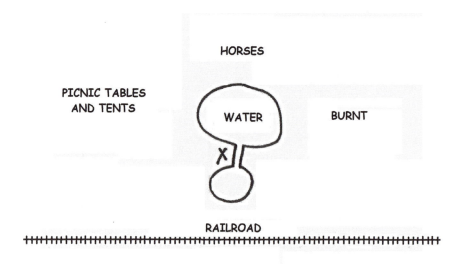

Reproduction of Ann Gehman's Map. (Courtesy of the author)

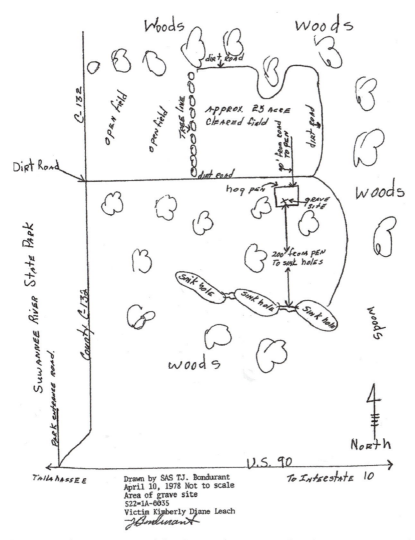

Terry Bondurant's Map of the Scene. (Courtesy Florida Department of Law Enforcement)

how she could have described "Ed Brady's" (or "Ted Bradley's") van and the use of stolen credit cards. Even if she didn't read the paper, the news was so full of those details that she could have picked up that much through the process of osmosis. But how about the map? The diagram on page 66 is my reconstruction of her map; the diagram above reproduces a diagram drawn by Terry Bondurant, one of the

FDLE agents at the scene. Are they close? I'm willing to say they are. How did she do it? One possibility is that she used "cold reading" and inductive reasoning. Psychics who specialize in telling you about your life history do it by the process of "cold reading."[12] They interview you, pick information out of you, and then make educated guesses based on the information you provide. Gehman could have done that with the officers who went to see her. Or she could have done something similar to what Edgar Allen Poe did when he solved the real-life mystery of the murder of Mary Rogers by reading newspaper accounts of the killing and then writing his short story "The Mystery of Marie Roget."[13] I offer one final explanation: as my grandfather used to say, even a blind hog will find an acorn every now and then. Back in the 1970s, a railroad ran parallel to US 90 all the way from Lake City to Tallahassee, so Gehman performed no remarkable feat by drawing in the highway and railroad. Anyone knowledgeable of Bundy knew he hid his bodies in rural areas. Campsites, picnic tables, horses, and burnt fields are common features of rural North Florida. Pick out a place at random in a wooded area along US 90, and you would be bound to find most, if not all, those features nearby.

The pertinent question to me is, did her information help us find Kim? We can answer that question from Gehman's own words. She told Cyndie Zahner, "What I tell the officers is helpful, but it doesn't solve the case. They work 24 hours a day for weeks to locate missing persons."[14] If we had never spoken to Gehman, Doug Barrow would still have sent us to the Suwannee River State Park, and we would have found Kim's body. Gehman's information helped to this extent: When we saw the sinkhole that looked so much like her drawing, we decided to search around that sinkhole first.

# Crime Scene Investigation

The morning after our reconnaissance, I attended the briefing of the search crew at the Suwannee River State Park. After the briefing, I went to the office. We had agreed on a code message to be transmitted if they found the body, "10–42," the police signal for "home." I hadn't been at the office long before Larry Daugherty radioed our office with the message "10-42½." I asked where, and Daugherty told me to come and I would be guided in. Upon arriving at the park entrance, I met a parked FHP cruiser. The trooper standing by the car waved me into the entryway and down Stagecoach Road. At the first dirt road to the right, I saw another FHP cruiser and another trooper, who waved me onto the dirt road. At the fork in the dirt road sat another cruiser and trooper directing me to the left fork. Not far down the left fork, I saw several cruisers and a crowd of troopers milling around in front of a fence adorned with yellow crime scene tape. I got out and asked where the body was. Sergeant Talmadge Pace, who had headed the search team, pointed to a collapsed shed across the fence and a short distance into the woods. I walked over to the shed, looked under the collapsed tin roof, and got my first glimpse of the girl we had been trying to find for the past two months.

I didn't get a good look at her, but I didn't want one. I just wanted to satisfy myself that we had truly found her. Official identification would come from dental records, but there was no doubt in my mind. The search was over, and the criminal investigation could begin in earnest. Most criminal investigations have two stages—in stage one, the "whodunit" stage, you determine who is responsible for the crime; in stage two, the "how-prove-it" stage, you assemble the evidence into a winnable case. This investigation had three stages, with the first being the "where-is-she" stage. We had worked on "whodunit" simultaneously with "where-is-she," but we gave little thought to "how-prove-it." With the discovery of Kim's body, we had solved not only "where-is-she" but "whodunit." From this point forward, we would work to prove Bundy guilty of murder.

In a way, we were lucky not to have found Kim's body immediately. If we had found her sooner, we would have had no strategy for what to do next. During the long, dreary search, we had hammered out such a strategy. Back in those days, when someone found a body in the Third Circuit, the local sheriff's office or police department would dispatch officers to secure the scene and collect the evidence. The quality of the investigation varied widely from one agency to the next. I once prosecuted a murder case where a deputy had worked a scene by (1) using a knife to dig a bullet out of the victim, and (2) taking four blurry photos of the scene. I worked another murder scene where the sheriff's office disassembled the front porch of the defendant's house so that it could be rebuilt in the courtroom for the jury. Nobody would have ever thought to ask the FDLE Crime Lab to send technicians to process the scene. J. O. Jackson suggested it for this case, and everyone agreed we should prearrange for the crime lab to send a crew of technicians when we found the body.

The issue of who would do the autopsy had also arisen, and it presented a thorny question. Our medical examiner was a very good hospital pathologist, but he was not a forensic pathologist. As a hospital pathologist, he refused to look at any evidence outside the examining room. He also had trouble making a call on decomposed bodies. He once told me that absent visible wounds on a decomposed body, he could only x-ray it and check for bullets. We expected that when we found Kim, simply x-raying for bullets would not be good enough. Forensic pathologists look outside the examining room to the crime scene and beyond. We needed a forensic pathologist. My boss, Arthur Lawrence, called Dr. Peter Lipkovic, a well-regarded forensic pathologist who served as the medical examiner in Jacksonville, and asked if he would be willing to perform the autopsy when we found Kim. Lipkovic agreed. That began a 25-year association between Lipkovic and our office that ended only with his retirement.

Lipkovic actually came to the scene to examine the body before it was moved. Jack Duncan headed up the crew from the crime lab, and he was assisted by a tall, thin young lady named Lynn Henson. I had never met Henson before, but I would come to know her quite well before the case was over. If you asked me to pick the one person whose testimony did the most to convict Bundy, I wouldn't hesitate in answering. Lynn Henson.

I stood outside the crime scene tape and watched as the analysts approached the hog pen. First they photographed the pen and the parts of the body visible from the outside the pen. Next they removed the roof and one wall of the shed. They photographed the body, and then Lipkovic began his examination. He found the body resting on its left side with the left thigh and knee drawn close to the chest. The left arm was stretched out straight and resting underneath the left thigh. The only clothing item on the body was the turtleneck. The rest of Kim's clothing lay on the ground immediately next to the body. Lipkovic noted a tan leather-like jacket, denim trousers, panties, and brown shoes. Lipkovic didn't see it, but Kim's jersey was also in the pile of clothing.[1]

When Lipkovic finished, Duncan began his work in earnest. Duncan marked off a 10-foot by 10-foot grid so as to accurately record the evidence he collected. He carefully collected and cataloged every article of clothing in the $10 \times 10$ grid and sifted the soil looking for clues. Scattered on the ground he found most of Kim's teeth, which had detached from her jawbone. These teeth proved crucial to a positive identification.[2]

While the lab crew worked slowly and methodically, a horde of reporters gathered at the gate leading into the scene. Somebody had to go deal with them, so I went out and gave an impromptu news conference. Never before or since have I been the center of such intense media attention. Fame is fleeting, however, and when the hearse came out carrying Kim's body, I lost most of my audience. They scampered to their cars and set off to chase the hearse. I was somewhat intoxicated by our success, and I probably said too much to the media. I told them that searchers had found some tangible evidence (I didn't say what) in the area of the body, and that lab analysis had given us a good investigative lead to go back to that area and search some more. Although I was tight-lipped about what led us to Kim's body, others were happy to misinform the press. One officer told them that dirt and leaves in the back of the FSU van provided the necessary clue. This officer went on to tell the press that "You could see where leaves and debris were caught up under the rear doors of the van, and you could see that something heavy was dragged from the vehicle."[3] The media tried to get me to say that Bundy was responsible for the killing, but I refused to play along. One reporter told me that I had been quoted by a high-ranking official in Tallahassee as saying that Bundy was our prime suspect. I heatedly replied, "Nobody connected with this Task Force said Ted Bundy was a prime suspect."[4] I went on to tell them, "There is too much speculation on Ted Bundy being involved in this case. There are a number of possibilities." I didn't share my opinion that, other than Bundy, alien abduction was the most likely possibility. I asked them to go away and leave us alone. I told them, "The publicity is killing us. I read the paper and sometimes I want to cry. We want to try this case in the courtroom, not the press."[5] One of the reporters who hadn't chased the hearse wandered off and slipped into the woods, trying to sneak up on the crime scene. FHP troopers intercepted him and escorted him back to US 90.[6] We were able to stop incursions into the crime scene on the ground, but soon an airplane was circling overhead taking photographs, which were published in the Suwannee County *Independent Post*.[7]

We didn't prepare for one thing, and it proved costly. We didn't coordinate ahead of time with Sheriff Katsaris to interview Bundy. If we had ironed out those details ahead of time, things would have run more smoothly over the next few hours. As I recall, we were standing on the crime scene waiting for the lab crew to arrive when Jackson said we needed to tell Bundy about our discovery and try to interview him, and we needed to do it quickly, before he got the information from other sources and got himself steeled for an interview. I said it sounded like a good idea to me, and we conferred with Lawrence. He okayed the mission, and Jackson called his supervisor in Tallahassee to make arrangements.

It was about 1:00 P.M. when Jackson's supervisor, Eddie Boone, received the call. Boone detailed Special Agent Ray Frederick to do the interview. Frederick talked to Jackson and Daugherty and got a description of the scene. Jackson instructed Frederick to give Bundy enough information about the scene to convince Bundy that we had really found Kim.

FDLE is a state agency, and state agencies are bureaucracies. Frederick couldn't run right out to the Leon County Jail and conduct the interview. They had to get authorization from up the chain of command. Boone and Frederick told FDLE Director Robert Kilfeather and Deputy Director Jack Dawkins of the request made by Jackson.[8] After discussing the matter thoroughly, they decided to have Frederick and Special Agent Ken Bridges interview Bundy. Boone contacted Katsaris by telephone while Frederick and Bridges traveled to the Leon County Jail. When they got to the jail, they were told to telephone Boone. Boone told Frederick to return to the office. Boone said Katsaris thought it was premature to question Bundy at this stage of the investigation. Katsaris felt unless we had more information as to Bundy's involvement, Bundy would not talk to them.

Katsaris asked Boone to call Lawrence to make sure that was what they wanted to do. By the time that Boone got through to Lawrence it was 5:00 P.M. Lawrence reiterated his request that FDLE interview Bundy as soon as possible. Frederick and Bridges went back to the Leon County Jail, while Boone again telephoned Katsaris requesting permission to interview Bundy. As Frederick and Bridges reached the Leon County Jail, they received a radio call from Boone, advising that Katsaris was making contact with Lawrence, and after talking with Lawrence, Katsaris would speak to Frederick and Bridges.

When Frederick and Bridges entered the Leon County Jail, they met Sergeant Qually Spencer. They told Spencer that they were waiting for a call from Katsaris to approve an interview with Bundy. Spencer pointed to a man making a call on the pay telephone in the waiting room. Spencer told them the man was Joe Aloi, an investigator for the public defender's office, who had requested to see Bundy. Aloi went up to Bundy's cell and remained there for approximately 45 minutes while Frederick and Bridges waited for Katsaris's call.

At 6:15 P.M., Frederick asked Spencer to call Katsaris to determine if he was going to approve the interview of Bundy. Spencer called Katsaris and put Frederick on the phone to talk to him. Katsaris said he had not been able to reach Lawrence to advise him of his concerns about trying to interview Bundy. Fredrick told Katsaris that Aloi was with Bundy as they spoke and he felt sure Aloi was telling Bundy about the finding of Kim Leach. He told Katsaris that he and Bridges had heard radio reports about the discovery. Katsaris gave Frederick permission to interview Bundy.

Finally, at 7:00 P.M., Frederick and Bridges got to interview Bundy in a conference room. They identified themselves to Bundy and advised him they wanted to talk to him reference Kimberly Diane Leach. Bundy appeared nervous. Frederick read Bundy his rights from an FDLE rights form. After reading the rights to Bundy, Frederick asked if he understood his rights and Bundy said yes. Frederick then dated the rights form and asked Bundy to sign the form only as to understanding his rights. Bundy signed the rights form but refused to waive his rights. Frederick then advised Bundy that Kim had been found at approximately noon that day. Frederick gave Bundy a brief description of the scene. Bundy listened carefully but did not ask any questions. Frederick asked Bundy if he had anything to say. Bundy said he would not discuss the investigation without the advice of his court-appointed attorney. Frederick and Bridges then made small talk with Bundy for approximately 15 minutes. Bundy asked Frederick and Bridges about FDLE and their jurisdiction and the FDLE Crime Laboratory, and the officers answered his questions. Before leaving, Frederick and Bridges asked Bundy if he wanted to say anything about the Leach girl. Bundy again stated he had nothing to say, that he had an attorney who was handling his case. Frederick asked Bundy if Aloi had informed him of the finding of the Leach girl. Bundy smiled and stated he and Aloi were discussing his case. Frederick and Bridges concluded the interview at 7:30 P.M.

When Spencer went to get Bundy for the interview with the FDLE agents, he noticed that Bundy was extremely nervous. After taking Bundy to the interview room and leaving him with Frederick and Bridges, Spencer searched Bundy's cell. He discovered nothing useful but did see that Bundy had burned papers and disposed of them in the toilet.[9]

The next morning, Daugherty and I drove over to Jacksonville to attend the autopsy. I had never met Lipkovic before, but I was well aware of his sterling reputation. After meeting with Lipkovic and exchanging pleasantries, we followed him into the examining room where Kim rested on a table. In the examining room I met Richard Stephens, a forensic serologist from the Tallahassee Crime Lab, who was present to take charge of any evidence found. On first sight, we had a partially mummified, partially decomposed body with the eyes, ears, nose, and mouth clean and intact. The decomposed parts of the body were those that had touched the ground, while the upper parts of the body were mummified. Two parts of the body that had not touched the ground were missing—the neck and the groin. Extensive evidence of maggot activity covered the body. Lipkovic completely disassembled the skeleton, thoroughly examined the interior of the chest cavity, and identified numerous desiccated organs. The only internal organs that he could not find were the uterus, ovaries, vagina, and trachea. It was fascinating watching him work, but from what I saw, I couldn't fathom what might have killed Kim.

After he finished, Lipkovic took us into his office and explained his findings. He said that Kim died of homicidal violence to the neck area, but due to the missing tissues, he could not say exactly what type of violence. There had also been violence of some type to the vaginal area. He could say one more thing about the violence to the neck and groin—it was accompanied by copious bleeding. Lipkovic explained how he came to such a conclusion. He said that insects usually attack dead bodies through the path of least resistance, normally the eyes, ears, mouth, nose, and anus. If, however, there is an open, bloody wound, the insects will find that place a more attractive gateway and will ignore the normal routes. Since Kim's neck was missing but her eyes, nose, ears, and mouth were intact, she must have suffered an injury to her neck that provided a better entryway for the insects. I was underwhelmed by his reasoning and debated with him about the cause of death. Lipkovic was adamant that the manner of death was homicidal, although he would admit that he might be "sticking his neck out" on the diagnosis of homicidal violence to the neck. Medical examiners often have a somewhat warped sense of humor. I don't remember Lipkovic ever saying anything to me about the possibility that Kim had been strangled, but the media reported him as saying that strangulation was possible. He went on to tell the paper, "There is no way of establishing now or in the future what type of instrument was used," but he did say that whatever it was, it tore the flesh of her neck.[10] I theorized it was the gigantic hunting knife John Farhat had sold Bundy the day before Kim's death.

Several years later, I confronted another mummified body with a missing neck. We took that body to the C. A. Pound Human Identification Laboratory at the University of Florida, where it was examined by Dr. William Maples, a distinguished forensic anthropologist. Maples diagnosed the cause of death as homicidal violence to the neck area, just as Lipkovic had with Kim, and gave the same reasons Lipkovic had given with Kim. Maples was at the University of Florida back in 1978. Had we consulted with him, he could have given Lipkovic some valuable backup.

We anticipated a vigorous attack on Lipkovic's opinion as to cause of death, and we were a little uneasy about how to word the indictment. The customary wording would have read something like this: ". . . did kill and murder the said Kimberly Diane Leach by cutting or stabbing her with a knife or other sharp instrument. . . ." We did some legal research and found an old case that allowed an indictment to plead that the grand jury didn't know how the murder occurred,[11] and we drafted our indictment accordingly.

Lipkovic did not immediately give an opinion as to time of death. It would take some analysis of the evidence of maggot activity to tell how long she had been dead. Maggots go through several stages in their growth from egg to fly, and each of these stages leaves evidence. Maggot activity ceases below a certain temperature and resumes when the weather warms. By determining how many stages had been completed and factoring in how many days were too cold for maggot activity, Lipkovic could estimate time of death.[12] After a thorough study, he placed the time of death right around the date of Kim's kidnapping, give or take a week.

As I recall, two other significant items of evidence were taken from the autopsy. Stephens got some tissue samples to try to determine blood type, and he also took the turtleneck sweater. We were well on our way to putting a case together.

The funeral was held on April 13, and the school board authorized students to miss class in order to attend.[13] The media estimated that 600 to 700[14] people attended the funeral, including 40 to 45[15] highway patrolmen. Active pallbearers were drawn one each from the Florida Highway Patrol, Columbia County Sheriff's Office, Lake City Police Department, and Public Service Commission.[16] All law enforcement officers who attended were honorary pallbearers.

I felt duty bound to attend the funeral, but I was not particularly happy about it. I sat in Parkview Baptist Church that morning with a scowl on my face. Over the past three years or so I had attended a number of funerals for homicide victims. Almost invariably the preachers had chosen Romans 8:28 as their focal scripture—"And we know that all things work together for good to them that love God, to them who are the called according to his purpose." I wasn't in the mood to have a preacher tell me that the brutal, senseless killing of an innocent young girl was a good thing. I was going to be especially angry if the preacher told us about how the man who did this horrible deed could find forgiveness and eternal life. I tensed and leaned forward when the preacher stepped to the pulpit and opened his Bible. He read from Matthew 18:6, "But whoso shall offend one of these little ones which believe in me, it were better for him that a millstone were hanged about his neck, and that he were drowned in the depth of the sea." I immediately relaxed and sat back in my seat. This verse was much more to my liking than the one I expected. None of the local papers that wrote on the funeral included references to Matthew 18:6, but I tucked it away in my memory bank; and over the next two years I would periodically bring it out, look it over, and draw comfort from it, secure in the knowledge that I was going to be one of the men helping to tie the millstone tight around Bundy's neck. I might even get the chance to shove him off the end of the dock.

# 8

# Building a Case

---

Most state-level prosecutions are reactive affairs, with the prosecutor coming into the picture after the arrest. The police perform their investigation, put their case together, and then present the prosecutor with a suspect in custody and a case that is nowhere near ready to go to trial. An arrest triggers the running of numerous time limits: In Florida the accused must have a first appearance within 24 hours;[1] a probable cause determination within 48 hours;[2] the formal charge must be filed within 21 days;[3] and the defendant must be tried within 175 days.[4] The current speedy trial rule has a "recapture" provision for trial within 15 days if the 175-day time limit is exceeded,[5] but back in 1978 there was no recapture provision. Although the speedy trial time was a little longer (180 days), if the defendant wasn't brought to trial within that time period, he was entitled to immediate discharge. When the prosecutor gets the arrest report, the clock has begun ticking on these time limits, and the prosecutor must scramble to decide upon a charge, finish the investigation, and put the evidence together so as to have a reasonable prospect of getting a conviction. The Bundy case presented a rare opportunity—the opportunity to get the case ready before the arrest. Bundy sat in the Leon County Jail facing scores of felony charges, and he wasn't going anywhere. I wanted to take full advantage of our opportunity to take a leisurely approach to completing the investigation, marshaling the evidence, and preparing the case for trial. I told the press it would be six weeks to two months before we would be ready to proceed with a prosecution.[6] It actually took more than three months, and the delay was time well spent.

With the discovery of Kim's body, the task force was dead in fact if not in name. The highway patrol disbanded its search teams and reassigned the troopers it had detailed to assist with the investigation. The Columbia County Sheriff's Office ceased its participation. Only the Lake City Police Department continued to devote manpower to the investigation, and that manpower was reduced to one man, Larry Daugherty. Even at the state attorney's office, we sent our investigators back to their usual duties and left one man—me—on the case. The FDLE stepped into the breach and assigned a team of officers to work under J. O. Jackson's supervision. We had our first meeting at the courthouse in Live Oak, Florida. As I recall, Special Agents Dalton Bray, James Wolf, Joe Uebehler, Ray Frederick, Ken Bridges, and Jim Skipper attended the meeting. Jackson briefed them on the status of the investigation and assigned each of them to a different aspect of the case. Their first mission was to collect and review all currently available material, reinterview all known witnesses, and to pursue investigative leads suggested by the available information.

One of the first things FDLE did was to interrogate an alcoholic convicted felon. On April 11, an anonymous call came in to the Jacksonville office of the FDLE. The caller tearfully reported that a man named "Slim" had murdered Kim Leach. The caller warned that Slim was armed and dangerous. The report had surface plausibility because Slim was a convicted murderer. A team of special agents went to Slim's rented room. Special Agent Bobby Kinsey, one of the best homicide investigators I ever worked with, led the team. They found the "armed and dangerous" convicted murderer unarmed and dead drunk. Kinsey asked Slim to account for his whereabouts during February of 1978. Slim said he was drunk most of the time and had trouble remembering where he was at any time, but he was pretty sure he hadn't gone to Lake City in February. He told Kinsey they could check his time records with his employer. Slim said the only thing he knew about Kim Leach was what he had seen on TV. During the interview Kinsey learned that an anonymous caller had given the Jacksonville Sheriff's Office an almost identical report on Slim, except the caller said that the "armed and dangerous" ex-con was involved in an auto theft ring.[7] They never determined who hated Slim so badly as to try to get him arrested for crimes he had not committed.

Robert Carl Hohenberger presented a more viable suspect. Hohenberger was released from San Quentin Prison in August 1977 and went to live in Louisiana. While in Louisiana he abducted and killed at least three girls. The victims had been abducted on March 2, April 27, and May 11, 1978—all Thursdays. It was believed that Hohenberger's parents lived in the Lake City area, and that he had visited them during the first part of 1978.[8] When Hohenberger became a suspect in the three Louisiana murders, he fled to Tacoma, Washington, where he shot himself to death rather than submit to arrest.[9] Hohenberger seemed ready made for the part of Kim's murderer—he killed young teenage girls whom he abducted on Thursdays, and Kim was a 12-year-old girl abducted on a Thursday. We could have announced that the murder was solved, shut down our investigation, and gone on to other cases. The only problem was that Hohenberger had an ironclad alibi for February 8, 1978. Daugherty worked with Uebehler, Bray, and Captain James Manning of the Morgan City, Louisiana, Police Department to establish by work records that Hohenberger was at his job in Louisiana on Thursday, February 8, when Kim was abducted.[10]

While we tooled up to begin a thorough reinvestigation of the entire case, Bundy was amusing himself by acting as his own lawyer on the Tallahassee charges. He represented himself at a preliminary hearing in which 8 of the 10 witnesses failed to identify him. At the end of the hearing Bundy asked Judge John Rudd for permission to go to the law library three times a week in order to prepare his cases for trial. Rudd didn't immediately rule on the request.[11] Perhaps he recalled Bundy's use of the law library in Colorado.[12]

With the discovery of Kim's body, a floodgate of leaks opened. Someone told the press that we had found a bloodstained man's coat near the body.[13] If we did, I never heard about it. While I was telling the press that "nobody connected with this Task Force has said Bundy was a prime suspect," someone was telling them that Bundy would be questioned about the finding of the body. While I was refusing to identify the body as being Kim, someone else was telling them that the clothing found at the scene matched Kim's clothing perfectly. I said merely that we had been led to the scene by "clues put together by crime lab technicians," while others were saying that the dirt and leaves found in the FSU van led us to Kim.[14] Lipkovic held a press conference in which he revealed almost every important detail of his autopsy. It was exasperating, infuriating, and unacceptable. I determined to do something about it. Jackson and I decided to clamp as tight a lid as humanly possible on the flow of information. Because some leaks had come from Tallahassee as well as from the ranks of the task force participants, we decided that the only people who needed to know anything were Jackson and the other FDLE agents working on the case. This meant cutting off all local law enforcement agencies and all Tallahassee agencies. Almost everyone wanted to know what we had found at the crime scene, and I steadfastly refused to share that evidence with anyone. I believed that both the Tallahassee and the Lake City investigations had progressed to the point that they were no longer law enforcement investigations aimed at making an arrest but were now prosecutorial investigations aimed at making a case. I told the Tallahassee authorities that I had arranged for a meeting with Howard Holtzendorf, the assistant state attorney assigned to prosecute Bundy in Tallahassee, and that I would give him all relevant information concerning what was found at the Suwannee River State Park. I told them we had nothing that would help with the Chi Omega investigation. They countered that I didn't know the extent of their investigation, and only they could judge whether the information was relevant. They were certainly right that I knew next to nothing about the Chi Omega investigation, but that situation was about to change.

Our series of reinterviews began on April 11 when Frederick and Bridges began to investigate the theft of the Media Center van.[15] Jackson collected copies of a number of handwritten motions filed by Bundy for use in handwriting comparison to the forged credit card receipts.[16] Lab analyst John McCarthy determined they were useless for comparison purposes because they were written in print rather than cursive, but I learned quite a lot from them. Bundy had written the best "jailhouse lawyer" pleadings I had ever read. His "Motion for Aids Necessary to Prepare an Adequate Defense"[17] was legible, articulate, well organized, and supported by legal authority. He was no dummy.

Bray investigated Bundy's credit card frauds.[18] Uebehler investigated Bundy's auto thefts[19] and also Kim's disappearance from the junior high.[20] Wolf had the task of investigating Bundy's attempt to kidnap Leslie Parmenter.[21] One of the reinvestigation's first accomplishments was to clear Bundy of a kidnapping that had occurred in Orange Park, Florida, on February 13, 1978. Robert Alred of the Clay County Sheriff's Office contacted FDLE to get a photograph of Bundy for a photographic lineup to be used in connection with their investigation,[22] but FDLE told Alred that Bundy was hundreds of miles away at the Holiday Inn in Crestview, Florida, on the date of the kidnapping in Orange Park.[23]

On April 18, 1978, Jackson and I went to the Leon County State Attorney's Office for a meeting with Howard Holtzendorf, Captain Jack

Poitinger of the Leon County Sheriff's Office, and Captain C. S. Hooker of the FSU Police Department. There was somewhat of a chill in the air as the meeting began, but the frost thawed as we discussed the case, compared notes, and strategized the future course of the investigations. The two cases were linked like conjoined twins who shared vital organs. Each case had a life of its own, but a fatal blow struck to one case might very well kill the other. We decided to strive to schedule our grand juries to return indictments simultaneously. Bundy would be arraigned and tried on the Chi Omega case first, and we would follow with the Leach prosecution. With this agreement in place, the icy relationship thawed, the flow of shared information increased, and we worked diligently together to make both cases. It was obvious that the success of the Lake City case depended entirely upon the success of the Tallahassee case. A lot of evidence was vitally important to both cases. If that evidence got suppressed in the Tallahassee case, it would be lost to us in the Lake City case. As a result of this, I spent a lot of time in Tallahassee conferring with the Tallahassee prosecutors and sitting on the front row of the courtroom behind the prosecution table. As I brought myself up to speed on all aspects of the Bundy case, I learned that the investigators had achieved some inspired feats of investigation, but they had also made some serious mistakes. One inspired feat of investigation centered around the price tag found on the floorboard of the Media Center van. The tag bore the markings "Green Acres" and a price of $26.00.[24] On February 24, Sergeant Ted Rivenbark of the FSU Police Department undertook to find the origin of the price tag. He contacted the secretary of state and got the addresses of every store in Florida that incorporated Green Acres into its name. Taking the 50 names on the list, Rivenbark began to call every store attempting to find a Green Acres store that used that type of price tag. Eventually he called Green Acres Sporting Goods in Jacksonville, Florida. John Farhat told Rivenbark that he indeed used such price tags and that he had recently sold a Buck General hunting knife priced at $26.00, which he had marked up from $24.00. Farhat's description of the purchaser fitted Bundy.[25] Rivenbark did not stop, however, until he had verified that no other Green Acres store in Florida used the red price tags.

The task force duplicated Rivenbark's efforts. Trooper Leroy Tompkins called directory assistance in Jacksonville and asked for the telephone number of any Green Acres stores in Jacksonville. He got three names, Green Acres Nursery, Green Acres Poultry, and Green Acres Sporting Goods. Tompkins called the three businesses and determined that the store he wanted was Green Acres Sporting Goods. Tompkins and Al Williams immediately drove to Green Acres and took a taped statement from Farhat. They also collected blank samples of Farhat's price tags and the "Meto" marking machine Farhat had used to make the price tag for the hunting knife.[26] The next day Sergeant Jim Sewell of the FSU Police Department was at Green Acres Sporting Goods interviewing Farhat, who was unable to pick Bundy's photograph out of a photospread.[27]

The price tag from the van, the "Meto" marking machine, and the blank price tags all went to the FDLE Crime Lab, where John McCarthy examined them. First he examined the price tag from the van and determined it was actually two tags, with the $26.00 price tag stuck over another tag. Carefully separating the two tags, McCarthy determined that the lower tag read $2?.00—the units number was completely illegible. Despite this problem, everything about the tag corresponded to the tag on Farhat's Buck General hunting knife. McCarthy then used the "Meto" marker to mark a number of the blank tags and compared the tags known to come from Farhat's marker with the tag from the van.

In making such a comparison, an analyst can give one of three opinions: (1) The questioned item definitely did not come from the known source. (2) The questioned item definitely did come from the known source; or (3) The questioned item may have come from the known source. McCarthy gave opinion 3. Specifically, he wrote that "it cannot be demonstrated that the labels found in the van were prepared with the 'Meto' labeling device to the exclusion of all other similar devices which may exist."[28] McCarthy gave us a definite maybe.

When Thomas Wood, the Tallahassee medical examiner, performed the autopsies on the Chi Omega victims, he noted a bite mark on one of the victim's buttocks. Forensic odontology was in its infancy at the time, but the significance of the bite mark did not escape Wood. He cut the bite mark from the body and attempted to preserve it for possible comparison with any suspect who might later emerge. Unfortunately, the bite mark shrank and shriveled, rendering it useless for comparison purposes. Fortunately, Wood had the bite mark thoroughly photographed before he excised it. Unfortunately, when the photographs were developed and examined, he had no photographs that had been taken with a ruler. It was imperative to have a ruler in the photograph so that it could be blown up to life size for comparison with the life-sized impression that would be taken from any suspect's teeth. It might have been a good time to simply throw up your hands and say, "Well, we're stymied. We can't use that evidence." Fortunately, at least one prosecutor working on the case would not take no for an answer. Oftentimes in big cases, essential evidence falls through the cracks, much as the testimony of T. B. Houston did in the Leach case. Prosecutors who are aware of this phenomenon will diligently search for such evidence. Sometimes these diligent searches are fruitless, but sometimes they are spectacularly successful. This particular prosecutor visited every police agency working on the case, examined every article of tangible evidence, questioned every investigator working on the case, and hit pay dirt. Howard Winkler, one of the investigators who had attended the autopsy, had placed a small six-inch ruler next to the bite mark and snapped one photograph. The prosecutor found that photograph and saved the bite mark evidence.[29] We will meet that diligent prosecutor in the next chapter.

When I became aware of the minor fiasco with the photographs, the Tallahassee authorities were in the process of trying to decide how to obtain a plaster impression of Bundy's teeth for comparison. There were two ways in which they could obtain court authorization for collecting samples from the person of a defendant. The old-fashioned way was to apply for a search warrant. A more modern way was to file a motion for discovery pursuant to Florida's relatively new rules of criminal procedure. Which was the better way? If they filed a motion for discovery, they would have to serve a copy of the motion on the defense, set the matter for hearing, and argue the sufficiency of the motion before a judge. The defense would have an opportunity to be heard and might talk the judge into denying the motion. This had already happened with a motion for discovery filed in the forgery case against Bundy. Judge Rudd had found the motion to be legally insufficient and had denied it.[30] That minor setback had been remedied by simply filing an amended motion for discovery setting out more details about the grounds for the motion, but such a setback in a motion for dental impressions could be fatal. They might be able to go back and reformulate the motion so as to state grounds that the judge would approve, but Bundy would have been tipped off and would have an opportunity to break enough of his teeth to render the dental impressions useless. Even if the first motion were granted, the lag time between serving the motion on the defense and the actual hearing would give Bundy enough time to mutilate the evidence. A search warrant could be applied for without notifying the defense and could be served on Bundy without giving any prior notice. Confronted with such a surprise, Bundy could not mutilate his teeth before the impressions were taken. They decided to go with a search warrant. Working with Dr. Richard L. Souviron, one of the foremost forensic odontologists in the nation, they obtained the dental impressions and matched Bundy's teeth to the bite mark in the photograph. Some might say that they were lucky, but I believe it was Thomas Jefferson who said that the harder you work, the luckier you get.

One thing that always irritated me as a prosecutor was defense attorneys who told juries that their clients were at a disadvantage because the state had "vast resources" to make a case. I never worked for any part of the state that had vast resources. We were constantly pinching pennies and compromising on quality in order to stretch scarce tax dollars as far as possible. Sometimes our frugality wound up costing us a small fortune cleaning up a mess that would never have been made if we hadn't been trying to cut corners and stretch dollars. We had a situation like that in the Bundy case. When they were interviewing Bundy in Pensacola, they used a variable speed reel-to-reel tape recorder. The faster the speed, the better the sound quality, but the more tape you had to use. The slower the speed, the poorer the quality, but you used less tape. In order to save money on tape, they recorded the interviews on the slowest speed. The tapes turned out to be near unintelligible. They looked for, and found, an expert in Gainesville who would be able to enhance the tapes by removing the static, but it was going to cost dearly. They bit the bullet and hired the expert. They received back a pile of cassette tapes containing the enhanced interviews, and I got a set of copies. The copies were near unintelligible. I told myself, "If these are the enhanced tapes, I'd hate to have to listen to the originals." I diligently searched the tapes looking for the places where Bundy made the damning admissions that Norm Chapman had reported to us. I could never find them. Nor could Chapman. He offered two explanations: Maybe they were covered up in static on the copies we had, or maybe the admissions were made at one of the frequent times that they had the tape recorder turned off. Whatever the reason, I wrote the interviews off as a bad deal. How could we possibly go to court and ask a jury to believe that Bundy said everything Chapman reported when we couldn't point to the place on the hours of tape recordings where the statements were made? We did some more finagling with the tapes, but I will save that story for the account of the Chi Omega trial.

It wasn't until the middle of the Leach trial that I discovered one mistake that had been made. When we started interviewing people who may have seen Bundy in the Media Center van, we showed them a photographic lineup of white vans. They were all different makes and models, but one of them was the same make and model as the Media Center van. The only trouble was, it was not the Media Center van. Instead of going to the FDLE impound and photographing the actual van, they simply found another van of the same make and model and photographed it. No big deal, right? A white van is a white van, isn't it? This one slip almost torpedoed the Leach case, but I will save that story for the account of the Leach trial.

While we were methodically trying to build a case, certain elements in the news media were methodically tearing it down. For example, shortly before we discovered Kim's body, the *Florida Times Union* ran a story that asked, "How did Bundy become a mass-murder suspect?" The story's answer was that the police made up their minds Bundy was guilty and then "psyched themselves into believing that all the evidence pointed to him."[31] The story quoted Bundy's Utah defense attorney, John O'Connell, as saying that the police had created a mythical framework of unsolved homicides and then put Bundy in the middle of that framework. This, of course, was exactly what we had not done. Certain members of the task force may have zeroed in on Bundy, but we explored all possibilities and ran down every available lead. The reporters had somehow gotten a copy of a confidential psychological analysis done on Bundy when he was in prison in Utah. The story characterized Bundy as being normal, supporting that assessment with quotes from the report of Utah State Prison psychiatrist Vann Austin: "I do not feel that Mr. Bundy is psychotic. There is no evidence of a major mood, behavior, or thinking disorder at this time. . . . There is no evidence of impairment of any of his intellectual functions, impairment of his ability to use good judgment or impairment of his ability to show appropriate affect." Although the psychiatric report did not give Bundy a squeaky-clean bill of health, it certainly didn't paint him as a maniacal sex killer. One prosecutor spoke out against this coverage, and it wasn't Howard Holtzendorf or me. It was David Yocom, the Utah prosecutor who had convicted Bundy in the DaRonch case. Yocom opined that Bundy may have killed as many as 16 or 17 women, and he played armchair psychologist by giving his theory for why Bundy killed all those people. According to Yocom, each of

Bundy's victims stood in as a proxy for a woman who had jilted him years ago. Yocom said the woman had long brown hair parted in the middle.[32] Long hair parted in the middle was indeed a component of Bundy's preferred victim profile, and we made use of that victim profile in our prosecution of Bundy.

As both Lake City and Tallahassee worked diligently to put cases together, Howard Holtzendorf continued to bury Bundy under an ever-increasing mountain of theft and fraud charges. By April 6, the charges totaled 46,[33] and by April 7 they had ballooned to 66.[34] One of the auto theft charges involved the FSU van, and Holtzendorf got a discovery order authorizing the taking of samples of Bundy's hair and blood for comparison to the bloodstain found on the carpet in the rear of the van and to human hairs found in the van. As it turned out, Bundy's blood would do nothing to further the charge of stealing the van, but it would prove vitally helpful in making our case for the murder of Kim Leach.

Not long after the discovery of Kim's body, Jimmy Lee Smith was arrested in Marianna, Florida, and charged with two counts of murder. After his arrest, he confessed to killing a teenager and 20 others. Naturally the press wanted to know if we were going to look at him as a possibility. I told them, "We are checking out this individual to determine whether he may be connected to the disappearance and death of Kimberly Leach. We are doing this because we feel it should be done. At this point, we don't feel there will be any connection, but I may be wrong."[35] I wasn't.

By the end of May, my boss made an announcement to the press. Mr. Lawrence said, "It looks reasonably promising, although not certain, that toward the end of next month [June], I will probably petition the court to organize a new grand jury." He went on to say that "the new grand jury will probably meet the first week in July."[36]

By mid-June I was talking to the newspaper. I told the *Lake City Reporter* that we were "seeing a pattern emerging which is consistent with our theory of the case." I went on to say, "We have not turned up any credible evidence which would refute the theory of the case we are working on." I told the *Reporter* that we had uncovered "some new developments." I went on to say, "The new developments are not of an earth shattering nature, but they appear to be consistent and dictate that we move with deliberate caution in the further conduct of this investigation." When asked how much longer it would be, I said, "As things develop, it looks like it might take a little longer than we hoped. . . . Given the magnitude of this case and given the circumstances, we feel that to move before all the evidence is marshaled would be ill-advised." I estimated that we had collected some 250–300 pieces of tangible evidence and conducted some 1,000 interviews.[37] I was quite proud of myself. I felt I had talked extensively, told the absolute truth, and revealed nothing.

In mid-June we began to receive investigative summaries from all the agents who had reinvestigated the case. Each investigative summary spoke to a different aspect of the case, and each set forth the evidence and witnesses necessary to prove that aspect of the case. The documents were excellent examples of thorough police work. Each summary consisted of a narrative account of the crime and the investigation, a schedule of tangible evidence, and a list of prospective witnesses with synopses of their potential testimony. Robert Miley turned in the first investigative summary, which detailed Bundy's activities in the Jacksonville area;[38] Dalton Bray summarized the events surrounding Kim's disappearance from the junior high;[39] William Davis and Joel Norred reported on Bundy's credit card forgeries in Lake City;[40] and Jim Skipper, who would later make one of the most important discoveries of the investigation, wrote up the summary on Bundy's activities stealing cars and license plates.[41] It was an impressive body of work, but it wasn't enough. I wasn't discouraged, though.

We had known all along that the heart and soul of our case would be the work of the analysts at the FDLE Crime Laboratory. In the weeks and months following the discovery of Kim's body, I made several trips to Tallahassee to confer with the analysts working on the various parts of the case. John McCarthy would play a key role in the case if only we could get a handwriting sample from Bundy. The Tallahassee State Attorney's Office had an order for handwriting samples from Bundy, but he refused to give them.[42] Contrary to what I mistakenly told the newspaper about finding no human hair in the Media Center van, we did have some human hair from the carpet in the back of the van. Pat Lasko, the lab analyst who examined hair, could find neither Bundy's nor Kim's hair in the hair collected from the van,[43] nor could she find Bundy's hair on any of Kim's clothing.[44] Lasko eventually testified for the defense. We had high hopes for some sort of fingerprint evidence, but Doug Barrow couldn't find Bundy's fingerprints anywhere.[45]

Barrow's failure to find Bundy's fingerprints caused us to undertake another extreme investigative measure. The FBI Crime Lab in Washington had just started using laser technology to raise latent prints on surfaces where they had never been found before. Why didn't we ask the FBI lab to use its laser on the van? We made a quick call to the FBI and found out that the laser equipment was immobile. You had to bring the items to the laser; you couldn't take the laser to the items. To compound the problem, the laser was not on the first floor of the building. I can't recall whether it was on the third or fifth floor, but I can recall that the elevator wasn't large enough to accommodate a van. What to do? Take the van apart and send the pieces to the FBI. I met with Lynn Henson at the impound lot where the van was being held and stood by watching as she examined the interior of the van. She looked for likely places where fingerprints might collect and removed every place. Because the van had previously been given a control number of 35, Henson numbered the exhibits taken from the van as 35A through 35GG, more than 30 pieces in all. Some of the pieces could be unscrewed or unbolted; others had to be cut out with an acetylene torch. Henson bagged the pieces, and Barrow drove them to the FBI Crime Lab. It was a complete bust. Not only did the laser fail to find Bundy's prints, it couldn't find any identifiable prints at all.[46]

Richard Stephens gave us a glimmer of hope with his findings. Insofar as possible, he matched Kim's blood with the bloodstain on the van carpet.[47] He found blood and semen on Kim's panties. The bloodstain was too small to get any results, but he matched Bundy's blood type to the semen. This really didn't help much, because Bundy had Type O blood, the most common type. I spent several nights lying in bed, staring at the ceiling, and fretting over the inconclusiveness of this finding. Then one day I had a brainstorm. I met with Stephens at the crime lab, and as best I can recall, we had the following conversation.

"I have an idea. Everybody's got DNA, right?" Stephens had to agree. "Everybody's DNA is different, isn't it?" Stephens said that wasn't exactly true. Identical twins had identical DNA. Undeterred, I said, "Well, all we've got to do is to take a DNA molecule from Bundy's blood sample and a DNA molecule from the semen, set them side by side, and see if they match." Stephens laughed and patiently explained to me that the DNA molecule was too long and complex, the technology did not exist to examine it in detail, and it was impossible to do what I was asking.

More than a decade later I was sitting in Sonny's Barbecue at the intersection of I-75 and US 90 in Lake City having lunch and staring at a man at another table who looked a lot like Stephens. He was staring back. Finally he asked, "Bob, is that you?" I admitted it and said, "Dick, is that you?" He said yes. I learned he was traveling south on vacation, and we had a cordial discussion about the weather and other trivialities. Then Stephens said, "Do you remember the question you asked me years ago on the Bundy case?" I told him I didn't think I'd ever forget it. "Well," he said, "we can do it now."

The most encouraging reports came from Henson, the analyst who was doing shoe track and fiber analysis. She found three shoe tracks in the dirt thrown onto the van carpet and one shoe track on the rear bumper of the van. She was able to match the shoe track on the bumper with a pair of Bass shoes taken from Bundy's Volkswagen in Pensacola. She also matched two shoe tracks from the carpet with a pair of Adidas tennis shoes taken from the Volkswagen. Unfortunately, she could not positively match the tracks to the shoes. She would only say that the shoes could have made the tracks.[48]

The fiber examination was even better than the shoe tracks analysis. The van carpet had been swept for foreign fibers, as had Kim's clothing. Henson began to find all sorts of fibers on various articles of Kim's clothing that matched the van carpet. She could not say conclusively that the van carpet had come in contact with Kim's clothing, but the sheer number of matches was convincing. She found blue fibers on the van carpet that matched Kim's jersey and white fibers matching Kim's socks. She also found a loop of blue thread on the carpet. This loop of thread had an unusual number of strands—the same number of strands as in the thread of Kim's jersey. Bundy had a torn burgundy shirt with multicolored threads among his possessions when he was arrested. Henson found fibers matching that shirt on Kim's purse and one of her socks.[49] Microanalysis of fibers is a slow process of matching the size, shape, color, and chemical composition of miniscule scraps of fiber, and Henson had myriads of unknown fibers from the van carpet and Kim's clothing. She released her first interim report on July 19, 1978, and her final report on June 14, 1979.[50] I was satisfied that we were going to be able to put Kim in the FSU van. Tying Bundy to the van would be more problematical, but it looked as though it was time to go to a grand jury.

# 9

# The Grand Jury

We did not want to take the Bundy case to a grand jury until we were satisfied we had sufficient evidence to obtain and sustain a conviction. Of course, we could never amass a sufficient quantum of evidence to guarantee a conviction—no case, no matter how strong it looks, is ever a lead pipe cinch. I had seen too many juries acquit too many obviously guilty defendants to be under any illusions about building an open-and-shut case against Bundy. We would, however, build as strong a case as possible before we went to the grand jury. The grand jury could be more than just a charging vehicle; we could use it as a tool to continue to build the case. The burden of proof before the grand jury is probable cause, not reasonable doubt, and probable cause is a very light burden. Because of this most prosecutors don't put on a full-blown case before a grand jury; just a skeleton case will do. I, however, wanted to use the grand jury proceeding as a dress rehearsal for the trial. I wanted to put all our evidence before the grand jury and see how it played out. We could gain valuable insight into how the witnesses would perform at trial and how a petit jury would react to the evidence. State Attorney Arthur Lawrence agreed. Our presentation before the grand jury would be as close to a trial presentation as possible.

We had a new prosecutor in Tallahassee. Howard Holtzendorf had taken a job with another state attorney, and Larry Simpson, the prosecutor who saved the bite-mark evidence, inherited the case. I wasn't really happy about the change. Holtzendorf was a good prosecutor, and he was very easy to work with. Simpson was an unknown quantity. Relations were a little stiff to begin with, but I soon came to realize that Simpson was not just a good prosecutor, he was an excellent prosecutor. The best thing about Simpson was that he readily accepted me as an ex officio member of the Chi Omega prosecution team.

I don't remember exactly why it happened, but for some reason we were not able to coordinate the grand jury proceedings. The Lake City grand jury would meet and render its presentment the week before the Tallahassee grand jury was impaneled. We decided that it wouldn't be a problem because a grand jury's indictment is always sealed if the defendant has not been arrested. Although Bundy was under arrest in Tallahassee, he was not under arrest for the murder of Kim, and we could seal the indictment until the Tallahassee grand jury indicted.

By the end of June, Lawrence told the press that he expected to convene a grand jury in mid-July. "It will not be July 5 as we had anticipated. It is going to be later on in the month, but we are not certain of a date right now." Lawrence said the delay was partly occasioned by the fact that we had not yet received an expected "package of reports."[1]

Patti Roth of the *Lake City Reporter* buttonholed me the week before the grand jury met. I wouldn't tell her what the grand jury was going to consider, but I did admit, "I think it is safe to assume that if a grand jury meets it will be looking into the disappearance of Kimberly Leach." Roth wanted to know the name of the potential indictee, but I refused to name anyone.[2] Not long after that the *Lake City Reporter* obtained copies of our grand jury subpoenas and published the names of all our witnesses in the paper.[3]

Finally the big day came, and we convened a grand jury. The potential jurors gathered in the courtroom, and Judge Wallace Jopling took the bench. Jopling was a relatively new judge, but he was a very experienced and highly respected trial lawyer before he ascended to the bench. While in law school I had clerked for Jopling in his law practice. I knew him to be an astute analyst, a careful reasoner, and a formidable civil trial lawyer. Jopling was also the epitome of the Southern gentleman. No judge was more courteous to litigants or more proper in his relations with the lawyers appearing before him. My only criticism was the fact that he held the State to a very strict burden of proof. He was not at all afraid to dismiss a charge if he felt that your proof was lacking. No other judge would have held us to a higher standard.

Jopling first swore the jurors to tell the truth and then asked them the standard questions asked of all potential jurors. Having qualified the jury, Jopling took a box containing the names of the potential jurors, shook it to mix the names, and pulled 18 names from the box. As he pulled each slip of paper, he called the name written on it and directed the juror to sit in the grand jury box.

A grand jury box is something of an anachronism. Modern court-rooms do not have them, but the Columbia County Courthouse did not have a modern courtroom. As you walked through the back door of the courtroom, you would see a gigantic judge's bench immediately in front of you. Against the left wall, you would see the petit jury box where the trial jury sat, and over against the right wall was the grand jury box. The petit jury box had 12 chairs, but the grand jury box consisted of two pews behind a jury rail.

Once the grand jurors were in the box, Jopling swore them. The oath he administered is one of the most impressive oaths you will ever hear in a courtroom. It is centuries old and was administered to grand juries under the common law of England.[4]

You, as grand jurors for Columbia County do solemnly swear (or affirm) that you will diligently inquire into all matters put in your charge and you will make true presentments of your findings; unless ordered by a court, you will not disclose the nature or sub-stance of the deliberations of the grand jury, the nature or sub-stance of any testimony or other evidence, the vote of the grand jury, or the statements of the state attorney; you shall not make a presentment against a person because of envy, hatred, or malice, and you shall not fail to make a presentment against a person because of love, fear, or reward. So help you God.

Jopling then instructed the grand jury on the general law applicable to their deliberations and allowed them to retire to the grand jury room to begin consideration of those matters brought to them by the state attorney.

The room where the grand jury met served multiple purposes. It was the law library, the petit jury room, and the prisoner holding cell. The walls were lined with books, the door was armored with mesh and a huge jailhouse lock, and the room always smelled of cigarette smoke and the unwashed bodies of prisoners. A huge conference table sat in the middle of the room surrounded by 20 or more chairs. Once you got the grand jurors, the court reporter, the prosecutors, and the wit-ness in the room, there was hardly space to move around. We spent almost a week in those cramped quarters taking the testimony of doz-ens of witnesses.

As the oath says, grand jury proceedings are secret, and it is a crime to reveal the substance of those proceedings.[5] Some jurisdictions have softened the secrecy requirement, but Florida has not. Consequently, I cannot reveal the testimony before the grand jury. I can, however, tell what the newspapers wrote about the proceedings. According to the paper, we called 15 witnesses the first day, including Morris Williams, the assistant principal at Lake City Junior High; Tom Leach; John Bishop; and six of Kim's classmates. We finished with the witnesses by 3:30 p.m. and recessed for the day. I got stopped as I left the courthouse and asked how things were going. I said, "Fine. Things are going well. It looks like it will be a week or possibly longer before we finish what we're doing." When asked what we were doing, I refused to say.[6] You might ask, "If the grand jury is secret, how did the paper know who testified before the grand jury as witnesses?" The answer is very simple. The reporters stood outside the grand jury room and watched who went in and out the door.

On Tuesday we fell behind our schedule. We had 12 witnesses slated to testify, but we got through only half of them. Norman Chapman came from Pensacola to testify, and the other witnesses were all task force members—Dale Parrish, Larry Daugherty, Kenneth Boatright, Harold Scott, and J.O. Jackson. Lawrence told the *Lake City Reporter* he thought we could make up for lost time on Wednesday, get back on schedule, and possibly finish as early as Friday.[7]

As we reconvened on Wednesday, Warren Goodwin, the chief assistant state attorney in Tallahassee, announced that they would begin their grand jury probe of the Chi Omega murders on July 24. We called 18 witnesses before the grand jury on Wednesday, but the *Lake City Reporter* emphasized that Leslie Parmenter and her brother Danny testified that day. The *Reporter* speculated that they testified about Bundy's attempt to kidnap Leslie.[8] We wrapped up the grand jury on Thursday after calling witnesses from the medical examiner's office and the FDLE Crime Lab. Jopling ordered that the indictment be sealed, and we were now in a holding pattern awaiting developments from the Tallahassee grand jury. The next week, Bundy was indicted for the Chi Omega murders.

We intended to arraign Bundy on our charges on August 14,[9] and I saw no need to unseal the indictment until that time. Jopling had other ideas, however. His reasoning followed this path: (1) The purpose of sealing an indictment against an unarrested defendant is to prevent the defendant from learning that he has been indicted and fleeing the jurisdiction. (2) Bundy, being in jail, wasn't going flee the jurisdiction. (3) No real purpose could be served by keeping the indictment sealed. He ordered the indictment unsealed.[10]

There was a time when the criminal law was steeped in ritual. You had to say and do certain things in certain ways in order to effectuate legal process. Some might say that the criminal law is still highly ritualized, but not nearly so much as it was in times past, and not nearly as much now as it was when I began practicing law. There was a time when, if a defendant didn't come to court, the prosecutor had to loudly say, "Dan Defendant, come to court as you are required to do by law or a capias will issue for your arrest! Dan Defendant, come to court as you are required to do by law or a capias will issue for your arrest! Dan Defendant, come to court as you are required to do by law or a capias will issue for your arrest!" If and only if the defendant did not answer that call could the defendant be arrested. I used to equate these required litanies with performing magical incantations—the desired event wasn't going to happen unless you said "abracadabra."

One of the ritual requirements involved reading legal process to the defendant. At one time, if you arrested the defendant, he was entitled to have the warrant or capias read to him. That custom had pretty well died out when I started practicing law, but two others hadn't. If you served a search warrant on the defendant's premises, you had to read the search warrant to him. If he wasn't home, you had to read the search warrant to the empty house. I have stood at the front door of many an empty house waiting for the officer serving the warrant to read the warrant to the house. When a defendant was arraigned in court, the prosecutor was required to read the charging document to him. After reading the charging document, the prosecutor then asked the defendant how he pled to the document—guilty or not guilty. Most defense attorneys waived the reading of the formal charges and entered pleas of not guilty on their clients' behalf, but the defendant was not allowed to waive the reading of a first-degree murder indictment.

As I said, the ritual of reading arrest warrants to defendants had largely gone out of practice by the time I started practicing law. The arresting officer simply told the defendant he was under arrest, advised him of the charge, and took him to jail. If the defendant was already in jail, the officer simply noted on the warrant that it had been served, notified the defendant that he had picked up another charge, booked him in on the new charge, and made arrangements to have the defendant appear before the committing magistrate for setting of bond on the new charges. That's not quite what happened when Bundy got arrested for the Chi Omega murders.

Something else that sometimes happens when defendants are arrested on high-profile charges is the "perp walk." Someone from the arresting agency tips off the media that so-and-so has been arrested and that he is being taken to jail. The arresting officer takes enough time getting to the jail to allow the media to set up their cameras and film him walking the perpetrator into the jail. It's quite a spectacle, with defendants hanging their heads in shame, hiding their faces, and folding their coats over their handcuffs.

When Bundy got arrested on the Chi Omega murders, something occurred that was a sort of hybrid of the ritual reading of the arrest warrant and the "perp walk." Bundy's arrest in the bowels of the Leon County Jail was televised. Sheriff Katsaris led a number of reporters, including at least one with a television camera, into the jail and to an elevator door. The door opened, the sheriff said, "Step out, Mr. Bundy," and an officer led Bundy off the elevator and into the presence of Katsaris and the media. Bundy said, "Gentlemen, I'm not going to be paraded for Sheriff Katsaris's benefit." Katsaris produced a copy of the indictment, and Bundy asked, "What do we have here, Ken? Let's see. It's an indictment. Why don't you read it to me? You're up for election, aren't you?" Bundy turned his back on Katsaris as Katsaris began to read the indictment. Bundy then said, "Okay then, you got an indictment. That's all you're going to get." Bundy asked, "Is this my chance to talk to the press? I'll plead not guilty right now. Can I talk to the reporters? We've had our chance. We've displayed the prisoner. Well, listen: I've been kept in isolation for six months. I've been kept from the press. I've been buried by you. You've been talking to the press for six months. I think it's my turn now." Katsaris handed Bundy the indictment and said, "We've got a court order. There won't be any press interviews." Bundy replied, "Sure, there won't be any press interviews. You've given them out. I'm gagged. You're not. I will be heard." Bundy tore up the paper Katsaris had given him and said, "This is what I think of your indictment." The shredded papers fluttered to the floor and Bundy got back onto the elevator to be returned to his cell. "You never know what you'll have in the way of a reaction when you charge them," Katsaris observed.[11] Katsaris's words were prophetic, but not as he meant them. Andy Anderson, who had been fretting over what he saw at the junior high that cold February morning, saw the arrest on the news. He could deny it no longer. The girl he had seen was Kim

Leach, and the man was most likely Ted Bundy. He decided to come forward with his information.[12]

The *Lake City Reporter* wanted to know if Lawrence was going to go to Tallahassee to read our indictment to Bundy. Lawrence replied, "I don't want to give Mr. Bundy any room for argument." He then went on to say, "I'd think it would just be a clown act."[13] Lawrence would eventually read the indictment to Bundy, but it would be in a courtroom during a regular court proceeding. Bundy's arrest on our charges occurred without the benefit of any press coverage. Jopling signed an order to bring Bundy over to Lake City for arraignment, and he was formally arrested in the booking room of the Columbia County Jail. Chief Deputy Luther Fralick did tell me about one interesting event that occurred as Bundy was being booked in at the jail. Bundy announced that he was not going to allow them to take his fingerprints. Fralick told Bundy they were going to take his fingerprints whether he wanted them taken or not; Bundy just had to decide whether they were going to be taken the easy way or the hard way. Bundy opted for the easy way.

# 10

# Bundy's Dream Team

Before identifying himself for his captors in Pensacola, Bundy wanted to call a lawyer. It seems strange that he would call a lawyer living more than 300 miles away in another state, a lawyer who had never before appeared on Bundy's behalf. Why would Bundy do such a thing? Why would the lawyer respond and eventually undertake to represent him? Depending on your point of view, Millard Farmer was a famous, or infamous, Atlanta criminal defense lawyer affiliated with an organization called Team Defense. It never was as famous as O.J. Simpson's "Dream Team" nor did it make quite as much money. Team Defense specialized in representing the poor and underprivileged in capital litigation. Its avowed purpose was to oppose racism and capital punishment and champion the cause of the oppressed and underprivileged. Bundy was definitely not underprivileged, and any "oppression" he might have experienced he brought on himself. Nevertheless, when Bundy was arraigned in Lake City, Florida, he had been consulting with Farmer since his arrest for the murder of Caryn Campbell in Colorado.[1] How did the dauntless defender of underprivileged minorities hook up with a Republican college graduate?

The only answers I ever got were based on little better than rumors. I was told that Bundy had wanted Farmer to represent him in his murder trial in Colorado. Supposedly Farmer was the best of the best as a criminal defense attorney and Bundy's ego would settle for nothing but the very best. There was, however, an insurmountable barrier to Farmer's representing Bundy—Colorado's death penalty had a history of less than vigorous enforcement. Farmer felt his time was better spent defending capital murder defendants in jurisdictions where the death penalty was more than a quaint, seldom-used statute. All this is little more than scuttlebutt. It does, however, form the basis for an intriguing conjecture—did Bundy come to Florida to continue his murderous rampage so that Farmer could defend him if he got caught? Farmer might have been engaging in rhetoric when he called Florida the "buckle of the Death Belt,"[2] but it is a fact that Florida has diligently sought to enforce the death penalty. Whatever motivated Bundy to come to Florida, it is clear what motivated him to call Farmer—he was in a world of trouble and he needed the best defense he could get.

When someone is arrested in Florida and does not immediately post a bond, the prisoner must be brought before a judge within 24 hours for first appearance.[3] At first appearance the accused is advised of his rights, advised of the charges, and asked if he can afford a lawyer. When Bundy appeared before Judge Charles McClure the morning following his arrest for murder, he had a lawyer by his side—Farmer. But Farmer wasn't licensed to practice law in Florida, and McClure refused to allow Farmer to represent Bundy. Later that day, Circuit Judge John Rudd refused to allow Farmer to appear for Bundy at his official arraignment in Circuit Court.[4]

On August 2, Farmer was back before Rudd armed with a motion to appear *pro hac vice* and a motion to disqualify Rudd as trial judge. In the sound discretion of the trial judge, an out-of-state lawyer may appear *pro hac vice* ("for this occasion") to represent a client in a single case. The lawyer must be a member in good standing of some other bar, and the judge can deny the application for good cause. Rudd again refused to allow Farmer to appear for Bundy. Farmer took the motion to disqualify, scribbled out his signature, and had Bundy sign the document.[5] When trying to practice *pro hac vice,* attorneys are often unfamiliar with the strict rules of procedure of a new jurisdiction. The motion to disqualify might have been a fine piece of legal draftsmanship in Georgia, but it was insufficient under Florida law. Rudd denied that also. The next day he entered a written order explaining his reasons for refusing to allow Farmer to represent Bundy. Rudd had two main reasons for denying Farmer's request: Farmer had been held in contempt by a judge in Georgia, and Farmer had, in Rudd's opinion, misbehaved when he appeared before Rudd. He explained himself by writing:

First, Mr. Farmer's conviction for criminal contempt by a Georgia trial court has recently been upheld by a Georgia Appellate Court. . . . A thorough reading of that opinion must lead one to the conclusion that Mr. Farmer's conduct during the trial in question, by studied design, intended to provoke the trial judge into intemperate remarks or precipitous acts which might result in a mistrial. This court simply cannot, and in fairness to the Defendant, will not allow these proceedings to become a bizarre circus where Mr. Farmer can play ringmaster for an audience that could not possibly include a jury.

Second, the attached transcripts of the experience that this court has had with Mr. Farmer will show to any fair minded person that Mr. Farmer's concept of a trial is grounded on some perverse principle of maximized obfuscation. . . . Mr. Farmer is incapable of a simple yes or no response, regardless of the simplicity of the question. This sort of conduct is dilatory and disruptive and in no manner advances the cause of a defendant, justice or respect for law.[6]

Farmer was not amused by Rudd's comments. He fired back in the press. Farmer called Rudd a "two-faced son of a bitch," characterizing him as being "in the middle of a lynch mob" and said, "If there were a statue of Justice in Leon County, she wouldn't only be blindfolded, she'd be holding her nose over what's going on in this case."[7] Rudd and Farmer were as far apart as East and West. Rudd was a common sense, no nonsense judge who maintained decorum in his courtroom with an iron hand. Farmer was a flamboyant lawyer whose courtroom maneuvers drew the ire of judges and prosecutors alike. He frequently filed motions to disqualify trial judges and prosecutors, and rumor had it that some judges would automatically grant his motions to disqualify so they wouldn't have to put up with him.

Farmer may not have been licensed to practice in the state courts of Florida, but he was licensed in the federal courts. He took his quest to represent Bundy to Federal District Court seeking an injunction requiring that he be allowed to appear for Bundy. Judge William Stafford was no more sympathetic to Farmer's request than Rudd had been. Farmer took his quest further by filing an appeal with the Fifth Circuit Court of Appeals, but that court summarily affirmed Stafford's order. There was only one court left that could overrule Rudd, and Farmer took his case to it. The United States Supreme Court also summarily denied his request.[8]

There was one other way Farmer could help Bundy. Because Bundy posed such an escape risk, Katsaris had taken extra precautions in providing for his security. Bundy's cell contained one 150-watt light bulb covered with a translucent shield and wire mesh, and he was heavily shackled during the few times he was allowed outside his cell for exercise.[9] On August 4, Farmer sued Katsaris for $300,000.00 alleging inhumane conditions at the Leon County Jail.[10] By Wednesday, August 30, Farmer had Bundy before the federal magistrate testifying to the hardships he was enduring in the Leon County Jail.[11] On Friday the magistrate announced his decision. He would recommend to Stafford that Katsaris: (1) Give Bundy more exercise time. (2) Give him additional lighting. (3) Stop opening and photocopying his mail. Farmer was only moderately satisfied. He told the news media, "I think it's a first step in alleviating the problems there. But you've got to be sick to be happy with an order granting this kind of minimal relief."[12]

I viewed the developments in Tallahassee with mixed emotions. I couldn't generate much sympathy for Bundy's plight in the Leon County Jail. He earned those severe conditions by making himself an escape risk. I didn't feel very good, though, about what was happening in Farmer's quest to get admitted *pro hac vice*. I discussed my misgivings with Larry Simpson, and he assured me that we didn't want any part of Farmer, that Farmer would make a full-blown nuisance of himself, and the case was going to be hard enough with congenial counsel on the other side. I had dealt with nuisance lawyers before, and although they made my life miserable, they didn't get many acquittals at trial. The reason for this is not hard to discern—there is no need to make a nuisance of yourself if you have a viable defense. Regardless of how I felt about keeping Farmer out of the Bundy case, our path was clear. We had to be consistent. We had to take the same position taken by the Tallahassee office.

I kept my opinions to myself, sharing them only with Lawrence and Simpson, but there was another Lake City lawyer who didn't mind speaking out. Milo Thomas, the public defender for the Third Judicial Circuit, said that he did not think his office would handle the case. "There are personal reasons—conflicts. We don't have the facilities and manpower for something that would take so much time. . . . It's a little premature . . . and I think he would be better off with someone else. . . . I think that [Rudd] ought to let [Bundy] have Farmer. If a lawyer is willing to represent a man, and the man wants him, then they ought to let him have the lawyer."[13] I found it hard to argue with Thomas's logic. Thomas might be reluctant to represent Bundy, but there were others who appeared quite willing to step into the breach. A public defender from Miami told the news media he would be willing to take the case on. Michael Von Zamft told the *Lake City Reporter* that someone had contacted him on Bundy's behalf. He said, "If the conflict is there and I understand it is a deep conflict, then yes, I would be willing to handle it."[14]

As the date for Bundy's arraignment in Lake City approached, it became clear that Lawrence was going to handle the litigation over Farmer and I was going to be relegated to the role of gofer. Bundy came over from Tallahassee under a heavy guard and was first taken to the county jail to be booked in on the murder charge. They then took him the few blocks that separated the jail and the courthouse and surrounded him as they escorted him into the courthouse through a crowd of onlookers. It really didn't register with me at the time because I didn't realize its significance, but Bundy was wearing the blue blazer he had worn the day he kidnapped Kim.[15] The first order of business at the courthouse was to have Bundy's first appearance hearing before County Judge Vernon Douglas in the courtroom on the second floor. The agenda for first appearance was simple. Douglas took the bench, Bundy was escorted before him, Farmer stood at Bundy's side, and Douglas allowed Farmer to enter a "limited appearance" on behalf of Bundy for the sole purpose of representing him at first appearance.[16]

The formalities of the first appearance having been tended to, Douglas left the bench and Judge Jopling took over. Lawrence called the case up for arraignment. Again, Farmer was allowed to put in a "limited appearance" on behalf of Bundy, pending resolution of the State's objection to his motion to appear *pro hac vice*, which Lawrence had reduced to writing and served on Farmer that morning.[17] Farmer interrupted Lawrence several times during the short proceeding, but Jopling took no notice.[18] At the appropriate point in the proceedings, Lawrence, who had a deep sonorous voice that could fill a courtroom, read the indictment to Bundy. The reading of a first-degree murder indictment at an arraignment was always an impressive proceeding, and the reading of Bundy's indictment was no exception. Bundy stood silently looking over Lawrence's shoulder as the indictment was read, and when asked, "How do you plead?" He said, "Because I am innocent, I plead not guilty,"[19] anticipating O. J. Simpson's arraignment plea of "absolutely 100% not guilty"[20] by more than a decade and a half. I think such pleas are absolutely 100% grandstanding stunts. They contribute nothing to the courtroom defense of the case, but they do tend to make nice headlines and sound bites. Jopling set the hearing on Lawrence's written objection for August 22, 1978.[21] Because of scheduling conflicts the hearing actually didn't begin until the middle of September.[22]

The heart and soul of Lawrence's objection consisted of two contempt citations against Farmer during the trial of a capital murder case in Georgia. The first incident occurred during some pretrial hearing at which the defendant testified and was cross examined. During the direct examination of the defendant, Farmer addressed him by his first name. During cross examination, the prosecutor also addressed the defendant by his first name. Farmer objected, saying that "we will refer to our client George Street by his first name, because that's an affectionate way that we feel about him. And, we've known him a period of time. But, we would insist that when he is referred to by the prosecutors that he be referred to as Mr." The prosecutor then asked the defendant, "Do you have any objection to me calling you George?" and Farmer objected again.[23] What happened next appears to me to have been an unfortunate display of obstinacy on the part of three grown men. The prosecutor refused to comply with Farmer's wish, the judge refused to order the prosecutor to comply, and Farmer refused to let the matter lie. He kept interrupting both the judge and the prosecutor even after the judge had told him that he had a "continuing objection" to the prosecutor's action. The proceeding degenerated into a contest of wills between lawyer and judge. The hearing continued:

> The Court: Overruled. Now, don't make that objection again. You have a continuing objection. I mean about the calling him by the name of George.
>
> Mr. Farmer: Your Honor, do you object to me calling you Elie? [The judge's first name].
>
> The Court: Mr. Farmer, do not ask the Court any such question as that. That is a direct confront of the Court of its authority. If you do that again I will consider it as a contempt of this Court.
>
> Mr. Farmer: What, Your Honor, may I ask the Court. I want to inquire . . .
>
> The Court: You are to be quiet at this point and we're going to proceed with the cross examination.
>
> Mr. Farmer: When may I make an objection?
>
> The Court: Are you going to allow us to proceed with the cross examination of this witness?

Mr. Farmer:   Your Honor, I feel like in representing my client . . .

The Court:   Mr. Farmer, this Court finds your continual interruption of the Court, your refusal to allow us to continue with examination of this witness to be in contempt of the Court. This Court so finds you in contempt of Court. It is the judgment of the Court that you are in contempt of Court. It's the judgment of the Court that you be sentenced to the common jail of this county for a period of 24 hours. Mr. Sheriff?[24]

The second contempt citation came eight days later and netted Farmer three more days in jail. Despite repeated warnings, he persisted in accusing the judge of making "malicious and arbitrary rulings" and engaging in a "cover up."[25]

In August Bundy made multiple court appearances in state court in Pensacola, Tallahassee, and Lake City, and also in federal court in Tallahassee. His blue blazer was getting ripe for cleaning, and it was getting noticed. Lynn Henson told J. O. Jackson that she was finding lots of distinctive blue fibers of the type used in making coats. Did Bundy have any blue jackets in his wardrobe? Yes. He often wore a blue blazer to make his court appearances. Shortly after Bundy's arraignment in Lake City, Jackson spoke to me about seizing the blue blazer. I thought we would probably be within our rights to simply remove the blazer from Bundy's property at the jail, but I wanted to do a little research on the issue to make absolutely sure. While I was researching the issue, Jim Skipper had an interesting conversation with Bundy's girlfriend, Carol Boone.

On the afternoon of September 5, Carol Boone came into FDLE's Tallahassee Regional Operations Center and said she wanted to talk to an agent about Bundy. Skipper met with her. Boone wanted to expound on Bundy's innocence, especially of the charges that had been brought against him in Utah and Colorado. Boone said she really didn't know why she came to FDLE, other than she had been told by others that she would get a fair hearing from them. Skipper listened to her patiently, and at the conclusion of the interview she made a request. She had Bundy's blue blazer with her, and she needed to get it dry cleaned. Did Skipper have any idea where she could get it cleaned? He recommended the Big B Cleaners on 324 North Monroe. Boone thanked him and left, and Skipper immediately called Jackson. Jackson started the process of getting legal authority to seize the blazer while Skipper went to the Big B to make sure Boone had carried it there. She had.

Jackson called me and advised me of the developments. I offered to come to Tallahassee to help with the warrant, but he said they could solicit the help of two local prosecutors, Jim White and Jim Gillis. Real-world law enforcement is quite different from television. On television, an officer could get a search warrant at the drop of a hat—in the real world it just didn't work that way. Back in the 1970s, without computers, and using electric typewriters, real-world search warrants took hours to prepare. Working through the night, Skipper, Jackson, White, and Gillis put together an application for a search warrant. When they finished, they called me and read it to me over the phone. It sounded good to me, and I agreed that it should be taken to Rudd. Rudd signed the search warrant at 6:00 A.M. on September 6, and by 7:12 A.M., Jackson and Skipper were at the Big B seizing Bundy's blazer.

At approximately 9:15 A.M. Jackson and Skipper went to the Leon County Jail. Jackson read the search warrant to Bundy and handed him a copy of it. Then he gave Bundy his Miranda warning and Bundy waived his rights. Jackson asked Bundy, "Do you understand that the item seized is your dark blue blazer that Carol Boone took to the cleaners for you?" Bundy replied, "Uh huh." Jackson tried to question him further, but Bundy refused to talk further. The case against Bundy had just improved by a quantum leap.

When we went back to court on September 14, litigating the issue of whether Farmer should be admitted *pro hac vice,* there had been a sea change not only in case quality but also in the prosecution team. Lawrence was now a circuit judge elect and in January he would embark upon a distinguished 22-year career as a trial and appellate judge, and I was interviewing for other positions. I had lost my bid to succeed Lawrence as state attorney, and a former law school classmate of mine, Jerry Blair, was state attorney elect. We had been friends in law school and friends as colleagues in the state attorney's office. Because we had both run clean campaigns, the relationship between us remained cordial, though not as warm as before. We discussed my continued employment under him as state attorney, and Blair had invited me to test the waters by staying on for the duration of the Bundy trial. No other job really appealed to me, and I had a strong sense of commitment to see the Bundy case through. We agreed that I would continue for the duration of the Bundy case. Blair and I had been trial partners in our practice court class in law school and had been the only prosecution team in our class to achieve a conviction. We worked well together in law school, and that translated to the real world as we worked on the Bundy case together. It was not long before I told him I would like to stay on with him permanently, and he graciously accepted. Over the next 26 years we partnered to try many high-profile cases.

When the hearing began on the afternoon of September 14, we were flying under the radar screen of the state and national media. They were all too busy covering Farmer's attempts to have Katsaris held in contempt for allegedly defying Judge Stafford's order[26] to pay any attention to what was going on in the backwater of Lake City. Although we didn't have the state and national media to contend with, we did have another lawyer to contend with. Albert Krieger, a Miami defense attorney, came in for the limited purpose of handling the hearing on behalf of Farmer and Bundy. Krieger was an impressive man. By his size and demeanor he dominated the courtroom while at the same time being the very model of civility. The newspaper described him as being a Kojack lookalike.[27] I took an instant liking to him, and before the hearing was over I had come to admire and respect both his abilities as a lawyer and his demeanor as a gentleman. Lawrence served as lead prosecutor, and I carried his briefcase and acted as gofer. We had certified copies of the contempt citations, a transcript, copies of outlandish motions signed by Farmer, and two crusty Georgia prosecutors to make our case. On the other side they had 10 attorneys aligned to testify about Farmer's superlative abilities as a criminal defense lawyer.[28]

The hearing, which we expected to last a few hours on the afternoon of September 14, stretched out over three days. Jopling observed that it had become more like a trial than a motion hearing. Our first witness was Farmer, whom Lawrence called to authenticate the pleadings bearing Farmer's signature. I don't think that Farmer really scored any points with Jopling when he steadfastly refused to admit that he had signed the pleadings. He admitted that signatures on the papers certainly bore some resemblance to his handwriting, but he could not swear under oath that he signed them. This proved only a minor obstacle to authenticating the documents and getting them into evidence, because prosecutors Vickers Nugent and Marion Pritchett identified the pleadings as Farmer's. Listening to them describe Farmer's tactics, I began to think that maybe keeping Farmer off the case might not be such a bad idea after all.

One rather amusing aspect of Nugent's testimony came when Krieger cross examined him in an attempt to use the *tu quoque* (you too) defense. Although it is sometimes a valid defense, *tu quoque* is considered a logical fallacy. Someone under criticism uses the *tu quoque* defense by saying that his accusers are guilty of the same sort of misconduct.[29] The defense has a strong visceral appeal, but as we all learned in kindergarten, "Two wrongs don't make a right."

Nugent's "misconduct" involved a murder trial in Lakeland, Georgia. Farmer had succeeded in getting more than half a dozen judges to disqualify themselves, and Nugent despaired of ever getting a judge to agree to stay on the case and put up with Farmer. The fad of burning American flags had not really caught on in 1978, but the Vietnam War was not long over, and people could still remember the war protesters who publicly burned their draft cards. Nugent called a press conference and burned a law book on the courthouse lawn.[30] When questioned about this by Krieger, Nugent was unapologetic, saying that the next judge assigned to the case refused to disqualify himself. When Krieger asked him if he would do something like that again, Nugent replied that the next time "I might burn two."[31]

After Lawrence rested, it was Krieger's turn, and one lawyer after another took the stand to laud Farmer's abilities to the skies. Michael Von Zamft went into great detail about how Farmer had helped him successfully avoid the death penalty in a high-profile Miami prosecution.[32] Another witness, Dade County Judge Steven Robinson, described how he witnessed a voir dire conducted by Farmer. "It was the most fascinating voir dire I ever saw, almost spellbinding." Robinson went on to say that Farmer "was almost able to go into their souls."[33]

The prosecution and defense were trying two different cases. The prosecution posed the question "Can Millard Farmer behave?" and proposed the answer "No." This issue was not congenial to the defense, so they redefined the issue as "Is Millard Farmer a talented lawyer?" and proposed the answer "Yes." The media bought in to the defense definition of the issues but couldn't quite grasp the State's definition. Lawrence was able, on cross examination, to bolster the State's case with the testimony of not only the defense witnesses, but Farmer himself. As Jopling noted in his final order, many of the defense witnesses had to admit that they did not approve of some of Farmer's tactics.[34] Farmer was the last witness to testify for the defense. He said, "Some of the things that came out, I am ashamed at what they look like and that these people have these perceptions."[35] When the testimony concluded, we recessed the case and came back on September 24 for final arguments and the judge's ruling.

My admiration for Krieger soared to new heights when I heard his argument before Jopling. Taking as his theme the tricolon: "Ultimate crime, ultimate punishment, ultimate defense,"[36] Krieger gave a superlative argument, probably the best I ever heard. If he convinced nobody else in the courtroom, he convinced me. He failed, however, to convince his most important audience. Jopling denied Farmer's petition to appear in a ruling that he announced from the bench and later set down in written form. In his order, Jopling wrote, "Millard C. Farmer, Jr., has set a past pattern for insulting, contemptuous, contumacious, dilatory, and disruptive misconduct of the type designed to directly impede the orderly administration of justice, and which provides ample grounds . . . for the denial of the motion to appear pro hac vice." He went on to say "Millard C. Farmer, Jr.'s apologies for past misconduct and promises to do better in the future are an insufficient guarantee that he will conduct himself properly at the trial of this cause."[37]

Having disposed of Farmer, Jopling then inquired of Bundy as to his wishes. Bundy said, "I will do my best to be respectful to the court. The decision was not expected nor desired. I continue to desire the defense of Mr. Farmer as he is the only one I know with the skills necessary to help me."[38] Upon finding Bundy indigent, Jopling asked Krieger if he would consent to represent Bundy. I don't know who was more horror-stricken at the suggestion, me or Krieger. He swallowed hard and told Jopling that his schedule would not permit it.[39] Krieger's consternation and mine came from different sources. He was probably thinking, "I'll go broke defending this case for the peanuts that they pay appointed counsel." I was thinking, "He'll kick us around the courtroom like a football!"

Bundy refused appointed counsel and asked to represent himself. Jopling inquired into his competency, and Bundy said he had a BS from the University of Washington and two years of law school. Bundy summed up with a statement of the law that was essentially correct,[40] "The U.S. Supreme Court has said legal background is not an issue. . . . I don't think any background is needed, other than that I knowingly and voluntarily take this step."

Of course, the media wanted comments from the parties involved in the hearing. They buttonholed both Krieger and Farmer. Krieger merely said he was disappointed, and that there were no immediate plans to appeal the decision as had happened in the case involving

Rudd. Farmer had a little more to say. He told the news media, "History will look back on this decision as they look back on the witch trials of Salem."[41]

Bundy later touched off a volley of motions and orders when, on November 14, he filed another motion to disqualify Rudd. This one was much better worded, and it cited to numerous purported *ex parte*[42] communications between Rudd and several prosecutors and law enforcement officials.[43] Without having a hearing, Rudd entered an order finding the second motion legally insufficient, but after finding it insufficient he undertook to respond to the allegations. He went on to explain, and in some instances contradict, the factual allegations in Bundy's motion.[44] Bundy, on the same day, returned fire on Rudd with a motion for reconsideration, attaching an affidavit that essentially denied that Rudd's explanations were truthful. Rudd fired off a counter barrage with another order denying the motion for rehearing and responding to the factual allegations in the motion and affidavit.[45] You will recall that Rudd had refused to allow Farmer to appear because he felt Farmer's tactics were such as to goad the judge into making an unsound ruling. Bundy's motion to disqualify had done just that. A judge presented with a motion to disqualify may not speak to the factual allegations contained in the motion. He must simply rule on its legal sufficiency.[46] By answering the allegations, Rudd had disqualified himself. Bundy filed a petition for writ of prohibition in the Florida Supreme Court. It ruled quickly. On December 22, the Supreme Court said: "When a judge has looked beyond the mere legal sufficiency of a suggestion of prejudice and attempted to refute the charges of partiality, he has then exceeded the proper scope of his inquiry and on that basis alone established grounds for his disqualification."[47] Rudd was out.

The Supreme Court appointed Circuit Judge Edward Cowart, the chief judge in Miami, to replace Rudd. Cowart was a big man with a jovial demeanor who kept firm control in his courtroom but still was the picture of courtesy toward lawyers and litigants. He also had something of a flair for giving the media good sound bites. He presented himself as a Southern gentleman with a superb sense of humor. He had an excellent legal mind, but sometimes his rulings were convoluted and hard to follow. I took an instant liking for him, which is a good thing because I saw a lot of him over the next few months. Whenever major issues were litigated in the Chi Omega case, I tried to be there sitting on the front row behind the prosecution table. Cowart treated me with the utmost courtesy, inviting me into his chambers to audit *in camera* proceedings,[48] and occasionally asking my opinion on legal issues.

Whenever a judge gets disqualified, all his rulings on any legal issues become suspect, and the new judge can, in his discretion, reconsider any and all of those rulings. This reconsideration may take the form of simply reviewing the record of the previous hearing, or it could be a full blown *de novo*[49] reconsideration of the matter. The defense insisted that Cowart reconsider Rudd's ruling that Farmer could not represent Bundy. There had been a new addition to Team Defense by the time the Farmer matter was reconsidered. Joe Nursey, a Tallahassee assistant public defender, had left that office and joined the team. Since Nursey had a license to practice law in Florida, there was no question that he could step into court and represent Bundy. Farmer sent him down to Tallahassee to handle some matters preliminary to the rehearing of the *pro hac vice* application, and that gave me occasion to witness another side of Cowart. Nursey used obstructionist tactics before Cowart. The judge didn't lose his temper, but Simpson and I could see that he was very angry about the disruptive tactics employed by Nursey. Simpson laughingly said to me that Nursey didn't understand the program—they needed to behave until Farmer got admitted and then begin using those tactics.

Simpson opposed rehearing Rudd's ruling, but Cowart didn't agree. He gave Bundy a full rehearing. Simpson brought in Marion Pritchett to testify, but he decided to replace Vickers Nugent with another Georgia prosecutor by the name of Robert Sparks.[50] The hearing wasn't a carbon copy of Jopling's hearing, but it was very similar. One distinctive feature was a motion to have Cowart disqualified, alleging that he had engaged in private talks with prosecutors on the case. Cowart summarily denied the motion, saying it was legally insufficient. Cowart displayed his proclivity for homespun one-liners during Farmer's testimony. "He can't be all bad with an accent like that. I kind of like that. He seems pretty tranquil to me." When, at the conclusion of the hearing, Judge Cowart allowed Bundy to argue for Farmer, Bundy told him that "dammit" he wanted a fair trial. "Bless your heart Mr. Bundy," Cowart replied, "I'm going to give you every right I can, but please don't use profanity in my courtroom."[51] Cowart took the case under advisement and the next day issued a five-page order explaining his grounds for refusing to allow Farmer to represent

Bundy. Cowart wrote, "While the court does not question the competency of Mr. Farmer, it does question the conduct previously engaged in by Mr. Farmer and his adherence to the practice of confusion and avoidance."[52] Farmer did not ride off into the sunset never to be heard from again. He came to court one more time, and when he did, we were happy to work with him—but that story must wait for another chapter.

# 11

# Bundy for the Defense, Part I

Once when I was a very young public defender, I defended an escape
charge against a man who called himself "Roble Noon." His real name
is irrelevant to this account, but his actions are instructive. Noon, a
professional robber who seemed to enjoy shooting police officers, was
serving multiple life sentences at Cross City Correctional Institution.
Noon escaped, pulled another string of robberies, and kidnapped a
law enforcement officer, whom he left handcuffed to a tree. Of all the
charges brought against Noon, the least important was the escape
charge. Because Noon wanted to raise an insanity defense, I got a copy
of the psychiatric report done in his kidnapping case. The psychiatrist
said that, although Noon was sane and competent to stand trial, he had
sociopathic personality disorder. I told Noon that, based on the psychiatric report, I could not raise a defense of insanity. On the morning of
trial, Noon physically attacked a deputy sheriff, verbally attacked me,
and engaged in such disruptive behavior that the prosecutor dropped
the charges. Noon's actions were typical of the sociopathic personality disorder. I represented a number of sociopaths as a public defender
and prosecuted even more as a prosecutor, and they were all difficult
to deal with. As we will see by the end of this chapter, Ted Bundy was
a sociopath, and his disruptive behavior in the Chi Omega and Leach
trials came chapter and verse from the sociopath's guide to courtroom
behavior. Sometimes, as in Noon's case, it works; but most of the time,
as in Bundy's case, it goes horribly wrong and the sociopath winds up
in a worse pickle than before he started acting out.

The sociopath often acts as his own counsel, and that's the very
first thing that Bundy did when he lost Millard Farmer. This can be

advantageous in a number of ways. The defendant who acts *pro se* (for himself) can get away with all sorts of misbehavior that would get a lawyer held in contempt of court. Bundy, however, was just a tad smarter than the average defendant, and his manipulations were more subtle than most. His manipulative behavior aimed at two objectives. First, he tried to create opportunities for escape. In his "Motion for Aids Necessary to Prepare an Adequate Defense,"[1] he asked that he be escorted by the Leon County Sheriff's Office to a complete law library once a week ostensibly to do legal research but more likely to reprise his first Colorado escape from the courthouse law library.[2] A second objective was to take a page from Roble Noon's trial handbook and be disruptive enough to derail the prosecution. This eventually led to Bundy's downfall, as we shall see.

Our first problem with the Bundy prosecution was a speedy trial issue. On April 7, when Kim's body was found, Ray Frederick and Ken Bridges went to the Leon County Jail to advise Bundy of his rights and talk to him. We never dreamed that such a procedure could ever be considered an arrest, but the First District Court of Appeals had other ideas. On July 10, just three months later, the court decided in *State v. N.B.* that when you read an incarcerated defendant his Miranda rights and tell him charges would probably be filed against him, you have arrested him for purposes of the speedy trial rule.[3] According to the court's opinion, Bundy was "arrested" on April 7 and would be entitled to discharge on October 4. The Farmer hearing ended September 21, which meant that we had 13 days to get Bundy to trial or the case would be dismissed. Eventually, in 1980, the Rules of Criminal Procedure were amended to overrule *State v. N.B.*,[4] but that did us no good in 1978.

From July until September 21, we had been rather busy getting Bundy indicted and Farmer fired, and we were blissfully unaware of *State v. N.B.* The year 1978 was B.C.—Before Computers—and there was no such thing as Lexis®, Westlaw®, or online posting of judicial decisions. When we became aware of *State v. N.B.*, we knew we had to do something, and we had to do it fast. The very next day we filed a "Motion for Extension of Time under Fla.R.Crim.P. 3.191" (the speedy trial rule).[5] We attacked the problem on two fronts. First, we argued that Bundy was different because, unlike N.B., nobody told Bundy that charges would probably be filed. As a fallback position we argued that exceptional circumstances justified extension of the speedy trial deadline. Rule 3.191 provided for several circumstances where complex cases merited extension of time, and we had almost all those circumstances in the Bundy case. Our third layer of defense would be to ask that the trial commence immediately, that we start picking the jury as soon as humanly possible, and by all means before October 4. We got a hearing date on our motion—September 30.[6] I also filed a motion for discovery and, quite foolishly, set it for September 30 as well.[7]

Bundy replied with a motion to continue the hearing on both motions, claiming he couldn't answer both of them on such short notice after having just suffered the trauma of being stripped of the protective shield provided by Farmer. He also complained that the sordid conditions in the Leon County Jail prevented him from adequately preparing for the hearings.[8] One thing he didn't mention in his motion—waiving his right to a speedy trial.

Bundy acquitted himself well at the motion hearing. We said we'd be glad to continue the hearings if he'd just waive speedy trial. He stubbornly insisted that he shouldn't be required to waive speedy trial as a part of his motion to continue. Of course, to continue the hearing without a waiver of speedy trial would mean that he would be entitled to a discharge on October 5. Judge Jopling denied his motion to continue the speedy trial hearing but granted the continuance of the hearing on the motion for discovery.[9] Jopling found as a matter of fact and law that Bundy was not arrested until August 14, but he also found that sufficient exigent circumstances existed for an extension of the speedy trial deadline. If the appellate court disagreed with him on the date of the arrest, they would certainly agree with him about the exigent circumstances. We had dodged a potentially lethal bullet.

We next went to court against Bundy on October 23. In the meantime, I filed an amended motion for discovery,[10] a motion to seal discovery,[11] and a motion for pretrial conference.[12] Bundy responded with a motion for continuance of the trial. We wanted two things from Bundy—handwriting samples and a saliva sample. The handwriting samples were necessary to connect Bundy to the credit card receipts he had signed. Most of the people who had taken the receipts could identify Bundy, but we wanted more. Eyewitnesses might be discredited by a vigorous cross examination; expert testimony identifying his handwriting would be less vulnerable. The motion for discovery explained why we needed a saliva sample:

27. FDCLE Crime Lab serologist[s] have determined that under garments found with the remains of KIMBERLY DIANE LEACH contain semen which they have utilized to determine that the male depositing said semen had a blood type of 0. They have

further determined that a blood sample taken from the Defendant pursuant to court order in Leon County Circuit Court Case No. 78–125-CF is identical with the blood type found in the semen.

28. The FDCLE Crime Lab serologist[s] have informed the undersigned that a saliva sample from the Defendant is necessary to determine whether the Defendant is a "secreter" or a "non-secreter," such that he would deposit his blood type in his semen. Such a determination would show:

(a) If Defendant is a "secreter", that he quite probably did contribute the semen on the underwear of KIMBERLY DIANE LEACH.

(b) If Defendant is a "non-secreter", that he definitely did not contribute the semen on the underwear of KIMBERLY DIANE LEACH.

Either determination would be helpful in establishing the guilt or innocence of the Defendant of the crimes charged in the above captioned cause.[13]

I also filed an answer to Bundy's demand for discovery, disclosing 277 potential witnesses, 44 written or recorded statements, 179 interview synopses, numerous oral and recorded statements by the defendant, 16 documents relating to seizures of evidence from the defendant's possession, 29 written reports made by forensic scientists, and numerous other items of tangible evidence divided into 11 categories.[14] Florida's discovery rule was more restrictive back in 1978 than it is now, and you could withhold a lot of information from the defense.[15] Whenever you got a demand for discovery, you looked carefully through all the reports and withheld much vital information. There was a lot of litigation over what could and could not be withheld, and quite a few cases got reversed because prosecutors withheld too much. We sidestepped that sort of litigation by engaging in "open file" discovery. We opened our file and gave the defense all police reports written in connection with the investigation. We thought the defense would not be able to complain that we were holding back anything, but Bundy found something to complain about anyway—we were giving him too much information!

Although Bundy felt it unreasonable to expect him to be ready for trial on November 6, the currently set trial date, he did not think he should be required to waive his right to a speedy trial. Eventually, the law came to recognize a motion for continuance as an implicit waiver of the speedy trial deadline, but back in October of 1978, the law hadn't been settled yet. Bundy hoped to get the case continued past the speedy trial deadline of February 10[16] without a waiver so that he could then move to dismiss the case. We wouldn't be ready for trial by November 6, either, but we needed that waiver. We were playing a high-stakes game of "chicken." Who was going to blink? Would Bundy cave in and enter a waiver or would we be the ones to chicken out and agree to continue the case without a waiver? Or would we slam into the brick wall of November 6, and both sides begin trial unprepared? If we hit that brick wall, I felt that we were better able to muddle through a half-prepared prosecution than Bundy was to mount an unprepared defense. When we got to the hearing, Bundy had a lawyer whether he wanted one or not. In an unprecedented move, the Chief Justice of the Florida Supreme Court, Arthur England, appointed Michael Minerva as counsel for Bundy.[17] Minerva was to act as counsel if Bundy would accept him or standby counsel if Bundy would not. Jopling took the matter of Bundy's representation as his first order of business and confirmed England's order appointing Minerva as standby counsel. The next order of business was my oral request to hold the hearing on our motion for discovery *in camera*. Bundy agreed with my request, and we went behind closed doors into the judge's chambers leaving the media standing in the hall wondering what we were doing. Bundy had to one-up us on the closing of the hearing. He made an oral request that I be ordered not to discuss what happened at the hearing with the media. I agreed to the request and asked that the gag order extend to Bundy as well.

Bundy contended our motion for discovery should be denied unless we supported it with live testimony. I argued that the motion for discovery was like an affidavit for search warrant. The law didn't require live testimony in support of an affidavit for search warrant, and the motion for discovery should be treated the same way. If it was sworn, and if it stated probable cause, it should be granted. Although Jopling was a highly experienced trial lawyer, most of his practice had been as a civil attorney. He almost bought Bundy's argument, which would have been disastrous. We would have had to call scores of witnesses to support the allegations in the motion for discovery, and the hearing would have taken longer than an ordinary jury trial. Jopling took the motion under advisement pending receipt of legal memoranda from both sides.

Bundy's motion for continuance came next. He steadfastly refused to waive speedy trial, and Jopling resolved the issue with a rather neat ruling. He continued the case to January 8, 1979, within the speedy trial time, but ruled that if and when Bundy entered a waiver, the case would be reset for March 12, 1979.[18] That very day Bundy agreed to sign a waiver of speedy trial. By some strange coincidence, I happened to have a waiver already typed out for his signature. Bundy signed it, and Sheriff Bailey witnessed his signature, as did Captain Poitinger of the Leon County Sheriff's Office. A few days later I filed a memorandum supporting my argument against live testimony on a motion for discovery.[19] Bundy asked for an extension of time to file his memo, and Jopling gave him until November 8 to get it filed.[20] Bundy never filed anything, and Jopling granted the motion for discovery without requiring live testimony.[21]

We sent Minerva and Bundy notice that we were going to collect the samples at the Leon County Jail on November 28, at the hour of 2:00 P.M. We anticipated trouble. Getting the saliva samples would be no real problem; you can forcibly remove saliva samples. You cannot, however, forcibly extract handwriting samples. Bundy had defied the Leon County court order for handwriting samples; he may very well thumb his nose at our court order. I attended the collection process. John McCarthy came over from the crime lab to personally collect the samples. They brought Bundy into a conference room at the jail and sat him down at a table across from McCarthy. McCarthy provided him with writing materials and then began to dictate to him what should be written. We had to verify a number of signatures, and we needed 15 samples of each signature with Bundy's right hand, and 5 each with his left. Amazingly, Bundy complied up to a point. He refused to give us the right-handed signatures. McCarthy didn't insist. He thanked Bundy, gathered up his materials, and left the room. I walked out with him. "When can you finish your examination and tell us whether Bundy signed those credit cards or not?" McCarthy smiled. "He signed them. I've been working with those forged receipts for months now, and it wasn't hard at all to identify the signatures. Of course, I'll go through all the procedural steps for analysis and get out a report as soon as possible." On December 1, we received his report confirming what he told me at the jail.[22]

And then the case entered into a most unusual phase. All parties reached an agreement that the Lake City case would not be tried until after the Tallahassee case, but the Lake City case did not lie dormant as the Tallahassee case moved forward. Bundy started taking depositions. We immediately faced one hurdle—according to the rules of criminal procedure, a deposition must be taken in the home county of the witness being deposed. We certainly weren't going to repeatedly haul Bundy back and forth between Lake City and Tallahassee so he could depose the witnesses and devise escape stratagems. Where there's a will, there's a way, however, and we worked out a way for Bundy to depose witnesses from the Leon County Jail. A state attorney in Florida has a power few other prosecutors have—the power to issue investigative subpoenas.[23] We agreed that the defense would tell me who they wanted to depose, and I would subpoena the witnesses to appear at the Leon County Jail on the agreed date and time. The system worked fairly well, but on the first day of depositions, we hit a snag.

Bundy noticed me that he wanted to take 18 depositions over a period of five days, Monday February 5 through Friday February 9, 1979. The first round of witnesses was mostly police officers and lab personnel. On Sunday evening, I drove over to Tallahassee and rented a room in a fleabag motel near the jail. When I got to the jail Monday morning, I ran into Dick Hagood, a reporter for the *Florida Times Union* in Jacksonville. I asked him why he was at the jail, and he said he had come to attend the depositions. "No, sir, you're not going to do that." I was emphatic. "Yes, I am, Judge Jopling gave me permission to attend the depositions." He was emphatic. I told him we'd cancel depositions before letting him attend them.

About that time a jailer came out and ushered me in. Hagood got up to follow. I stopped. "Mr. Hagood, you must understand. You're not going to attend these depositions." Thinking that settled it, I started back for the door with Hagood on my heels. The jailer, a burly young man, grabbed him by the arm as we went in. I made it to the deposition room alone.

I explained the situation to Bundy and his standby counsel, and Bundy agreed with my attitude toward the presence of the press. We had hardly gotten that issued discussed when a jailer came in and told me I had a phone call. It was Jopling, and he wasn't happy. Brute force may have worked on Hagood, but it wouldn't work on Jopling. I explained to Jopling that if he allowed reporters into the deposition room, we'd not only have a circus, we'd have our entire case reported in the news. I offered to call off the depositions until we could get a definitive ruling, and he finally said, "No, go ahead with the depositions." Next I received a call from a lawyer representing the *Florida Times Union*. He insisted that Hagood be admitted to the depositions, and I refused. He said he was going to file a motion to intervene and compel us to allow the press into the deposition room, and I told him to file it as soon as possible, because we were going to hold more depositions beginning on February 26, and I wanted the matter to be resolved before we resumed the depositions.

Eventually, we started taking depositions. I felt somewhat strange sitting in a room with the defendant in a murder case, listening to him question witnesses. We had a lot of down time, when we had finished one witness and the next had not arrived, and eventually we started shooting the bull. We made small talk, carefully staying away from anything that might lead into a discussion of the merits of the case. Bundy proved to be likeable, witty, and a good conversationalist. Bundy also proved to be a good questioner. The job he did wasn't on par with the more talented lawyers, but he covered all the bases and got most of the pertinent information from the witnesses. When he overlooked a vital area, I stepped in and asked a few questions calculated to lead him down the right path.

My helpfulness led to an interesting occurrence during Doug Barrow's deposition. Bundy thoroughly questioned Barrow on all the work he had done examining fingerprints from the van, Bundy's apartment, and other locations. It was a long story, but you can summarize it in one sentence—Barrow didn't find Bundy's or Kim's fingerprints anywhere. The longer Barrow's deposition went on, the greater the look of smugness on Bundy's face. He concluded his questioning on a tone of "Well, you certainly haven't been much help to the State, have you?" I decided to put my oar in the water.

I asked Barrow about his comparison of the cigarette butts. We went over his findings that the driver of the Media Center van had smoked the cigarette butts found at the Suwannee River State Park, and I had him describe how that finding led to the discovery of Kim's body. It was interesting watching the emotions play across Bundy's face while I was asking the questions. He first looked concerned. Then he was nervous. Finally he was horrified. I decided to be merciful and asked Barrow a few more questions. I had him explain that his examination was highly speculative and that he could not testify to his findings. Bundy breathed a sigh of relief and immediately recovered his aplomb. There was only one conclusion that could be drawn from Bundy's reaction. He realized he had made a mistake by stopping so close to where he had left Kim to clean out the van. He thought Barrow's findings were going to put a noose around his neck. I really enjoyed watching him sweat.

I hoped that the *Times Union* would file its motion to intervene before our next round of depositions began on February 26, but as time passed it looked less and less likely that the motion would be filed until we were again in depositions. I took the bull by the horns and filed my own motion for a protective order barring the press from depositions.[24] The *Times Union* immediately responded with a petition to be admitted to depositions,[25] and (since the same lawyer represented both papers) the *Miami Herald* weighed in with a pleading opposing the motion for protective order.[26]

We held the hearing on February 23. Bundy was present with an assistant public defender from Tallahassee, and Harold Wahl represented the *Times Union*. I presented an affidavit[27] and a brief[28] in support of the motion, and called eight witnesses, mostly law enforcement officers and local lawyers. Wahl called only one witness, Don Caldwell, the publisher of the *Lake City Reporter*.[29] Bundy couldn't just stand idly by, so he filed a motion to prevent his being photographed in handcuffs.[30] Jopling took the matter under advisement, saying he would rule by February 28, and ordering that no depositions could be held until he made his decision.[31] Despite my best efforts, depositions had been derailed by interference from the media, but they would not be derailed again. On February 27, Jopling entered a protective order barring the press from attending depositions.[32] It wasn't until 1987 that this issue was definitively settled, when the Florida Supreme Court ruled that depositions were not public proceedings, that members of the press had no right to attend them, and that it was not necessary to obtain a protective order to keep the press out.[33]

We went back to the drudgery of depositions. Day after day, week after week, I went through the routine of going to the Leon County Jail to sit through hours of testimony, leaving the jail and going to eat supper by myself at a restaurant, going back to my room at the Fleabag Hilton, sleeping eight hours, then getting up and doing it all over again. One day when Mike Minerva came and sat through depositions with Bundy, he and I left the jail at noon to go eat lunch together. As we sat eating barbecue in a restaurant not far from the jail, Minerva leaned over the table and said to me, "I sure would like to plead this case out." John Spinkelink had recently become the first man executed in Florida since the reinstatement of the death penalty, and Minerva felt that this event might have made Bundy more willing to consider the possibility of a plea. I told Minerva I would make some inquiries and get back in touch with him. The first people I spoke to were Larry Simpson and Jerry Blair. Simpson was amenable and agreed to make inquiries of his boss, the heads of the various Tallahassee law enforcement agencies, and the victims' families to get their feelings on the matter. Simpson's boss was Harry Morrison, the elected state attorney. Morrison, who had been a prosecutor since the year I was born, wasn't at all sure that taking a plea from Bundy was the right thing to do, but he grudgingly went along with the idea.

Blair and I had a long talk about the quality of our case and the advisability of a plea. We agreed that the prospects of losing at trial were very good. We also discussed and dismissed the possibility that taking a plea could mean the end of our careers as prosecutors. The political backlash of such a plea might very well finish us, but we could not let that possibility enter into the calculus of whether to take the plea. We ultimately decided to take the plea. Now we had to go on a round of shuttle diplomacy, talking to the various heads of our local law enforcement agencies. They all agreed that we should take a plea if we could. Blair and I then went to talk to Tom Leach, and we had a most interesting conversation.

Leach was a short-distance truck driver, so we didn't have any real difficulty tracking him down. We found him not far from the Holiday Inn where Bundy had spent the night. He was clearing some land near the Quail Heights Country Club, and we wound up squatting under the shade of an oak tree as we discussed the matter. We laid it all out to him as objectively as possible, telling him that he had full veto power over the plea. Although we didn't have to have his blessings to take the plea, we weren't going to take it without them. Leach then told us he had recently made a delivery at the Reception and Medical Center in Lake Butler, where all men entering prison were first sent. "An inmate came up to me and asked me if I wasn't the father of that little girl over in Lake City who had been kidnapped and murdered. I told him I was. He said, 'We've been following that story here in prison, and we don't like what happened one little bit. I just want you to know that when Bundy gets here, we'll take care of him for you.'" Leach wanted to know if there was any possibility that the inmate had told him the truth. Blair let me field that question, and I spoke circumspectly. My family had been in corrections since before World War II, and I felt I knew prison culture fairly well. "You can never know for sure," I said, "but prisoners don't like child molesters, and it is quite likely that

Bundy will live longer on death row than he would if you just dumped him out in the general population of a maximum security prison." Leach agreed to the plea.

Getting back in contact with Simpson, I learned that everyone on his end of the case was agreeable. Now we had to decide what the terms would be and how the plea would be entered. We also had to get the plea entered as soon as possible, and we had to get it entered as cleanly as possible. If there were any glitches in the plea inquiry, they could form the basis for a motion to vacate the plea or a collateral attack on the plea. Bundy could act out, infect the plea with error, sit back for several years until he was satisfied that our case had deteriorated beyond repair, then get the plea vacated and proceed to a sure victory at trial. Simpson, Blair, and I decided we would take nothing less than a plea of guilty as charged on all counts with an agreement that the three life sentences for murder run consecutively. Each life sentence for murder carried a 25-year mandatory minimum, and we wanted it clear that Bundy would serve 75 calendar years before becoming eligible for parole. Then I dropped a bombshell. I thought we ought to insist that Bundy's plea include a confession to exactly what he did in all three homicides. My colleagues unanimously shouted me down on the point. I believe what Simpson said was, "Good Lord, Dekle, do you want to get us run out of town on a rail? If Bundy described exactly what he did in those murders and that description went public, can you imagine what they'd do to us for taking the plea?" I reluctantly agreed, but I did insist that the plea offer include a bare bones confession to the murder of Kim Leach. Next, we went to Minerva with our conditions, which were included in a written plea of guilty that we expected Bundy to sign. Minerva looked them over and pronounced them doable, but Bundy had to have some concessions. After getting booted off the case, Farmer had continued to consult with Minerva and Bundy behind the scenes, and Farmer had been instrumental in persuading Bundy to plead. Farmer had to be involved in the plea. We said fine, they could resurrect Clarence Darrow and bring him to court if they wished, we were willing to bend to get the plea taken.

What Minerva didn't tell us was how Farmer had sold Bundy on the plea. I learned years later that Farmer had convinced him it was a good tactical move. Farmer told Bundy he could enter the plea, wait for the case to deteriorate beyond repair, and then file a postconviction motion to set aside the plea.[34]

We needed to discuss two final points. Bundy had to behave himself in court. If he acted out, there was going to be no plea. Minerva understood and assured us he would exert his utmost power to rein Bundy in. Finally, I expressed some concern to Minerva over the issue of Bundy's competence. Minerva told us a psychiatrist had examined Bundy, and the psychiatrist had told him that if Bundy had enough sense to enter the plea, he was competent to proceed. I don't recall if it was then or later that Minerva showed us the report by Dr. Emanuel Tanay.

Tanay believed that if Bundy was too out of touch with reality to comprehend what a great case we had against him, his inability to understand the magnificence of our case rendered him incompetent to stand trial. If, on the other hand, he had enough brainpower to figure out that his only chance of avoiding execution was to cop a plea, then he was competent to plead. Simpson and I had a good laugh on that one. It seemed to us that Bundy understood the quality of our cases much better than Tanay.

Next, we had to enlist the judges. Both Jopling and Cowart were willing to go along with the plea, and they were ready to do it sooner rather than later. We set up a plea for the next day. We hoped that we could sneak into court in Tallahassee, get the plea taken under the media's radar, and get out of town as quickly as possible. We believed that the bigger the audience, the more likely Bundy was to do some grandstanding. There's an old saying that three people can keep a secret if two of them are dead, and the mechanics of setting up the plea guaranteed that far more than three people knew the secret.

When we got to the courthouse the morning of the plea, pandemonium greeted us. Reporters swarmed all over the courthouse, and the courtroom was full to capacity. Blair and I got a sinking feeling in our stomachs when we saw a rather unique seating arrangement. Three chairs had been set up against the back wall of the courtroom next to the judge's bench. These chairs were occupied by Ken Katsaris, Eldridge Beach, and Ed Blackburn, interim director of FDLE. Each of those men had played an integral role in the case, and it was fitting that they be there for the plea, but we really wished that they had found different seating accommodations. Given Bundy's high regard for Katsaris, merely seeing the man in the courtroom might set Bundy off. Things were beginning to unravel, but we soldiered on.

I asked Minerva if Bundy had signed the paper. He had. "Show me the paper." Minerva showed me the plea offer. There on the last page was Bundy's signature. Then we got some more disconcerting news. One of the jailers assigned to escort Bundy told us that Bundy had spent all night typing in his cell, and that Bundy was acting like he was wired that morning. Everything was set, however, and the only thing we could see to do at that point was hold our noses and jump off the high dive before all the water drained out of the pool.

We entered the crowded courtroom and took our places at counsel table. I sat on the far end of the State table and was elbow to elbow with Minerva. The atmosphere was electric. Jopling and Cowart assumed the bench, and Minerva began to announce the plea. Then our dive hit bottom—and the pool was dry. Bundy stood up, handed motions all around, and began to berate Minerva for everything but a competent lawyer. I glanced at the papers Bundy had served on us. They were captioned in both the Tallahassee case and the Lake City case and were a motion for continuance[35] and a motion to replace appointed counsel.[36] The gist of both motions was that Minerva was providing ineffective assistance of counsel. As Bundy continued to rant about Minerva, I slipped out of my chair and went behind counsel table to where Blair was sitting. We briefly discussed how bad this was and how we could not now under any circumstances take a plea. I moved over to Simpson, and we had an almost identical conversation. I returned to my seat at Minerva's side and started listening carefully to what Bundy was saying. It seemed to me that he was leading up to something. Bundy reached down and picked up some papers. They looked very much like the written plea offer. I asked Minerva, "That silly bastard isn't fixing to try to plead guilty is he?" Minerva said he thought so. I replied, "Tell him to sit his ass down, we ain't taking no pleas." Minerva tugged on Bundy's coat sleeve and Bundy bent over. Minerva whispered in his ear, and the transformation in Bundy's appearance was almost immediate. He went from a self-assured lawyer to a surprised layman. Bundy managed to get off a few more sentences and then sat down. I was so fired up that I don't really recall what the judges said at that point, but it wasn't long before we were in recess. I immediately accosted Minerva and demanded that he return the written plea offer. He did, but it was mutilated when I got it. Bundy had torn his signature off the paper. That suited me fine. I completed the job of tearing the paper into the tiniest fragments possible. That wasn't the most exasperating and humiliating day I ever spent in court, but it easily ranks in the top 10.

I really felt bad for Minerva. He was an excellent criminal defense attorney who had served as chief assistant public defender before becoming the elected public defender. As chief assistant, he handled all the public defender's most serious cases. He had a wealth of experience, a good legal mind, and a sterling reputation for competence, courtesy, and ethics. Bundy would have done well to let him take over the defense. Instead, Bundy treated him with scorn and disrespect. When the Chi Omega case finally went to trial down in Miami, Minerva handed the case off to his assistants and for the most part stayed in Tallahassee. Bundy had succeeded in driving off the one member of the public defender's office most capable of saving him. Before Minerva completely washed his hands of Bundy, there was one more thing he could do, and he did it.

One of the things I really liked about being a prosecutor as opposed to a defense attorney was the fact that as a prosecutor, you are in charge of the case. Of course, you must consult with various interested parties, for example, the victim and the police, but in the final analysis, you call the shots. As a defense attorney, you don't make the decisions, your client does. You may advise, counsel, and encourage, but your client is in the driver's seat. You might have a perfectly good defense, but if your client does not want you to raise it, you can't. Minerva really wanted to raise an insanity defense in the Chi Omega case, but he was stymied on two fronts. First, he was merely standby counsel, and second Bundy wouldn't hear of it. There was, however, one mental health defense that could be raised without Bundy's consent, and Minerva raised it.

In criminal law, there are two broad areas where mental health issues can be raised to thwart a prosecution. First is the defense of not guilty by reason of insanity. This defense raises a historical question. Was the defendant, at the time he committed the crime, so insane as not to be held accountable for his actions? Depending on what jurisdiction you are in, there are different tests for this form of insanity. Florida applies the most stringent form of the insanity defense—the M'Naughten Test.[37] M'Naughten provides for such a stringent standard of proof that someone could have a severe mental illness but still not be insane in the eyes of the law.

Second, the defendant may raise a question as to his competency to proceed—either to trial or to sentencing. This question is not a historical question. It deals with the defendant's current mental status. And the standard for a finding of incompetence to stand trial is quite different from the standard for a finding of insanity. The test used to determine competency to proceed is "whether the defendant has a sufficient present ability to consult with his lawyer with a reasonable degree of rational understanding—and whether he has a rational as well as factual understanding of the proceedings against him."[38] If he is so mentally ill that he can't help his lawyer defend the case, then he can't stand trial. If he is so mentally ill that he can't understand what is happening to him when he gets sentenced, then he can't be sentenced. Where insanity can completely stop a prosecution, incompetence can only delay it. A defendant who is found incompetent is usually hospitalized until such time as he regains his competence, and then the trial proceeds. Although Bundy could prevent Minerva from raising an insanity defense, he couldn't prevent him from raising an incompetency defense. If Bundy was incompetent, he didn't know what he was doing, and somebody else had to make the decision for him.

Minerva made the decision for Bundy and filed a suggestion of incompetency to proceed. This did not make Bundy happy. He was a vain man, and any suggestion that he was subpar in any category was anathema to him. When a suggestion of incompetency is made, the trial court almost automatically appoints experts to examine the defendant. The experts make their written reports to the court, and a hearing is held to determine the defendant's competence to stand trial. In my experience, if the doctors all agreed that the defendant was incompetent, we simply stipulated the reports into evidence and the judge made a finding of incompetence. If there was disagreement, then we went to a full-blown evidentiary hearing on the issue. There was disagreement among the experts.

Tanay was the star witness for the defense at the competency hearing. He found that Bundy suffered from sociopathic personality disorder, which today is called antisocial personality disorder. According to the American Psychiatric Association, someone who has antisocial personality disorder exhibits three or more of the following characteristics:

1. Failure to conform to social norms by repeatedly committing crimes.
2. Deceitfulness.
3. Impulsive behavior or failure to plan ahead.
4. Irritability and aggressiveness, as indicated by repeated physical fights or assaults.

5. Reckless disregard for safety of self or others.
6. Repeated failure to sustain consistent work behavior or honor financial obligations.
7. Lack of remorse, indifference to harming others, or rationalizing having hurt, mistreated, or stolen from others.[39]

I once had a psychiatrist ask me if I wanted a definition of sociopath in layman's language. When I replied that I'd like that very much, he said, "Bum, hobo, criminal." Tanay wrote a report that pegged Bundy as exhibiting all the APA criteria. He emphasized Bundy's narcissism, poor judgment, and manipulative behavior. Among other things, Tanay wrote:

> Mr. Bundy is guided by his emotional needs, sometimes to the detriment of his legal interests. The pathological need of Mr. Bundy to defy authority, to manipulate his associates and adversaries, supplies him with "thrills," to the detriment of his ability to cooperate with his counsel. . . . I would anticipate that in the unlikely event that the prosecution's case against him would weaken, he would through his behavior bolster prosecution's case. I have much less doubt about Mr. Bundy's capacity to assist prosecution than his ability to assist his own counsel.[40]

According to Tanay, Bundy's narcissism, manipulative behavior, and lack of judgment prevented him from cooperating with his lawyers and therefore rendered him incompetent to stand trial. I agreed with almost everything Tanay had said about Bundy—except for the bottom line. As I saw it, Bundy was able to cooperate with his lawyers, he just didn't want to.

The outcome of Minerva's attempt to have Bundy declared incompetent in the Chi Omega case was vitally important to the Leach case. If Bundy was found incompetent there, then he was certain to be found incompetent in the Lake City case as well. I went over to Tallahassee and conferred with Simpson as he prepared the case for hearing. Tanay was a big name in psychiatric circles; did Simpson have anybody who could go against him? Simpson told me that one of their investigators, Dale Croy, had a psychiatrist friend from Georgia. It seems the two men were fishing buddies. At any rate, Croy's fishing buddy was willing to come to Florida and testify on behalf of the State. I wasn't especially encouraged by the fact that the State's case was going to rest on the shoulders of somebody's fishing buddy. When I talked to the doctor I was somewhat reassured, but not much. Dr. Hervey Cleckley was a likeable old fossil who exuded common sense from every pore of his body, but he was obviously out of date. When he referred to Bundy, he used the antiquated term "psychopath" instead of "sociopath."

When the hearing began Tanay took the stand. He testified quite convincingly as to his findings and rendered the opinion that Bundy was not competent to stand trial. On cross examination Simpson got him to admit that his opinion represented a minority view, that most psychiatrists would say a sociopath was competent to stand trial. Simpson asked Tanay if he relied on any particular literature in arriving at his diagnosis. Tanay said that there was one book that was an excellent reference on the subject. The book was entitled *The Mask of Sanity*, and it was written by America's foremost authority on the subject of sociopathy. Who might that be? Dr. Hervey Cleckley from Georgia. Would Tanay defer to Cleckley's judgment? Tanay readily admitted that Cleckley was far more knowledgeable about sociopathy than he was.

When Cleckley took the stand, Simpson asked him if he was the Hervey Cleckley who had written *The Mask of Sanity*. Cleckley admitted that he was indeed the author of that book, and from that point forward in the hearing we had smooth sailing. Cowart recessed before hearing arguments, and I got an opportunity to ask Simpson if he had known that Cleckley was such a renowned expert in the field. Simpson assured me that, no, he didn't know. All he knew was that Cleckley was a friend of one of their investigators who had agreed to come help out. I swallowed that line at the time, but later decided that Simpson was pulling my leg. It wasn't until many years later that he finally admitted he was indeed kidding me. Cowart found Bundy competent to stand trial. I really don't see how he could have arrived at any other decision. Sociopaths aren't incompetent to stand trial; they're egotistical manipulators who think they can con anybody. When they come into contact with the court system, they can sometimes manipulate themselves into a winning situation. More often, however, they wind up like Bundy, who had manipulated himself onto a collision course with Old Sparky in the death chamber at Florida State Prison.

# 12

# Marshaling the Evidence

If you were to ask the average millionaire how much money was enough, you might get the answer, "Just a little bit more than I already have." If you were to ask the average prosecutor how much evidence was enough, you'd probably get the same answer. As the prosecutor works through the evidence, she finds deficiencies that she wants to correct; questions occur that beg for answers; she thinks of things to do to shore up the case; and sometimes new evidence falls upon her like manna from the sky. Not long after Bundy's indictment the manna came down. Larry Daugherty called me and told me that a new witness had come forward, a lieutenant and paramedic with the Lake City Fire Department named Andy Anderson. I knew Anderson. We were classmates in high school but not really close friends. Anderson had always seemed like a stand-up guy, and I was interested to learn what he had to say.

We met at the police department, which was in the same building as the fire station, and Anderson told us his tale. I turned on the tape recorder and placed him under oath. He began by saying, "Well, this morning when I was watching the news, I saw Theodore Bundy on TV and when I saw him, he turned sideways and I saw a profile of him. He looked an awful lot like the man that I saw put a dark haired girl in his white van in front of the Lake City Junior High School."

Could he tell us when he saw this? "I can't remember the exact date." Could he give us any kind of a time frame for when he saw it? "It was a very short time, probably less than a week before ya'll found out there was a girl missing and started searching for her."

I asked him, "Alright, now you say you saw a man who looked very similar to Bundy put a girl in a white van? Tell me where it was you saw it?" He replied, "In front of the Junior High School. It was on West Duval Street, almost at the corner of Second Street and Duval Street. It was a little bit west of Second Street."

"About what time of day was this?" I wanted to know. "It was morning . . . mid-morning between 9:00 A.M. and 10:00 A.M. roughly," he replied.

"What were you doing over there at that time?" Anderson thought a moment, "Ah . . . I think I had come up to the Fire Station for overtime, and I was going home."

What exactly had Anderson seen? "Ah, there was a white van parked in the street against the curb and had traffic backed up, several cars had pulled around it and I was . . . that's when I saw a man and young girl. The man had the girl by the, let's see, he had her by the left arm. And she had an unhappy look on her face. I thought at the time you know some little girl had got in trouble and daddy had come to take her home. He led her across the street in front of the van and opened the door on the passenger side and helped the girl get in the van and slammed the door of the van and ah . . . just drove on."

"Alright, did she resist him in anyway? Pulling back or . . ." Anderson interrupted me. "She wasn't pulling back but she seemed reluctant to go. Like he wasn't actually dragging her or you know forcing her . . . he was walking ahead of her, and had her by the arm. She was lagging behind. Kind of dragging her feet."

I asked, "You say this van had traffic backed up?" Anderson replied, "Yeah. One or two cars between me and the van, maybe." I asked Anderson to describe the people he saw, and he gave a description of the man that could have fit Bundy or any other white male between the ages of 25 and 35. His description of Kim was little better. What he did say about the two people he saw was this: The man looked like a prominent young lawyer in town by the name of Tom Brown—and by golly, Bundy did look like Brown. He said the girl looked like his niece. We got a photograph of his niece, and again she looked very much like Kim.

Anderson said he followed the van approximately five blocks and then turned off to go home. I asked him why he had not come forward before. "Well, I first heard they were looking for a white car and then later on I heard they were looking for a white van and this was when it really began to bother me about what I'd seen. But I still wasn't sure enough to really mention it to anybody. I did mention to Frank Moore [another fireman] and then but I can't remember exactly how I said it and I said there's one slight chance it could have been the guy that I saw."

Anderson continued, "I've seen pictures of Bundy in the papers and seen where there was a resemblance but until this morning when I saw the news and I seen him turn sideways, well when I seen his profile, I knew I had to come tell somebody about it, cause it looks an awful lot like the man."[1]

There were a number of problems with Anderson's testimony, some obvious, some not so obvious. It seems bizarre that a kidnapper would stop a car in the middle of the street and march across a school campus to accost a girl. The sheer improbability of such a thing told heavily against Anderson's story. Except—what possible motive could Anderson have had for making it up? I thought Bundy was crazy enough to do exactly what Anderson said he did, and the FBI Behavioral Sciences Unit corroborates my belief. It teaches that as serial killers become more experienced, they begin to feel bulletproof and often engage in illogical behavior that winds up getting them caught.[2]

Another factor weighing against Anderson's testimony was the inordinate length of time between his observation and his report. Why would someone wait so long to tell something so significant? Anderson's explanation was that he didn't want to send us on a wild goose chase. My explanation is that he didn't want to believe that he had seen what he had seen. As the saying goes, denial is not just a river in Egypt.

The third problem with Anderson's testimony was that he was too fuzzy on his dates and he was wrong about his work schedule. He thought he was going home to bed when the work records showed that on February 8 he had been called back to work two shifts the day before the kidnapping, and when he saw Bundy kidnapping Kim he was just beginning his regular shift.

If we could identify the drivers of the cars stopped behind Bundy, we might get some corroboration for Anderson. All we needed was the license numbers of the other cars. Thinking that hypnosis might help him remember the tag numbers, we arranged for Anderson to be questioned under hypnosis. Imogene Keene, a psychiatric social worker with the VA Hospital in Lake City, performed the hypnosis later that afternoon, and the results were nil.[3] Keene said that Anderson might relate better to a male hypnotist and suggested that we enlist the aid of Jack Burnette, another psychiatric social worker from the VA. We set up another time for the second hypnosis.

On the date of the second hypnosis, Anderson came in and told us he had done some serious thinking about when he saw the incident, and he had decided that it was February 9. He said the night before he was supposed to take his daughter to see "Smokey and the Bandit" for her birthday but had to disappoint her because of his callback. He said when his shift began on February 9, he had been working so furiously on rescue runs that he needed to change his clothes and take a bath. He got permission from his supervisor to run home for a few minutes and freshen himself up. He left the fire station, drove to his home, and saw the incident on the way. When he got home, he ate a piece of his daughter's birthday cake, showered, changed clothes, and went back to work. Anderson underwent the second hypnosis session, and it did no more good than Keene's hypnosis session had done. Burnette suggested a third hypnosis session,[4] but I was beginning to think we may have already done too many sessions.

Anderson's testimony was the next-to-the-last major piece of evidence we uncovered in the Bundy case. The last major piece of evidence will require a little explanation. In order to fully understand the significance of this last piece of evidence, we must look back some 20 years before Bundy came to Florida to the infamous case of *Williams v. State*.[5]

Around 7:30 on the evening of November 5, 1957, 16-year-old Judy Baker arrived at Webb's City in St. Petersburg, Florida. She parked her black Plymouth in the parking lot and went shopping. When she carried her shopping bags back to the car, she opened the door and saw the head of a man hiding on the floorboard of the back seat. She screamed, and two auxiliary policemen came to the rescue. The man jumped out of her car and ran, but he didn't get far. The officers apprehended him and learned that his name was Ralph Williams. Williams explained that he had mistaken Baker's black Plymouth for his brother's car and had crawled in the back seat to take a nap.

Some six weeks later, around 7:30 P.M. on December 18, 1957, a 17-year-old young lady known to legal history only as "the Prosecutrix" parked her green Buick in the Webb's City parking lot very near the place where Miss Baker had parked. The Prosecutrix did some shopping and returned to her car around 9:15 P.M. Not being lucky enough to have noticed Williams hiding on the back seat floorboard of her car, she got in, cranked up, and drove off. She drove a short distance before Williams came up from the back seat, reached over her, and planted an ice pick in her chest. He then climbed over into the driver's seat and took control of the car. Williams drove her around St. Petersburg, threatening to kill her if she did not do what he wished. During this time he "criminally assaulted"[6] her twice. Finally, he let her go, and she was able to get herself home around 11:00 P.M. Her parents took her to a hospital where medical examination confirmed the sexual assault as well as the severe ice pick wound in her chest. The finger of suspicion immediately pointed at Williams, and he was arrested the next morning. He told the investigator that he saw the car driven by the Prosecutrix and, thinking it was his brother's, crawled in to take a nap. He said nothing about having had any kind of sexual contact with the victim. At trial he changed his story, testifying that he and the victim were longtime lovers, and that she had accidentally stabbed herself with the ice pick when he slammed on brakes while she was threatening to kill herself because he wanted to break up with her.

At the time of Williams's trial, Florida courts held that evidence of uncharged misconduct by the defendant was inadmissible and could not be heard by the jury unless the evidence fell into several narrowly drawn exceptions to that rule. Evidence falling within these exceptions was known as "similar fact evidence" because it usually involved evidence that the defendant had committed a crime that was very similar to the one for which he stood trial. Florida also recognized that "non-similar fact evidence" of uncharged misconduct was admissible against a defendant "where it is impossible to give a complete or intelligent account of the crime charged without referring to the other crime."[7] In Williams's case, the Florida Supreme Court reversed its longstanding rule of excluding such evidence and held that evidence of other crimes committed by the defendant was admissible if relevant to prove any material fact in issue, except bad character or propensity to commit crime.[8] It held that the trial court properly allowed the testimony of Judy Baker to be heard by Williams's jury and affirmed Williams's conviction. Forever after in Florida, evidence of uncharged misconduct on the part of the defendant has been called "Williams Rule" evidence. Courts have been very wary of allowing such evidence before the jury, but when the requisites are met, such evidence can be the difference between conviction and acquittal. You may recall that the Colorado prosecution of Bundy was built in large part on such evidence, and when the judge ruled most of the evidence inadmissible, it dealt the prosecution a severe blow.

Our case was built largely on "non-similar fact" Williams Rule evidence. We could not have made the case at all without extensive evidence concerning Bundy's theft of cars, car tags, and credit cards. Without this type of evidence "it would be impossible to give a complete or intelligent account of the crime charged."[9] I believed the case would benefit from some "similar fact" Williams Rule evidence showing that Bundy had tried to kidnap and kill under circumstances very similar to Kim's disappearance. The uncharged misconduct would have to be so similar to Kim's abduction that it constituted a sort of "behavioral fingerprint" that unerringly pointed to Bundy as Kim's killer. Of course, we already had one such similar fact incident—Bundy's accosting of Leslie Parmenter near her school—and that evidence was doubly relevant as both "similar fact" Williams Rule evidence (showing an attempted abduction) and "non-similar fact" Williams Rule evidence (tying Bundy to the 13d-11300 tag and the Media Center van). We needed more, and I thought I knew where we might find it. Bundy was a suspect in more than three dozen cases in the western United States. Surely one or more of those cases would provide us with the "behavioral fingerprint" we needed. I talked to J. O. Jackson about the issue, and he agreed to analyze all the western cases to see if he could find one or more that fit our specifications.

It wasn't long before Jackson came back and reported his findings. He had found one disappearance from Bountiful, Utah, that might fill the bill. A young girl by the name of Debbie Kent had disappeared leaving a high school auditorium where she was attending a play. Interestingly, the disappearance had come almost immediately upon the heels of Bundy's failed attempt to kidnap Carol DaRonch in Salt Lake City. Might there be a pattern here? A failed abduction in one city almost immediately followed by a successful abduction from the campus of a secondary school in another city. It was worthy of a detailed investigation. Jackson and I flew to Utah along with Tom Trammel, who had just come to work for us from Harry Morrison's office.

If memory serves me correctly, our first stop was with Jerry Thompson, the Salt Lake City police investigator who had worked on the DaRonch case. We talked with Thompson, got copies of reports, read transcripts of statements, and came away from our meeting feeling that we were really on to something. Bundy's approach to Carol DaRonch and his approach to Leslie Parmenter had some striking similarities. Probably the most striking similarity was his posing as an authority figure—a police officer. There was no Danny Parmenter in the Sears parking lot to prevent Bundy from getting DaRonch into his car, but when he tried to handcuff her, she put up a determined fight. Eventually, she broke free from him and escaped his automobile, taking with her the handcuffs that he had managed to get onto one of her wrists.

The very evening of his failed attempt to kidnap DaRonch, Bundy was at Viewmont High School in nearby Bountiful, where a play was being put on in the auditorium. At the play he approached a number of women who had their hair parted in the middle. It appeared that he was "coming on" to them, trying to get one or more of them to accompany him to his automobile on some pretext. He was seen in the company of, or at least standing near, Debbie Kent shortly before she disappeared. Kent left the play early on an errand and was never seen or heard from again. After collecting all available reports, speaking to as many witnesses as possible, and thoroughly digesting the information we had gathered, it seemed clear that we had our "behavioral fingerprint." The similarities between the DaRonch/Kent incidents and the Parmenter/Leach incidents were too many and too telling to be mere coincidence. We tabulated all those similarities, and I was very satisfied with the results. In the DaRonch/Kent incident we had four victims, two actual and two potential, in the Parmenter/Leach incident we had two victims, one actual and one potential. We tabulated the following similarities:

1. All victims in all cases were attractive, young white females.
2. All victims had shoulder-length hair parted in the middle.
3. Five victims, including Kim, had brown hair.
4. Five victims, including Kim, had pierced ears.
5. All victims wore coats with fur collars.
6. Four victims, including Kim, wore jeans or slacks.
7. With five victims, Bundy was described as wearing a blue coat; with one it was described as a dark coat.
8. In the Utah incidents, Bundy wore a moustache. In the Florida incidents, he was beginning to grow a moustache.
9. In Utah, the first victim was accosted in a Sears's parking lot; the later victims were entering and leaving a high school auditorium. In Florida, the first victim was accosted in a K-Mart parking lot, and Kim was entering and leaving a junior high auditorium.
10. In Utah, Bundy approached his first victim posing as a police officer. In Florida he approached his first victim as a fireman.
11. In all incidents Bundy's attack came at a time and place where large numbers of people were gathered.

12. All attacks came in town connected by an interstate to a state capital where Bundy was attending or living near a college.
13. Both the Utah and the Florida incidents followed the same pattern: Bundy, posing as an authority figure, accosted a girl in a department store parking lot. When this abduction attempt failed, he went to a secondary school campus in another town and accosted girls entering or leaving the school auditorium. Through all the transactions ran the thread of luring or taking victims to his automobile.

I overlooked one thing in assessing the DaRonch/Kent evidence. When Bundy got to the Lakeview High auditorium, he made such a nuisance of himself that it's surprising some man didn't undertake to run him off from the auditorium. This gives us another similarity that I did not catalog—after a failed abduction attempt, Bundy became reckless in his attempts to find a substitute victim.

We disclosed all the witnesses necessary to prove the DaRonch/ Kent incidents, and the defense filed a motion in limine[10] seeking to suppress all our Williams Rule evidence. Specifically, they wanted to suppress:

(a) Evidence relating to the DARONCH abduction case in Utah:
(b) Evidence relating to the various searches conducted in Utah of Defendant's automobile and apartments;
(c) Evidence relating to any investigations in Utah which have not resulted in charges being filed against Defendant, including the disappearance of DEBRA KENT;
(d) Evidence relating to the murder charge pending in Colorado involving the death of CARYN CAMPBELL;
(e) Evidence relating to [Bundy's] June 7, 1977 escape and related cases arising in Colorado;
(f) Evidence relating to [Bundy's] escape from Colorado which occurred on or about December 30, 1977, and related cases.[11]

Suppression of all the evidence from Utah and Colorado would not be fatal to our case, but they did not stop there. They also wanted to suppress evidence of Bundy's criminal activities in Florida, including:

(a) Evidence relating to his arrest on or about February 15, 1978, in Pensacola, Florida and the charges arising therefrom, including testimony of DAVID LEE;

(b) Evidence relating to the various burglary and auto theft charges currently pending in Leon County, Florida, including the orange Volkswagen and white Florida State University van;

(c) Evidence relating to the various credit card thefts which allegedly occurred in Florida, including the cards owned by WILLIAM R. EVANS, RALF B. MILLER, MARK F. LABADIE and THOMAS N. EVANS;

(d) Evidence relating to the unauthorized use of the credit cards specified in item (c);

(e) Evidence relating to the theft of a Florida license tag, number 13d-11300, including the testimony of RANDALL RAGANS;

(f) Evidence relating to the alleged purchase of a buck knife from the Green Acres store in Jacksonville, including the testimony of JOHN FARHAT;

(g) Evidence relating to the purported identification of Defendant as the operator of a white van bearing the license number 13d-11300 in Jacksonville, including the testimony of LESLIE PARMENTER, DANNY PARMENTER and LESTER PARMENTER.[12]

We could survive the suppression of the western activity, but if the judge suppressed Bundy's illegal activity in Florida, we were sunk. The litigation of the motion to suppress the Williams Rule evidence would prove to be one of the most important aspects of the pretrial phase of Bundy's prosecution.

Now that we had amassed all the available evidence, it was time to put that evidence together into a winnable case. Most of the cases I had handled before Bundy had been simple affairs with no more than a dozen or so witnesses and a few pieces of tangible evidence. My usual "trial brief" consisted of a legal pad onto which I scribbled the names of the witnesses to be called and a list of the items of tangible evidence to be used.

To try the Bundy case in such a way would be to court disaster. Where most criminal files in that day and age were considerably less than one-inch thick, the Bundy file soon ballooned to three file cabinets jammed full of paperwork and possibly a dozen banker's boxes equally full. All this information had to be assimilated in some fashion, its probative value assessed, and then it had to be assembled into a persuasive presentation. Armed with a supply of ballpoint pens, legal pads, 3x5 cards, a two-drawer card catalog, and an electric typewriter, I began my work.

The initial task was to separate the wheat of good information from the chaff of irrelevance. Sitting down with the files and reports, I began laboriously reading every page, taking notes onto 3x5 cards and arranging them alphabetically in the card catalog in three sections. In section one, each witness, no matter how seemingly irrelevant, had a card with contact information and a one- or two-sentence synopsis of the witness's significance. In section two, each item of tangible evidence had a card describing it, giving a statement of its significance, stating the authority for its seizure, and documenting its chain of custody. Section three contained any other relevant comments, thoughts, or ideas. I started this process in the early days of the search for Kim, and it continued until we went to Orlando to try the case.

It soon became obvious that the card catalog was not very portable, and I needed something a little more manageable that I could take with me and use as a ready reference wherever I went. I transcribed the information on each 3x5 card onto two lists written on letter-sized paper placed in a three-ring binder. The first list named each witness, gave the witness's contact information, and described the witness's relevance. The second list did the same for each item of tangible evidence. The lists, however, were not as comprehensive as the card catalog. They contained only witnesses and evidence that appeared to be necessary for use at trial.

After compiling the lists, I began to organize the case. I saw the Media Center van as the key to the case. Put Bundy in the van, put Kim in the van, put Bundy and Kim together, and we would have a conviction. How could we best arrange the evidence to do those three things? Could we amass any additional evidence to help with the task? I decided that the case was too massive to treat as a single case. The best way to analyze and present the case would be in a series of "mini-trials." Each mini-trial would prove up one important aspect of the case and would dovetail with the other mini-trials in painting a persuasive picture of Bundy's guilt.

The first step toward organizing the mini-trials was to decide what they would be and to fall back on the old reliable yellow pad in mapping out a rudimentary "trial brief" for each mini-trial. I named each mini-trial and gave it an acronym and a Roman numeral, which were written at the top of a sheet of legal paper. Underneath the name I listed all the witnesses relevant to that particular mini-trial, and below the witness list I recorded all the tangible evidence relevant to the mini-trial. The contemplated mini-trials were:

I. DFS: Disappearance from School—Of course, it was essential to prove that Kim had disappeared, and to give a sufficient description of the disappearance to negate any chance of her having run away.

II. DB/CS: Discovery of Body/Crime Scene—After proving Kim was lost, we had to show how she was found. Again we wanted to present this evidence in such a way as to negate any suggestion that her death was anything but a homicide. It was also necessary in this stage to lay the groundwork for the scientific analysis with which we intended to close the trial.

III. AUT: Autopsy—Essential elements of every homicide case are proof of the identity of the victim and proof of manner of the victim's death. Additionally a number of items were recovered from the body that would prove essential in connecting Bundy to Kim.

IV. LCG: Lake City Gulf—We needed to put Bundy together with Kim, and to do so we needed to put Bundy in Lake City around the time of Kim's disappearance. The evidence of his purchase of gasoline in Lake City could help to do this.

V. LCHI: Lake City Holiday Inn—Even more important than Bundy's purchase of the gasoline was his sojourn at the Lake City Holiday Inn the night before the abduction. The Holiday Inn was less than 2 miles west of the junior high on US 90.

VI. CCT: Credit Card Thefts—Bundy had paid his hotel bills and gasoline purchases with stolen credit cards in the names of a number of people. It was important to demonstrate how Bundy got hold of those cards and prove it was he who used them.

VII. VAN: Media Center Van—The huge bloodstain in the carpet on the rear floor of the van indicated that the interior of the van was our crime scene. We had to wrap that van around Bundy's neck to show that he was the person who committed the crime.

VIII. TAG: 13d-11300 Tag—Almost everywhere Bundy went in the van, it bore the same stolen license plate. The tag was essential to tying Bundy to the van. When we finally went to trial, we consolidated this mini-trial with the VAN mini-trial.

IX. PAR: Parmenter Incident—The incident with Leslie and Danny Parmenter firmly placed Bundy in the FSU Media Center van, but it did more. Leslie bore a striking resemblance to Kim, and his method of approaching Leslie was highly suggestive of how he had approached Kim.

X. A/VW: Arrest/Volkswagen—The fact that Bundy resisted arrest was evidence of guilty knowledge, and the stolen Volkswagen he was driving proved to be a treasure trove of evidence. We found all the stolen credit cards in the Volkswagen, and we found even more. There was a torn burgundy shirt that we matched to fibers found on Kim's clothing and on the van carpet; and there was an assortment of shoes that matched shoe tracks found in and on the van.

XI. BB: Blue Blazer—The blue blazer Bundy brazenly wore to court was, in my estimation, the most important aspect of the fiber evidence. It had four different types of blue fiber—singed and unsinged blue polyester, and singed and unsinged blue wool. All four of these fiber types were found all over the van carpet and Kim's clothing.

XII. LAB: Crime Lab Results—Our final salvo would be the findings of the FDLE Crime Lab. John McCarthy would identify the forged signatures on the various credit card receipts as having been authored by Ted Bundy. Richard Stephens would identify the blood on the van carpet as being the same type as Kim's blood and the semen stain on Kim's panties as being the same type as Bundy's. Finally Lynn Henson would match Bundy's shoes to the shoe tracks in the van and would describe the myriads of fiber transfers between Bundy's clothing, the van carpet, and Kim's clothing.

XIII. WMR: Williams Rule evidence—Evidence of the abductions of Carol DaRonch and Debbie Kent could seal Bundy's fate, but we might not get it before the jury.

At this stage of the preparation, it was time to share my work with Jerry Blair. He had been very busy establishing himself as the newly elected state attorney and organizing the office to his specifications, but he wanted to be kept informed about the progress of the investigation and trial preparation. I brought my ideas about the mini-trials to him and shared my thoughts about how the mini-trials should best be organized. We had a spirited debate about how to order the mini-trials but finally worked things out. We wholeheartedly agreed that the lab testimony was a sledgehammer best saved for last.

Each witness for each mini-trial warranted a folder into which we placed copies of every document pertaining to that witness—interview reports, statements, and depositions. I arranged these folders alphabetically into two banker's boxes. Finally, it was time to write the trial brief, which I broke into three volumes. Volume one was the trial brief proper, containing typed testimony synopses for each witness arranged in the order in which we anticipated calling them. Volumes two and three were more like trial preparation workbooks, into which went annotated police reports, handwritten notes, preliminary drafts of testimony synopses, and an overall evidence inventory listing the tangible objects we intended to introduce into evidence. All three volumes ran to more than 1,700 pages, with the testimony synopses taking up 169 pages. I made two copies of volume one, giving Blair a copy and taking a copy for myself.

I did one final thing. The case was not as massive as some I have since tried, but it was the biggest, most complex case I had ever confronted at the time. I needed some way to wrap my mind around all the evidence and the interrelationship between the individual items. It called for a chart of some kind, and I devised one. On an 11x17 sheet of paper, I drew three boxes, one in each upper corner and one in the middle on the bottom edge. The upper left box I labeled "Bundy," the upper right "Kim." The lower box was labeled "Van." I drew lines between the boxes and on each line wrote an item of evidence tying each of the boxes together. After several reworkings, I had three sets of 12 lines signifying 12 separate items of evidence connecting each of the three boxes. That diagram disappeared long ago, but I have a record of the 36 items of evidence.

(A) Tying Bundy to the van:
1. The 13d-11300 tag was stolen near Bundy's apartment.
2. The van was stolen and recovered near Bundy's apartment.
3. Bundy bought gas in Lake City on February 7 while driving the van.

   4. Bundy bought gas in Jacksonville on February 7 while driving the van.
   5. Bundy bought the knife in Jacksonville, its price tag was found in the van.
   6. The Parmenter incident.
   7. The sightings by Anderson and Edenfield.
   8. Daws detained Bundy near the van.
   9. Shoe tracks in the van matched Bundy's Adidas shoes.
   10. A shoe track on the van's bumper matched Bundy's Bass shoes.
   11. Fibers in the van matched Bundy's blue blazer.
   12. Fibers in the van matched Bundy's torn burgundy shirt.

(B) Tying Kim to the van:
   1. Anderson saw Bundy putting Kim in the van.
   2. Bloodstains in the van carpet matched Kim's blood type.
   3. Blue and white fibers in the van matched Kim's jeans.
   4. Six colors of fibers in the van matched Kim's purse.
   5. White fibers in the van matched Kim's fur collar.
   6. White fibers in the van matched Kim's socks.
   7. Blue nylon loops in the van matched Kim's jersey.
   8. Fibers on Kim's purse matched the van carpet.
   9. Fibers on Kim's bra matched the van carpet.
   10. Fibers on Kim's socks matched the van carpet.
   11. Fibers on Kim's jersey matched the van carpet.
   12. Fibers on Kim's jeans matched the van carpet.

(C) Tying Bundy to Kim:
   1. Bundy bought gas in Lake City on February 7.
   2. Bundy spent the night in Lake City on February 8.
   3. Clinch Edenfield saw Bundy at the junior high.
   4. Anderson saw Bundy with Kim.
   5. Semen on Kim's panties matched Bundy's blood type.
   6. Green fibers on Kim's socks matched Bundy's torn burgundy shirt.
   7. Burgundy fibers on Kim's socks matched Bundy's shirt.
   8. Blue polyester fibers on Kim's socks matched Bundy's blue blazer.
   9. Blue wool fibers on Kim's socks matched Bundy's blue blazer.

### DEFENDANT TO KIMBERLY DIANE LEACH

1. Defendant buys gas in Lake City on 2/7/78
2. Defendant spends night in Lake City on 2/8/78
3. Clinch Edenfield sighting
4. Andy Anderson sighting
5. Semen stain on Kim's panties matches defendant's blood type
6. Green fibers on Kim's socks match burgundy shirt
7. Burgundy fibers on Kim's socks match burgundy shirt
8. Blue polyester fibers on Kim's socks match blue blazer
9. Blue wool fibers on Kim's socks match blue blazer
10. Blue polyester fibers on Kim's jeans match blue blazer
11. Blue wool fibers on Kim's jeans match blue blazer
12. Parmenter incident

### KIMBERLY DIANE LEACH TO WHITE FSU VAN

1. Andy Anderson sighting
2. Bloodstain on van carpet matches Kim's blood type
3. Blue & white cotton fibers in van match Kim's jeans
4. Six colors of cotton fibers in van match Kim's purse
5. White fibers in van match Kim's fur collar
6. White fibers in van match Kim's socks
7. Blue nylon loops in van match Kim's blue jersey
8. Fibers on Kim's purse match van carpet
9. Fibers on Kim's bra match van carpet
10. Fibers on Kim's socks match van carpet
11. Fibers on Kim's blue jersey match van carpet
12. Fibers on Kim's jeans match van carpet

### DEFENDANT TO WHITE FSU VAN

1. 13d-11300 Tag taken and recovered near Oaks Apts.
2. Van taken and recovered near Oaks Apts.
3. Defendant buys gas in Lake City driving white van with 13d-11300 tag on 2/7/78
4. Defendant buys gas in Jacksonville near Jeb Stuart School on 2/7/78 with 13d-11300 tag
5. Defendant buys Buck General knife in Jacksonville, price tag recovered in van
6. Parmenter incident at Jeb Stuart School on 2/8/78
7. Sightings by Anderson, Edenfield and Moore
8. Defendant arrested in orange Volkswagen taken three blocks from abandoned van
9. Two partial shoe tracks in van match defendant's Adidas shoes
10. Partial shoe track on van bumper matches defendant's Bass shoes
11. Fibers in van match defendant's blue blazer
12. Red fiber pills in van match fiber pills on burgundy shirt

The Relationship Triangle. (Courtesy of the State Attorney's Office of the Third Judicial Circuit, Florida)

10. Blue polyester fibers on Kim's jeans matched Bundy's blue blazer.
11. Blue wool fibers on Kim's jeans matched Bundy's coat.
12. The Parmenter incident.

I showed the triangle to Blair, and he liked it. Blair thought that the triangle was not just an excellent graphic for helping us understand the evidence. He thought it would be an excellent graphic for demonstrating the evidentiary connections to the jury. I said I would get some butcher paper and make a larger triangle to use in final argument, but Blair had a better idea. He took the triangle to a graphic artist, and the artist produced a gigantic visual aid for use in final argument. When it was finished, I had to admit that it looked better than anything I could have done on butcher paper.

# 13

# Bundy for the Defense, Part II

Judge Cowart was no stranger to high-profile cases. He had presided over 12 capital murder trials and ordered three men to death row. It is rare for appellate judges to make public comments, but Chief Justice Arthur England told the press he had appointed Cowart because "I wanted somebody who was obviously competent in criminal law." Michael Von Zamft, Bundy's would-be lawyer from Miami, called Cowart "the best judge I've ever seen."[1]

Cowart was probably one of the shrewdest judges I have ever seen in being able to stay on the right side of the media. He called himself a cowboy because he once owned quarterhorses,[2] and played the role of a bluff and blustery country philosopher with a genuine sense of humor. Despite his frank and friendly façade, he ruled his courtroom with an iron hand, brooking no nonsense from lawyers and litigants alike.

One thing was certain from the day Cowart took over the case. Bundy was going to be tried in Miami. It would have been foolish to try the case in Tallahassee. Somewhere in the appeals process or postconviction proceedings, a Tallahassee trial would most certainly have caused massive problems defending the conviction. Where, then, to go? Back home to Miami where Cowart could sleep in his own bed at night. Almost every change of venue I ever got in a murder case resulted in the case being moved to some venue convenient to the judge. Either the judge had a relative living in the new city, or the new city was the judge's hometown, or the judge had some other personal reason for wanting to go there.

Cowart went through the motions of actually considering the possibility of trying the case in Tallahassee, and the prosecution team tried manfully to keep it in Tallahassee. Cowart agreed to try to select a jury in Tallahassee. The voir dire examination of potential jurors began, and Cowart considered the testimony of five potential jurors, dismissing four of them for cause on grounds of pervasive publicity. He threw in the towel on the testimony of potential juror Richard Linkhart, who said he would do his best to put the publicity out of his mind, but warned, "I can't guarantee that I can do that." With Linkhart's testimony, the curtain fell on the Tallahassee voir dire, and the prosecution and defense teams began preparing for the trek to Miami. Ed Harvey, one of the senior members of the Bundy team, called the decision "extremely good for the defense," and Bundy called it "excellent."[3] It was. Every community is different, and death penalties are harder to come by in certain parts of Florida. At that time, Miami had a reputation as being a place where it was rather difficult to get a death penalty.

Minerva sent three lawyers, two law student interns, a secretary, and an investigator to Miami, but he stayed home.[4] As I saw things, the best lawyer standing between Bundy and Old Sparky was Minerva, and Bundy had driven him off. Why? It seems that Bundy believed that Minerva thought he was guilty.[5] In the final analysis, it makes no difference what the defense attorney believes. The prosecutor attempts to establish the truth, and the defense attorney attempts to test the proof. That duty to test the proof is not changed one iota by the defense attorney's personal opinion, and a lawyer acts in the highest degree of professionalism when she attempts to demonstrate to a jury that the proof is lacking even though she believes the defendant is guilty. Minerva was a good enough professional to not let his personal feelings interfere with his sworn duty.

Of the three lawyers Minerva sent to Miami, I knew two. As I saw it, Ed Harvey was the natural leader of the group. He was an experienced, level-headed, competent lawyer capable of doing a good job for a cooperative client. Lynn Thompson, who had the distinction of being the only lawyer to serve on both Bundy trials, was every bit as experienced as Harvey and a very good trial lawyer. I didn't know Margaret Good, an appellate attorney who handled legal briefs and arguments before the higher courts, but I felt she was a good choice for the role of the defense team's legal arm. Bundy still had a shot at winning if he would just let them do their jobs. Simpson's case was more than sufficient to prove Bundy guilty, but it did have flaws that could have been effectively exploited by a defense team free to exercise their own legal judgment. The sociopathic murder defendant, however, often does not allow his defense team the freedom to properly defend him.

Preparations for the Miami trial continued apace. Five hundred potential jurors were summoned; Bundy's cell was "escape proofed."[6] Two hundred fifty media representatives were expected at the trial.[7] Eleven Florida television stations formed a consortium to film and report on the trial, and another consortium of Florida PBS stations went together to broadcast late-night recaps of the trial.[8] The courtroom was ballyhooed as the very courtroom where the infamous Ronnie Zamora "TV Intoxication" case had been tried.[9] I wasn't impressed with the courtroom. Accustomed as I was to the spacious courtrooms of rural North Florida, I found it disappointingly small.

State Attorney Janet Reno gave the prosecution team some space in her office, and it was soon equipped with four filing cabinets full of files and four banker's boxes full of depositions. Katsaris came to Miami for the trial, and everything appeared in readiness.[10] Simpson went to Miami with a retinue also. Although he had been pretty much a Lone Ranger in the pretrial stage, it was time to call in the cavalry. It came in the form of his boss, Harry Morrison; Dan McKeever, a trial lawyer with a wealth of experience; and Lyndia Kent, a sharp young prosecutor who specialized in research. I had known McKeever as both an adversary and a colleague. Arthur Lawrence had hired McKeever while I was still a public defender, and I had opposed him in numerous trials. After moving over to the prosecution side, McKeever and I worked together on several trials before he left the office and took a job with Morrison. McKeever was smooth as silk before a jury and had a very good ability to evaluate and present cases. Simpson and McKeever made a good team. Kent went on to become a much-feared federal prosecutor who bore the nickname "The Steel Magnolia." Rounding out the prosecution team were Investigator Grady Smith and legal secretary Jan McCullers. They had one tag-along—me.

I had two basic reasons for going to the Miami trial. First, there were many legal issues to be resolved that were common to both cases, and I wanted to be there to do what I could to help see to it that they were resolved favorably. Second, I had never tried a case that lasted more than a day or two, and I wanted to pick up some pointers. I couldn't stay down there forever, so I limited my time in Miami to jury selection and the motion hearings.

When I got to Miami, I got a surprise. I naturally thought that the motion hearings would be held first, and we would then begin the jury selection. But something had to be done about the media. The lawyers wanted the motion hearings closed, and the media wanted them open to the public. A week or more of public motion hearings would wreck the jury selection process. The only solution I could see was to close the hearings, but Cowart found another way. He announced that he intended to pick, swear, and sequester the jury and then begin the motion hearings.

I didn't like Cowart's idea. Before the jury is sworn, if the judge makes a bad ruling, the State can take an interlocutory appeal and try to get the decision reversed. Although such an appeal might theoretically be possible after the jury is sworn, it would be highly impractical. Cowart could kill the case with a bad ruling after jury selection.

That wasn't my only surprise. The ranks of the defense team had swollen. They added a new lawyer, Robert Haggard, and a jury selection expert, Emil Spillman, an Atlanta psychiatrist and hypno-analyst who supposedly could quickly determine a person's character by interpreting Freudian slips, facial expressions, and body language.[11] Empowered by his success in driving Minerva off the case, Bundy took a highly visible role in the defense, dictating what he wanted done and not done. Nobody on the defense team knew how to handle him.

It might seem I have painted a dismal picture of an ill-coordinated, hamstrung defense facing the well-oiled machine of the prosecution team. Don't think for a moment that Bundy had no chance in Miami. There's an old chess proverb that says the winner of a chess game is the player who makes the next-to-the-last mistake. With a little modification, you could apply it to the courtroom—all other things being equal, the side that wins a trial is the one that best exploits the other side's mistakes. But the client must give the lawyer the tactical and strategic freedom to exploit those mistakes.

Jury selection began on a Monday and lasted until late the next Friday night.[12] Because the courtroom was so small, I spent a lot of time upstairs in the pressroom monitoring the voir dire on the numerous television monitors. Haggard seemed to be the man carrying the ball for the defense. I didn't think he had been on the team long enough to be fully versed in the case, but that is not the only strange thing that happened with the defense down in Miami. Haggard appeared to be a student of the talk-them-to-death school of voir dire, and he quickly incurred Cowart's ire. Spillman sat at counsel table with the defense team, and if I ever saw him in whispered consultation with any of them, I don't remember it. Finally the jury was sworn and sequestered, and we began the adventure of the motion hearings.

A disorganized army can inflict heavy casualties, and Bundy's defense team was able to score some major blows during the week of motions. I don't remember the order in which the motions were heard, but I do remember some significant incidents from the hearings and the preparation periods preceding them. One of the big motions, of course, was the motion to suppress the hours of taped statements Bundy made to Patchen, Bodiford, and Chapman. Simpson and McKeever put the trio in a hotel room to try to sort through the hours of tapes and make heads or tails of them. I pitched in to help and was immediately astonished. They were listening to the original tapes, which had far better sound quality than the "enhanced" tapes that I had been struggling with for months. What was going on? I got an explanation: You will recall that when they first made the reel-to-reel tape recordings, they ran them on the slowest speed to conserve money, at the cost of sound quality. When they sent the tapes off for the prohibitively expensive "enhancement" of sound quality, they didn't want to risk losing the originals in the mail. To safeguard the originals, they made cassette copies to mail to the expert for enhancement. The expert got virtually inaudible copies of the original tapes and did a marvelous job of enhancing them back to approximately 75 percent of the quality of the original tapes. Although both McKeever and Simpson were upset that Cowart suppressed the statements, my feelings weren't too badly hurt.

Another ruling that hurt us was Cowart's suppression of Utah state trooper Bob Hayward's testimony about his August 16, 1975, arrest of Bundy. It was around 3:00 A.M. when Hayward drove up on Bundy's VW parked on the side of the road and Bundy sped off in an attempt to evade Hayward. Hayward stopped Bundy and found some interesting things in the VW—a missing passenger seat, handcuffs, a jimmy, an ice pick, a ski mask, a pantyhose mask, several short lengths of rope, and torn pieces of a white sheet.[13] Bundy had an explanation for his odd equipment, just not a very good one. He said that he had found the handcuffs in a garbage dump near the apartment where he lived. Bundy went on to say that when he lived in Seattle, he had once made a "citizen's arrest" of a bicycle thief and had to scuffle with the thief until the police arrived. When he found the handcuffs, he decided to keep them for use on the next bicycle thief he encountered. His explanation of the pantyhose mask was even better: The previous year he had taken lots of night classes and it had been cold. In trying to decide how to cope with the severe cold, he remembered a story about Utah mountain climbers shielding their faces with nylon and ran right out and bought some pantyhose. He cut eyeholes and a mouth hole in them so that he could wear the pantyhose mask under his ski mask while changing classes in the frigid night air.[14] If you juxtapose these items with the handcuffs he used when attempting to carry Carol DaRonch off in a VW and the statement he made to Norm Chapman about taking seats out of VWs to "haul cargo," you might come up with a more rational explanation for why he had those things. Cowart wasn't comfortable with the legality of the seizure and suppressed the evidence. This hurt both cases, but the Lake City case suffered a far worse blow than the Chi Omega case. On that August night in Utah, Bundy was obviously doing exactly the same thing that he was that February morning in Lake City—looking for a victim.

I don't really recall much about the other motions—except the motions to suppress the in-court identification of Bundy by Nita Neary, who saw him in profile as he left the Chi Omega house, and Connie Hastings, who saw him in the vicinity of the Chi Omega house that evening.[15] Haggard went after them like a starving piranha and left their testimony in rags and tatters, but Cowart refused to suppress the identifications. I wished Simpson lots of luck when he got the two ladies before the trial jury, and he too expressed some trepidation, but when they actually testified before the trial jury, they performed like champions. Haggard's badgering had accomplished three things—it had removed their fear of cross examination, it had given them practice in weathering rugged cross examination, and it had fired them up to want to do their best before the jury. I was almost eager to get our eyewitnesses before Judge Jopling for such a hearing so that they could receive some pretrial training, but the Leach defense team was too smart for us. They filed no such motion and the witnesses' first experience of rugged cross examination came at trial before the jury. Every one of them performed poorly.

Most of the essential issues, though hotly contested, went the State's way, and then it was time for me to pack my bags and leave Miami. My work there was done, and the trial proper was ready to commence. The rest of my knowledge of the trial came from newspaper reports, phone calls with Simpson, and watching the late-night recaps on our local PBS station. I also kept in touch with Minerva, and he told me (without revealing any secrets) that the tide of battle ebbed and flowed. They would occasionally inflict major damage on the State's case, and Simpson would occasionally return the favor, but hardly any of this appeared in the paper or on TV. The media is more concerned with sensation than significance. Zeroing in on the sensational and ignoring the significant can give a very distorted picture of what is actually happening, and Bundy was ready, willing, and able to supply them with the sensational. As the trial opened the next week, one reporter confessed that he was "absorbed" by the Bundy case, saying it was made for TV, had flashy attorneys, a colorful judge, and the handsome Bundy himself.[16]

The media described how Haggard had vigorously objected to the "parade" of witnesses reciting gory details of the crime but noted that it was Bundy himself who elicited the goriest testimony of the day while cross examining a witness.[17] Objecting to gory photos is a staple of almost all murder cases everywhere, even when the photos are not gory. And self-destructive cross examinations conducted by sociopathic defendants aren't that rare, either. Bundy did, however, have a steep learning curve. His advocacy skills were much improved six months later when we tried him in Orlando.

Bundy's excursion into the world of cross examination bears description. One of the first officers on the scene at the Chi Omega house was an officer named Ray Crew. Bundy closely questioned Crew about whether he used his right hand or his left to open a door, but the significance of that line of questioning wasn't immediately apparent.[18] Nor were his questions concerning whether Crew put on gloves to open the door.[19] Bundy then walked Crew through a graphic description of first-aid attempts being made on a survivor,[20] and turned the witness back over for redirect examination. When Simpson began the redirect examination, one of the lawyers on the team leaped up to object, and within a few moments another defense attorney sprang to his feet to object. Cowart decreed that "The person who cross examines must do the objecting—that is the rule. Mr. Bundy, do you have an objection?" Bundy, somewhat nonplussed, stood up and replied, "Yes, your honor." He bent over to confer with his lawyers. After a brief whispered exchange, he rose confidently and announced "Immaterial," to which Cowart replied, "Overruled."[21] Some courtroom observers speculated that Bundy was acting as counsel before the jury so that they could see him in some light other than that of an accused mad-dog killer. According to this school of thought, the defense team wanted the jury to see Bundy the Barrister—instead they got Bundy the Bungler.

Then one day Bundy broke a light fixture in his cell and refused to come out for the trial. Cowart recessed the trial and sent officers to fetch the wayward defendant, but Bundy still refused to come. Cowart then ruled that "This court will reconvene and will continue whether he's here or not."[22] Bundy decided to come to court after all. And once again, his efforts to stymie his trial failed to equal the efforts of similarly situated, but less celebrated, sociopathic killers. I once represented a sociopath who actually slashed his wrists and overdosed on drugs trying to stop his trial.

Somewhere under all the hoopla, Simpson was slowly and methodically building as strong a case as possible; and the defense, when not encumbered by Bundy, were doing their best to chip away at it. Simpson saved his best evidence for last. Forensic odontologists Richard Souviron of Coral Gables and Lowell Levine of New York both testified that the bite mark found on the body of Lisa Levy matched Bundy's teeth and nobody else's. With that, Simpson rested, and the defense undertook to undermine the testimony. Mike Minerva, an expert on bite-mark evidence, came to Miami and conducted the cross examination of Lowell Levine. After conducting the cross, Minerva went back to Tallahassee. Bundy complained bitterly to Cowart that Minerva had abandoned him because Minerva "withdrew from the case without any discussion with me."[23] Either Bundy realized too late that he had driven his best defender off the case, or he was just complaining to try to make a record for appeal. He also complained about Haggard's cross examination of an FDLE expert, about lack of communication from his lawyers, and about Cowart's refusal to allow Millard Farmer onto the case.[24]

The first defense witness to attack the State's findings was an orthodontist who testified that Bundy's teeth patterns were "real common." Then came their big gun. Oral surgeon Duane DeVore from the University of Maryland brought in five casts of teeth that he said could have fit the bite marks. He said that four of the casts came from children 12 to 15 years of age.[25] Simpson devastated DeVore on cross examination. He got DeVore to admit that there was a sixth set of teeth that could have made those marks—Bundy's. Since there hadn't been any club-wielding 12- to 15-year-old children roaming the Chi Omega house the night of the crime, Bundy was the only candidate for being the killer. The defense did not collapse so much as it deflated. And to ensure that the air was completely squeezed from the case, Bundy dismissed Haggard and appointed Margaret Good to give his final argument.[26]

Appointing Good, who had never argued before a jury, to deliver the final argument was the last nail in the coffin of Bundy's defense. Haggard had been a nuisance, but he was much more qualified to give the final argument than Good. I watched the spectacle on television and felt sorry for both of them (Haggard and Good, not Bundy). Haggard had donated a month of his life without charging a cent to try to give Bundy a defense, and the last we saw of him he was walking out of the courtroom like a "Survivor" contestant who had just gotten voted off the island. But Good was in worse shape. She was an appellate lawyer. Arguing the law to a group of judges is a far cry from arguing the facts to 12 jurors. She was completely at sea and as ineffective as I would have been arguing an arcane point of Admiralty law before the United States Supreme Court. Somebody suggested that Bundy had made a great strategic decision. The jurors would have to think, "Look, there's a woman arguing for him. She'd never do such a thing if he were really guilty of doing those horrible things to other women." Jurors often show that they have far more horse sense than lawyers give them credit for having. When they returned with a verdict of guilty as charged on all counts, Simpson told the press, "It was a common sense jury and they used their common sense. We certainly will ask for the death penalty."[27]

As the dust settled and the smoke cleared, people were beginning to talk. Spillman, the defense jury consultant, said, "This guy is so self destructive it's unbelievable. I predicted from the start that he'd try to blow his own defense out of the water. And he did."[28] Bundy made the statement that got my vote for most incoherent comment: "I know I'm innocent, certainly the verdict hasn't changed my mind about that. I'm innocent, and that's what's going to keep me going through all this." His remark was like the bad joke about what O. J. Simpson allegedly said when the glove didn't fit, "Hey, maybe I didn't do it after all."

Then Bundy gave a jailhouse interview in the days leading up to the penalty phase of the trial. The reporter described Bundy as "alternately charming, witty and grave," and quoted him as saying: "The most important thing, what I want people to know, is that I'm innocent in this thing. I haven't lost any sleep about the verdict."[29] When asked what he thought Cowart would do in the penalty phase, he adopted a mock Southern drawl and said, "Ah can only hope that the judge looks at mah case with an open mahnd and considers all the evidence."[30]

Millard Farmer, speaking from Atlanta, weighed in with some comments that changed my mind about the wisdom of keeping him off the case: "[Bundy] has no chance in the Florida system. It's inevitable that this judge is going to sentence him to death. This judge has tried to deprive him of a fair trial in every way possible." Farmer went on to predict that Bundy would have no chance in the state appellate system, "The first time he'll have a chance is when he gets into the federal system. That's because of the Florida system of justice. They're going to disregard the law."[31]

By my lights, Farmer's comments about Cowart couldn't have been more wrong. It looked to me as though he worked as hard as he could to see to it that Bundy had every opportunity to get a life recommendation out of the jury. According to the newspapers, Cowart suppressed Carol DaRonch's testimony in the penalty phase and forced the State to put on a "highly sanitized" presentation.[32] Simpson called DaRonch to the stand in the presence of the jury, but before she could testify, the defense stipulated that Bundy had been convicted of attempting to kidnap her and that the crime was an aggravating circumstance warranting the death penalty. When the defense offered that stipulation, Cowart ruled that the State didn't need to present her testimony. Far from being a tyrant who, according to Farmer "tried to deprive [Bundy] of a fair trial in every way possible,"[33] Cowart actually worked hard to defang any prejudicial effect from the evidence offered by the State. Even though the judge required a "highly sanitized" presentation, the jury recommended death. As he was escorted from the courtroom, Bundy called to the press, "See you in the next trial."[34]

Ed Harvey made one last stab at trying to either get off the case or to get Bundy committed. Harvey alleged that Bundy suffered from a "debilitating . . . mental disorder," but Cowart refused to relieve Harvey or hold a hearing on Bundy's mental state. Cowart said, "I don't think there's any question in my mind that Mr. Bundy is competent from a legal standpoint." The judge went on to add, "He may be a miserable client. I can't answer that."[35]

And then, after sentencing Bundy to death, Cowart made what must have been one of the most misunderstood comments of his judicial career. Just before Bundy was led away, Cowart made this remarkable comment: "It's a tragedy for this court to see such a total waste of humanity. You're a bright young man. You'd have made a good lawyer. I'd have loved to have you practice before me. But you went another way, partner."[36] One commentator dismissed Cowart's statement by observing that the judge couldn't resist the opportunity to do a little "male bonding" with Bundy before sending him to death row.[37] In order to characterize the judge's remarks as "male bonding," you have to ignore the fact that Cowart prefaced his remarks by calling Bundy a "total waste of humanity." Like the commentator, I too misunderstood what the judge was saying. I thought he was grandstanding for the press, but

I have come to understand that his comment exemplified the highest standards of judicial conduct. It will take a moment to explain.

The roots of that comment go back centuries to a time when criminal jurisprudence and Christian theology were inextricably intertwined. How could Christian judges, themselves not that long ago subject to arbitrary execution, reconcile their official duty to impose the death penalty with their Christian duty to refrain from taking life? By the 13th century, Christian jurists had reconciled the dilemma. Canon law held that the judge could absolve himself of blood guilt by the simple expedient of following correct legal procedures. Although it has been stripped of its Christian context and somewhat modified, this is still a viable principle in modern death penalty litigation. In fact most post-conviction death penalty litigation doesn't involve asking whether the defendant is guilty and deserves to die, it centers upon whether proper procedures were carried out in order to obtain that death penalty. Christian theology was not satisfied that simply dotting all the Is and crossing all the Ts would be sufficient to save a judge from mortal sin in pronouncing a death sentence. There had to be more, and theology supplied the more—to be free of mortal sin, the judge must act without malice when pronouncing the sentence. Any death sentence pronounced with the least bit of anger, spite, or ill will rendered the judge guilty of mortal sin.[38] So what was Cowart telling Bundy? I think he was saying, "Son, although you are a total waste of humanity, I acted without malice when I imposed the supreme penalty upon you."

# 14

# Motion Sickness

When I got back to Live Oak from my sojourn in Miami, the prosecution team had a new member. Blair had hired Len Register, a young prosecutor from the Eighth Circuit State Attorney's Office. Register would assist me with the pretrial litigation and would sit "third chair" at the trial. The first thing I noticed about Register was his size—he was a good two or three inches taller than me. Register was no bean pole, looking more like an NFL lineman than a basketball player. He proved to be congenial, industrious, and a good legal scholar. In short, he was an excellent addition to the prosecution team. Register later went on to serve as the elected state attorney for the Eighth Circuit and as an assistant United States attorney. As the state attorney for the Eighth Circuit, Register investigated the Danny Rolling case, obtained an indictment against him, and commenced the prosecution, which was concluded by his successor in office, Rod Smith.

As the prosecution team began to take its final form, the defense team was also coming together. Bundy agreed to accept legal representation, and Judge Jopling appointed J. Victor Africano to be the lead defense attorney, assisted by Lynn Thompson. Don Kennedy would be the defense team's investigator. Kennedy had served for several years as an investigator for the Third Circuit Public Defender's Office in Lake City, and was an energetic, capable young man. He later became the executive director for the Third Circuit Public Defender. Oddly enough, Kennedy had to "interview" for his job on the Bundy defense team. When Milo Thomas assigned Kennedy to assist the Bundy defense team, Bundy didn't particularly want to have him unless he "passed muster," so to speak. Kennedy drove to Tallahassee to meet with Bundy and answer any questions Bundy may have had. The interview was a success, and Bundy accepted him onto the team.[1] Once the team was fully formed, they began to inundate us with motions. Africano said he was giving us "motion sickness," and he did. Before the case got to trial, more than 50 pretrial pleadings had been filed addressing alleged deficiencies in the evidence. Some of the motions were well founded, some were mere boilerplate. Probably the most important pretrial motion was the one the defense didn't file.

Not long after Judge Cowart held Bundy competent to stand trial, I spoke with Africano about filing a motion for mental examination in our case. Although I urged him to file the motion, Africano steadfastly refused, saying that Bundy was competent to stand trial. "I know that," I told Africano, "but this issue needs to be appeal-proofed." Africano replied, "There is no evidentiary basis for me to file such a motion. I can't ethically do it." Failing to convince Africano to file the motion, I talked to Blair about us filing the motion. After thoroughly discussing the issue, we decided that we shouldn't. If Africano had no basis to file the motion, then we certainly didn't. It might have been unethical to file the motion, but Africano later learned it was unwise not to file it. The question of Bundy's competence to stand trial in the Lake City case gave us all kinds of trouble in the postconviction proceedings, but that story must wait until Chapter 17.

Oddly enough, I fully agreed with Africano's first motion. He wanted permission to file sensitive pretrial motions under seal, and he wanted to hold the hearings on those motions in the judge's chambers with the press excluded.[2] I filed a notice stating that the prosecution agreed.[3] The news media quickly responded. The *Orlando Sentinel* was the first to oppose our motion,[4] followed closely by the Florida Publishing Company.[5] The *Lake City Reporter*, the *Gainesville Sun*, and the *Miami Herald* also filed a pleading in opposition to our joint motion.[6] The last thing that anybody on the prosecution or defense teams needed to do was to spend time in court fighting the news media. We had a case to get ready for trial, and time wasted on the media was time stolen from trial preparation. Something had to be done, however. If not, every last piece of evidence would be bandied about in the press before we conducted voir dire on the first juror. Jopling ruled with us, despite the impassioned arguments of the lawyers representing the media.[7]

Jopling's order should have settled the matter, but the media are a tenacious bunch. The Florida Association of Broadcasters filed motions seeking to be allowed to inspect the motions filed under seal[8] and to videotape the motions held *in camera*.[9] The broadcasters wanted to be allowed to inspect the motions and videotape the hearings in return for their promise that they wouldn't air any of the information until after the jury was sworn. At first glance, this might seem reasonable, but allowing the media to get hold of that information would mean surrendering control of the situation to them. Those weren't the only additional "media motions" filed. The defense filed another one seeking to bar all electronic media from the courtroom during the trial.[10] Jopling denied all three motions.[11]

One of the most hotly contested motions was the defense motion to suppress our Williams Rule evidence. I felt we had an excellent chance of getting Jopling to rule the DaRonch/Kent incidents admissible. The hearing on the motion was long, but the longer it went, the more sure I was that we were going to win. Jopling was very receptive to our arguments, making a number of favorable comments and asking Africano some tough questions about the similarities. Then disaster struck. We held the hearing in mid-October. The trial was set to begin on November 5. The defense had not deposed the DaRonch/Kent witnesses. As the arguments were winding down toward what looked like a favorable ruling for our side, Africano told Jopling, "If you rule this evidence admissible, we're going to have to move for a continuance so that we can go to Utah and depose these witnesses." We were sunk. There was no way that Jopling would allow anything to happen that would cause a continuance. He suppressed evidence of the DaRonch/Kent incident but allowed evidence of the Parmenter incident, holding that it was relevant to establish identity.[12]

Another hotly contested motion was Africano's motion to suppress the testimony of Andy Anderson.[13] If I were allowed to redo one thing about the prosecution of Bundy, I would go back and prevent the use of hypnosis with our witnesses. At that time hypnosis was a trendy tool for refreshing witnesses' recollection, and every reported case I could find upheld its use.[14] Little did I know that shortly after our use of hypnosis, the nation would be inundated by a tidal wave of opinions criticizing, restricting, and outright banning its use as a memory aid.[15] One common denominator in most of the reported cases from this era was the testimony of Dr. Martin Orne, who was highly skeptical of the usefulness of hypnosis.[16]

We accomplished several things with the hypnosis of Andy Anderson: we seriously harmed his credibility; we made him vulnerable to a scathing attack; we gave the defense a very good issue on appeal; and we caused ourselves untold wasted hours dealing with the issue of hypnosis. One thing we most emphatically did not accomplish—we did not enhance Anderson's testimony one whit.

The defense team did not retain Orne, but they did retain one of his disciples—Milton Kline. And they held off disclosing him until the last minute. Jopling had set October 3 as the hearing date for the motion to suppress Anderson's testimony.[17] The defense disclosed Kline as a witness on October 2. It came as part of our first formal discovery answer from the defense.[18] The defense had demanded discovery more than a year before.[19] Between that date and the day we received the defense's first "Response to Reciprocal Discovery," we had filed no fewer than 37 discovery exhibits,[20] and the defense waited until the day before an essential hearing to file its first discovery response. To say that we were caught flat-footed would be an understatement. In his report, Kline disparaged Imogene Keene's session with Anderson, but he savaged Jack Burnette's session. He wrote:

> The second hypnotic session involves a rather different kind of experience. The induction procedure itself is a more authoritative and somewhat overwhelming procedure. It involves a certain amount of confusion designed to lead to dissociation. The use of an attempt at age regression in which the witness recalls emotionally gratifying experiences from an earlier age, particularly in relation to a father with whom he had strong positive feelings and who is now dead, generally produces a very positive transference hypnotically.

We couldn't receive Kline's report on October 2 and then go to hearing on October 3. We got the hearing continued, and Register and I flew to New York City to depose Kline. We were the first to arrive at Kline's office. As we bided our time in Kline's lobby waiting on Africano and the court reporter, I examined the photocopied diplomas on Kline's walls. It struck me as odd that Kline would have photocopies of his diplomas, but I decided that he must work out of two different offices and the original diplomas had to be in the other office.

At the deposition, Kline was cordial and appeared cooperative. He testified that Anderson's hypnosis was flawed in a number of different ways. First, the hypnotists used the wrong model for describing to Anderson how memory worked. They told him that the eye was a video camera and that somewhere buried in his brain was a videotape of what he saw. Kline said this model gave Anderson a false understanding of how memory worked and caused a substantial likelihood of confabulation. I had to stop Kline and get him to define "confabulation" for me. It seems that memory is imperfect. We only remember portions of any observation, and our minds fill in the blanks with plausible details. In other words, witnesses subconsciously make things up to bridge the gaps in their memories. Confabulation is not lying. The witness believes that the confabulated details are bona fide memories. Everyone's memory works in this way, filling in the gaps with plausible conjectures. According to Kline, however, hypnosis supercharges the confabulation process and reinforces the confabulated details, making the witness more confident that they are real memories.

Kline went on to explain that you can't prevent confabulation, but you can try to minimize it. Kline said that the two hypnotists who worked with Anderson did not use proper measures to minimize confabulation and used techniques that increased the chances of confabulation. Kline gave the following guidelines:

1. The hypnotic session should be conducted by a licensed psychiatrist (M.D.) or psychologist (Ph.D. or Ed.D.) trained in the use of hypnosis. Kline emphasized that it was essential for the hypnotist to be a doctor like he was.
2. The qualified professional conducting the hypnotic session should be independent of and not responsible to the prosecutor, investigator or the defense.
3. Any information given to the hypnotist by law enforcement personnel prior to the hypnosis must be written or recorded so that the extent of the information the subject received from the hypnotist may be determined.
4. Before induction of hypnosis, the hypnotist should obtain from the subject a detailed description of the facts as the subject remembers them, carefully avoiding adding any new elements to the witness' description of the events.
5. All contacts between the hypnotist and the subject should be recorded so that a permanent record is available for comparison and study. Videotape should be employed if possible, but should not be mandatory.
6. Only the hypnotist and the subject should be present during any phase of the hypnotic session, including the pre-hypnotic testing and post-hypnotic interview.[21]

Kline said he couldn't guarantee that the absence of those safe-guards would produce confabulation, nor could he say that the presence of his safeguards would prevent confabulation. I came away from the deposition with the distinct impression that in the ocean of expert witnesses, Kline was a guppy.

Kline concealed some important facts. Despite the fact that I asked about his work on other cases, Kline never shared with us the fact that he was currently working on a New York case entitled *People v. Lewis*.[22] We would have been particularly interested to know that Kline had hypnotized the defendant, and that he had violated almost every one of his safeguards that he said were absolutely necessary. In criticizing Kline's work, Judge Benjamin Altman of the New York County Supreme Court had this to say:

> The hypnotic session in this case did not comply with the enumerated safeguards. There is no videotape of the interview session. There is only a tape recording of part of the session. There is no evidence of what transpired between the hypnotist and the defendant prior to the time hypnosis was induced. The defendant's attorney was present at the hypnotic session. This is clearly a departure from the accepted procedure.[23]

Judge Altman wasn't aware of Kline's most glaring departure from the protocol. We'll discuss that departure in Chapter 17. Had we known about Kline's failure to follow his own procedures we could have impeached his testimony with a devastating *tu quoque* defense. The gist of this defense would be that you can't trust someone who doesn't practice what he preaches. We first met this defense in Chapter 10 when Albert Krieger sought to impeach Vickers Nugent because Nugent had burned a law book on the courthouse steps. Although most books on informal logic recognize the *tu quoque* defense as fallacious,[24] it can sometimes be valid. Whereas in Nugent's case, his arguably contemptuous conduct did not exonerate Farmer, in Kline's case, his ignoring his own safeguards suggested he wasn't being candid.

Although we were unaware that Kline felt he was exempt from his own safeguards, I was confident that we could handle his testimony on cross examination. In my opinion, Kline's first "safeguard," that the hypnotist had to hold a doctor's degree, was ludicrous. A string of letters after your name means only that you are well educated, not that you are competent. Clearly, a hypnotist needs to know only two things—how to perform hypnosis and how to ask nonleading questions. A review of the hypnosis transcripts plainly showed that Burnette and Keene knew how to do both.

The second "safeguard," that the hypnotist be independent of the prosecutor, police, or defense attorney, is unrealistic. The moment you retain someone to hypnotize a witness, the hypnotist arguably loses her independence. The only way to ensure a completely independent hypnotist would be to ask the court to appoint the hypnotist without any input from the parties.

The third "safeguard," that the information given the hypnotist by law enforcement should be in writing, is overkill. It isn't important what law enforcement tells the hypnotist if the hypnotist doesn't tell it to the subject. With a recorded hypnotic session, you can determine whether the hypnotist is feeding the subject information by simply listening to the questions.

As for the fourth safeguard, we had a full and complete tape-recorded statement from Anderson taken before he was ever hypnotized, and its clear showing that hypnosis had no effect on his memory eventually saved our case.[25]

"Safeguard" five, that all contact between the hypnotist and the witness be recorded, is overkill. By Kline's lights, everything from the introduction of the parties to the farewells after the session should have been recorded.

Safeguard six, that only the hypnotist and the witness be in the room during the hypnotic session, is aimed at keeping the spectators from inadvertently giving the witness clues. It is reasonable that you should try not to give the witness inadvertent clues in any interview or interrogation.

At the hearing our guppy became a barracuda. We deposed Kline on October 15, and the hearing was held on October 19. It takes time to transcribe a deposition and distribute copies. We didn't have enough time to thoroughly digest the deposition transcript before the hearing, and soon after Kline started testifying, it became clear that he had sandbagged us at the deposition. It also seemed clear to me that he was blowing smoke. A really good expert can express complex ideas in simple language, while a bad expert seeks to hide behind a barrage of psychobabble, such as:

Confabulation is most frequently encountered within a positive hypnotic transference where an ego interject with the hypnotist is incorporated and frequently confused with a parental relationship.[26]

After the testimony, we argued the case to Jopling, and he took the motion under advisement, saying a written order would be forthcoming. Four days later we got his order. He had denied the motion to suppress,[27] but he denied the motion without prejudice, which meant that the defense could raise the motion again at trial. The hearing had settled nothing.

Kline was going to be the biggest gun in the defense arsenal at the trial. We had to do our homework to get ready for him. When we got back to the office, we began to take his CV apart. It gave us some fertile fields for investigation. He had written a number of interesting articles, including "A Note of 'Primate-like' Behavior Induced by Hypnosis."[28] If he had been hypnotizing people and making them act like monkeys, we might use that fact to make a monkey out of him. We began collecting copies of every one of his articles, and they proved very helpful indeed.

It would be tedious indeed to discuss all the pretrial motions filed by the defense, but a few more motions deserve our attention. One was the motion to suppress Bundy's blue blazer. The motion to suppress argued several grounds, but the most significant ground involved an attack on the judge who signed the search warrant. The United States Supreme Court had long ago decreed that search warrants must be approved by a "neutral and detached magistrate."[29] The defense motion to suppress argued that: Judge Rudd had issued the search warrant for the blue blazer; the Florida Supreme Court had found that he was not a neutral and detached magistrate; therefore the blue blazer should be suppressed.[30] The defense filed another motion seeking to suppress the blood sample Rudd had ordered be taken from Bundy. This motion also argued that Rudd was neither neutral nor detached.[31]

We could survive the granting of the motion to suppress Bundy's blood. All we needed to do was to make another application for a blood sample and use the blood obtained pursuant to the second motion. Getting the blue blazer suppressed would cripple our case. The fibers from that blazer were an essential thread in the web of circumstances with which we intended to convict Bundy. We argued that the grounds for disqualifying Rudd arose long after he entered the order and issued the search warrant. We also argued that it was obvious from the record that Rudd acted fairly and impartially. We pointed out that he denied the State's initial motion for blood samples, and that he required the State to file a second motion for body materials and an amended second motion for body materials before he would enter the order. Jopling denied the defense motions.

The defense also moved for a change of venue.[32] The motion claimed that publicity over the case had been so pervasive that it would be impossible to select a fair and impartial jury in Columbia County. Conventional wisdom holds that pervasive pretrial publicity makes it near impossible for a defendant to achieve an acquittal. In my experience, pervasive pretrial publicity has the opposite effect. America's ideal juror has no knowledge of the case, and pervasive publicity makes the pool of ideal jurors very small. As Mark Twain put it, "We have a criminal jury system which is superior to any in the world; and its efficiency is only marred by the difficulty of finding twelve men every day who don't know anything and can't read." What happens, then, when a case has pervasive publicity? Most of the intelligent, well-informed potential jurors get excused because they know too much about the case. You are left with jurors "who don't know anything and can't read." A prosecutor prosecuting a guilty defendant wants intelligent jurors who are capable of processing, analyzing, and evaluating great masses of evidence. Jurors who don't know anything and can't read are far more likely to acquit a guilty defendant. They become overwhelmed and confused by the mass of evidence and are easily led astray by specious arguments.

We should have agreed to the change of venue. We would have been able to conclude the trial in 1979, and we would have saved ourselves a lot of wasted effort, but we thought we had a procedural trick up our sleeves to keep the trial in North Florida.

In our memorandum opposing the motion for change of venue, we made three arguments:

1. The motion was fatally defective because it did not have supporting affidavits attached to it.
2. The motion did not make out a sufficient showing of necessity for a change of venue.
3. The defense had no right to a change of venue without first electing to be tried in Suwannee County, which neighbored Columbia County on the west.

Our first argument was a procedural "Gotcha" maneuver that the defense quickly remedied by filing supplemental affidavits. Looking back from the perspective of my 30-year career as a prosecutor,

I wonder how we could have made the second argument with a straight face. That we could and did argue the point with straight faces is a testament to how the zeal of advocacy can sometimes compromise your objectivity. The third argument, our ace in the hole (or up the sleeve), needs explanation.

We didn't really know where Bundy had killed Kim. We knew she had disappeared in Columbia County and had been found in Suwannee County. It was reasonable to conclude that the murder had occurred in one of those two counties, but which one? Because the accused has a right to be tried in the county where the crime occurred, it is necessary to charge and prove that a crime occurred in a particular county. Establishing the county in which the crime occurred is known as proof of venue. When we sat down to draft the indictment charging Bundy with Kim's murder, we had to be careful to properly charge venue. The Florida Constitution provided us with a margin of error for charging venue. Article I, Section 16 provided that:

> If the county is not known, the indictment or information may charge venue in two or more counties conjunctively and proof that the crime was committed in that area shall be sufficient . . .

The Constitution gave a margin of error, but it also conferred a privilege upon a defendant who was charged in two or more counties. The section went on to say:

> . . . but before pleading the accused may elect in which of those counties the trial will take place.[33]

Bundy had no need to move for a change of venue. He could move the trial out of Columbia County simply by electing to be tried in Suwannee County. Of course, the defense didn't want to have the trial in Suwannee County any more than they wanted it in Columbia County, but we argued that they couldn't in good faith move for a change of venue until after they had elected to be tried in Suwannee. Jopling reserved ruling on the motion for change of venue pending an attempt to select a jury. In the order, however, he specifically held that the defense had the right to elect to stand trial in Suwannee County.[34] The defense immediately elected Suwannee County.[35] Not long after electing to be tried in Suwannee County, the defense filed another motion, which they entitled "Motion for Change of Venue or in the Alternative to Abate Prosecution."[36] The defense contended that Bundy not only couldn't get a fair trial in Suwannee County, he couldn't get a fair trial anywhere. The remedy sought for this terrible state of affairs was that the prosecution be "abated" (suspended) until such time as everyone had forgotten about Bundy. If the defense had gotten their way, Bundy would never have stood trial. It's been more than 30 years, and Bundy still hasn't been forgotten. Africano argued that motion with as straight a face as we had when we argued against moving venue from Columbia County.

After the trial moved to Live Oak, we heard a few more irritant motions (including the motion to abate prosecution) and were finally ready to pick a jury. The most irritating motion was the motion to alter the seating arrangement. The Suwannee County Courthouse was a relic of another age. When I first walked into the courtroom as a fledgling attorney, I immediately thought of Clarence Darrow, William Jennings Bryan, and the Scopes Trial. Except for the fact that it had seen better days, the courtroom looked almost exactly as it had when the courthouse had been built. There was a crest up over the judge's bench bearing the date 1904, and a huge crack ran from the ceiling, through the crest, and almost to the floor. The gallery was huge, with two balconies on the right and the left. The jury box stood to the left side of the courtroom, and the prosecution table stood next to the jury box. Jopling had ordered that the television camera be set up in the right-hand balcony,[37] giving the camera a straight shot at the jury box and the prosecution table. Africano wanted to sit at the prosecution table. I sincerely believed that he wanted to sit there because the cameras would get a better angle on him. We didn't care whether the cameras were pointed at us or not, we simply wanted to sit at the customary table where prosecutors had sat since the building of the courthouse. We had a terrible wrangle over seating.

Africano argued that counsel tables were positioned so as to make it hard to see the jury and witnesses from the defense table. I tried dozens of cases as a defense attorney in that courtroom and never had any problem seeing. Jopling took us into the courtroom and had us rearrange tables and chairs to try to accommodate Africano's complaint. We huffed and puffed and pushed and pulled tables and chairs back and forth in the courtroom until Jopling finally settled on a diagonal configuration for counsel tables. Africano still wasn't happy.[38] Finally, Jopling made a ruling that would have made King Solomon proud. He ruled that the prosecution team could sit at the prosecution table for the first day of the trial, and each day thereafter we would alternate tables, with Africano getting to sit in front of the cameras every other day.[39]

Africano wasn't the only one who wanted the defense table to be in the direct line of fire from the video camera. On the first day of the trial the television camera crew, who knew that the defense customarily sat on the right, came in and began to set up their camera in the left-hand balcony. This directly defied Jopling's administrative order, which had been sent to all media outlets. I always tried to be the first person to the courtroom on trial days, and I was the first person in the courtroom that day. As if I didn't have enough real problems to deal with, I became incensed watching the camera crew set up in violation of Jopling's order. By golly, I was going to show them a thing or two. I accosted the head cameraman and told him that he was violating the judge's order; he had to set up in the right-hand balcony. He was almost as cordial to me as I had been to him when he told me to mind my own business. I told him, "We'll see about that." When Jopling and the court reporter got to the courtroom, we saw about it.

Jopling's first order of business was to listen to my complaint about the placement of the television camera. We went into the judge's chambers to settle the issue, and it was standing room only in chambers as news people crowded in to hear the arguments. When I had finished saying my piece, the head cameraman made his defense and concluded by saying to the judge, "Just tell me where to put the camera." I interjected, "I'll tell you where to put the camera!" The head cameraman asked me for further and better particulars concerning where I'd like to see him put his camera, but Blair put his hand on my shoulder and told me I'd said too much already. Jopling ruled that they could put the camera in the left-hand balcony. I was outraged that the judge had ruled against me until it became clear that Africano no longer wanted to sit at the prosecution table. We sat at the prosecution table for the duration of the jury selection in Live Oak.

Then we got down to the business of trying to pick a jury. The first day was long, tedious, and unproductive. At the end of the day, we had three jurors and had excused everyone else we had questioned.[40] The high percentage of excusals for cause wasn't necessarily for inability to sit as fair jurors. As a matter of fact, most jurors were quite willing to set aside everything they had heard and try the case solely on the law and evidence they heard inside the courtroom—until an incident that we called the "Kamikaze voir dire."

Blair became concerned that too few jurors were being excused for cause. He decided that he would give the panel some gentle encouragement to opt out of jury service. The nation was in the throes of the Iranian Hostage Crisis, and Blair decided to mention the Iranian hostages. When our turn to ask questions came again, he compared sequestration to being an Iranian hostage, painting a grim picture of the freedom they would lose and the inconvenience they would endure if selected. After his eloquent description of the horrors of juror sequestration, he returned to the issue of whether or not the jurors could be fair. The 12 jurors in the box immediately began to make excuses for why they couldn't serve. In the twinkling of an eye, Jopling had excused almost everyone in the jury box for cause. It was the St. Valentine's Day Massacre of voir dire. When Blair returned to counsel table after all the excusals, I told him, "I think you may have overdone it just a little bit." For the rest of the day, juror after juror claimed bias and asked to be released. We had been fortunate to survive the first day with any jurors in the box.

After the trial recessed, we went back to the office and strategized for the second day. We were tired and discouraged, but we planned as well as we could. One last mishap ended the day. I got into my car to drive home down US 90 toward Lake City. Blair, who lived east of Live Oak, followed me in his car. I drove one block to the stoplight on US 90 and US 129. The light turned red and I stopped. Blair didn't. He rammed the rear end of my car, giving it a good jolt. We got out and inspected our cars, determining that neither had suffered any major damage. I told Blair I would file my worker's compensation claim the next morning, got back into my car, and drove home.

The next day Blair, Register, and I got to the courthouse so early that the doors were locked and there was nobody to let us in. As we stood at the door with our arms full of briefcases and files, Register looked up to the second-story window of Bundy's holding cell. Bundy was already in the cell, looking refreshed and upbeat. He began to laugh at us, thinking it quite funny that we couldn't get into the courthouse. Register made a crude hand signal at Bundy. Blair cautioned him against making such signs while Bundy laughed even harder. It seems that Blair was forever restraining either Register or me. We stood there under Bundy's watchful eye for several minutes before we could get the attention of a custodian and get into the courthouse. The most memorable event of the second day came when Bundy, who was sitting at the defense table behind us, said in a stage whisper, "Psst! Register!"

Register looked around, and Bundy flashed the same hand signal back at Register. Bundy was very careful, however, to make sure that no one but Register could see it. By the end of the day we had seven jurors tentatively seated.[41] Prospects of seating a jury anytime soon were not good. Normally, in a capital murder case each side has 10 peremptory challenges, which theoretically allows them to strike 10 prospective jurors for any reason. Jopling had increased the number of allowable peremptory challenges to 20 per side. That meant we could excuse up to 40 jurors peremptorily. If we continued to seat jurors at the rate of 4 per day, and if both sides used all their challenges, that meant we could be in voir dire up to two weeks or more.

The third day saw us arrive at the courthouse bleary-eyed and downtrodden. I don't think we went past noon before Jopling was ready to throw in the towel. He granted the change of venue.[42] Apparently Jopling had done some prior planning, because he immediately named the new venue for the prosecution. We were going to Orlando, and the trial would commence January 7. Africano and Thompson immediately began complaining that Orlando would not be a good place to try the case. Thompson told the press that "It's going to be difficult to pick a jury anywhere in Florida."[43]

# 15

# Try, Try, Again

We tried to get a jury in Lake City and failed. We tried to seat a jury in Live Oak and failed. We were going to try to seat a jury in Orlando, and we were determined that we would not fail this time. We left for Orlando on January 3, 1980, shortly after eating lunch at a local steakhouse in Lake City. While we were at the steakhouse, Tom Brown came into the restaurant and noticed us sitting at a table. He walked over to us and said, "Well, are you heading off to prosecute my look-alike?" I debated whether to ask Brown to come to Orlando so we could use him to corroborate Andy Anderson. Larry Simpson had done that with Ronnie Eng and Nita Neary, and Tom Brown looked a lot more like Bundy than Ronnie Eng did. I decided that disclosing Tom Brown as a witness so close to trial would cause more problems than it solved.

When we concluded our meal, we loaded up in two cars and drove down to Orlando, arriving at the Harley Hotel before sundown. The Harley was within easy walking distance of the courthouse, meaning we did not to have to fight Orlando rush-hour traffic commuting to and from the courthouse. The Harley was also within walking distance of the First Baptist Church, which we attended during the trial. We all took separate rooms, and my room adjoined onto a studio that we used as our "war room" during the trial. We stored files and evidence in the war room, and every evening we used the war room to prepare the witnesses who testified the following day. Our prosecution team had grown by one member. Tony Wallace, a young criminology intern from FSU, acted as secretary. She saw very little of the trial, being cooped up in our tiny office behind the courtroom telephoning witnesses and arranging for their transportation to and from Orlando.

The public reaction to the second trial ranged from apathy to antipathy. The media was especially blasé about the trial. Author Ann Rule did not attend and confined her account of the Orlando trial to a few paragraphs in the epilog of her book, *The Stranger beside Me*.[1] Where 400 press credentials were issued for the Miami trial, by January 8 fewer than 60 had been issued for the Orlando trial.[2] Florida Public Broadcasting stations decided not to reprise the daily show that they ran for the Miami trial.[3] Dick Burdette, an *Orlando Sentinel* columnist, found the trial to be a source of amusement, saying that Bantam's just-released book, *Ted Bundy—The Killer Next Door*, was selling as well as tour trips to Afghanistan.[4] Actually the book sold well. Bantam sold out its January 1 run of 150,000 copies and by January 4 had printed another 150,000. Unsurprisingly, sales of the book were best in Seattle, Tallahassee, and Lake City.[5] Burdette also made sport of the enhanced security measures and wondered how the trial would "play in Peoria."[6] I was more interested in how it would play in Orlando. The less media attention we had, the better I would like it.

The sheriff planned to bring Bundy in on January 6, and he was to be housed in a seven-by-nine-foot cell on the sixth floor of the courthouse.[7] Two floors below was Courtroom E, the largest courtroom in the Orange County Courthouse. It had a seating capacity of 200,[8] which was rather paltry compared to the courtroom in the Suwannee County Courthouse. The workspace behind the bar was adequate. The judge's bench occupied the center of the back wall to the courtroom, with a small clerk's workstation in front. To the judge's right was the jury box, which sat with its back to the audience and at an angle to the rest of the courtroom.[9] The television camera was set up behind the jury box. On the back wall to the judge's left was a door that led to a rear hallway. In the hallway were doors leading to the judge's chambers, the prosecution room, and the defense room.

We had another issue over counsel tables. In Courtroom E of the Orange County Courthouse, the defense table sat nearest the jury and was positioned so as to make it difficult to be seen from where the television camera was located. The prosecution table was positioned so as to be easily seen by the television camera. Africano, who had wanted to sit nearest to the jury in Live Oak until it became apparent that the defense table was more visible to the television camera, suddenly wanted to sit at the prosecution table, which was farthest from the jury, in Orlando. We readily agreed to sit at the defense table, which put us in our customary position, closest to the jury. Africano assured us that the placement of the television camera had nothing to do with his choice of counsel table.

We faced a different sort of jury selection in Orlando than we did back home in Live Oak. In a small jurisdiction like the Third Circuit you would know many of the potential jurors. If you didn't know a prospective juror, you certainly knew someone who did. Most of the work of jury selection occurred before the jurors came to the courthouse. You'd get a copy of the jury venire and study it, looking for names you recognized and marking the venire with notes on their suitability to serve. You'd then pass the venire around the office for everyone else to review and mark. Finally you would take the venire to the sheriff and several other knowledgeable people and get their comments on the jurors. The questions you asked of the jurors in the courtroom weren't nearly as important as the answers you got about jurors before you ever went to the courtroom. Orlando was too large for our customary jury selection procedures to work. The chances that we would know someone on the panel were slim, and the only information we were going to get about the jurors was what we learned from the questions we asked.

Jury selection has been called more art than science, and the way some lawyers approach jury selection, it may be more voodoo or vaudeville than anything else. I've seen lawyers ask jurors some mighty silly questions. All lawyers have their pet superstitions about jury selection. Mine was the two-ponytail rule. I would tolerate one man with a ponytail on the jury, but I would not accept a jury panel that had two men with ponytails. Clarence Darrow supposedly said, "Every knowing lawyer seeks for a jury of the same sort of men as his client; men who will be able to imagine themselves in the same situation and realize what verdict the client wants."[10] In order to achieve a winning jury, Darrow leaned toward Irishmen, Englishmen, and Germans, but he did not like Lutherans, Presbyterians, Baptists, Scandinavians, or women.[11] In Darrow's day such stereotyping was permissible, and even as late as 1980 you could get away with excusing jurors for reasons smacking of discrimination, but nowadays you cannot excuse jurors based on considerations of race, gender, color, religion, national origin, or even economic status.[12] One old saw from the lore of prosecution holds that a good prosecution juror is "middle, middle, middle"—middle class, middle-aged, middle-of-the-road. Cicero said it best, however, when he characterized the ideal juror as attentive, receptive, and well disposed—attentive to the evidence, receptive to your arguments, and well disposed toward your side.[13] But you really have only minimal control on who actually sits on the jury. You can better control who doesn't sit. It's not jury selection as much as it is juror elimination.

I had scoffed at the Miami defense team's use of a jury selection consultant, but we decided that a consultant might help us in Orlando. We went to Sid Bradley, a local psychologist, and asked him to give us his insight. He produced a multipage report supported by a bibliography. Page one consisted of three columns titled "desirable," "neutral," and "undesirable." In each column he wrote down personality traits that he considered appropriate to each category. Page two gave profiles of the three most desirable jurors, and page four gave profiles of the two most undesirable jurors. Some of his information confirmed feelings that we already had, some of it was counterintuitive, and some of it was wrong. Bradley's most desirable juror was an older married female who was a mother. She was religious, traditional, moral, and politically conservative. She belonged to a social club and the PTA, but she was not a feminist. She was a college graduate and a professional or a homemaker. He went on to say that she was also uncertain, cautious, and fearful. Bradley told us that our most undesirable juror was a young, style-conscious, economically advantaged female with at least some college. She was a socially active jet-setter with weak family ties, a women's rights advocate, anti-establishment, politically liberal, and religiously indifferent. He listed one more trait for our nightmare juror—she was a critical thinker.[14]

I disagreed with Bradley on two points. We didn't want jurors who were uncertain and fearful. Uncertainty and fear are not attributes of someone who is going to find a man guilty of first-degree murder and then vote to recommend the death penalty. We did want jurors who were critical thinkers—as that term is used when discussing informal logic. We wanted people who were able to weigh and evaluate complex arrays of evidence. Jurors who couldn't think logically would get confused, and confusion is never good for the prosecution. As will be shown when we discuss the jury deliberations, we got a group of critical thinkers on our jury. It wasn't easy. Jury selection began at 10:40 A.M. on January 7, and ended around 2:30 P.M. on January 19, taking approximately 73½ hours.[15]

When jury selection began that first Monday morning, there were four men and one woman detailed as bailiffs to the courtroom. John Dame, a retired military man, served as the chief bailiff, and Kay Nead, a retired WAC,[16] was our lady bailiff. I don't remember the full names of the other two bailiffs, but one was named Alex, and the other looked like the Marvel superhero, Thor. Dame and Nead were in charge of the jurors, and it seemed that Alex and Thor were in charge of Bundy. Our court reporter was Ann Sage, a perennially cheerful lady who planned to build an addition to her home with the money she expected to make typing the transcript of the trial. She was shocked when I pointed out to her that we just might lose. "You're joking, aren't you?" she wanted to know. "I wish I were," I replied. Sage had good reason to want Bundy convicted. It was estimated that the trial transcript would run to 5,000 pages. At the going rate of $2.85 per page, that added up to $14,250.00.[17]

Voir dire is not the most exciting portion of the trial, and the media had to dig to find something to write about those first two weeks. They counted the number of observers in court;[18] they described the courtroom in detail;[19] they described Bundy's clothing each time he came to court;[20] they reported comments made by observers in the courtroom;[21] they interviewed observers in the courtroom;[22] they speculated about other spectators who wouldn't give interviews.[23] Laura Kavesh, writing for the *Orlando Sentinel,* reported that we had 24 observers the first day of jury selection,[24] but Patti Roth of the *Lake City Reporter* said the courtroom was one-third full (which would have been approximately 66 observers).[25] The *Orlando Sentinel* zeroed in on a spectator who was sitting with Carol Boone. The lady had a son on death row, and she said she had come to watch the Bundy trial in part because she couldn't go to her son's trial.[26] The *Lake City Reporter* was more interested in a mysterious young man seen periodically talking to Carol Boone. When Roth approached him, he only gave his name as Steve and wouldn't talk about what he was doing at the trial. He did say that he wasn't a member of the press. Roth nosed around and discovered that the man's name was Steve Michaud, and that he was supposed to be a ghostwriter for Bundy. Apparently Bundy intended to write a book with the proceeds going to a Would-Be Corporation. The corporation was a nonprofit enterprise intended to raise money to help defray the legal costs of indigents charged with capital crimes.[27] As things turned out, Michaud wrote his own series of books on Bundy.[28]

Jopling cleared up one thing early on in the jury selection process—he told the jurors that although they were going to be sequestered, they definitely were not going to be treated like the Iranian hostages.[29] He repeated that statement several times throughout jury selection, which he referred to as a "grinding" process.[30] The first week he excused a juror who said that Bundy would have to come forward with some evidence of innocence;[31] a juror who said that if Bundy was guilty, "they ought to kill him;"[32] a VISTA worker who could never vote for the death penalty; a computer programmer who could never vote for anything else;[33] and another juror who had speculated that she might sit on the Bundy case when she got her subpoena.[34] The second week he excused an AA member who said he was afraid that sitting on the jury would drive him back to drinking.[35]

Jopling also cleared up an issue that had caused us some grief leading into the trial. After Bundy got the death penalty in Miami, a lot of registered voters in our circuit thought we ought to drop the charges. They reasoned that Bundy was already going to be executed and to get a third death penalty on him would be a waste of money. Whenever someone accosted me about the "waste" of money, my standard answer was, "Okay, you go tell the Leaches that their daughter isn't important." The critic's fallback position would be, "Why don't you just put the case on hold and see if the Chi Omega case stands up on appeal? You can always try the case later if it gets reversed." My standard reply to that suggestion was to observe that, unlike wine, criminal cases don't get better with age.

A prospective juror voiced that criticism during voir dire, and Jopling told him that "The State of Florida has the right to have a criminal matter disposed of without unnecessary delay. The proceedings in other trials—although they are completed on the trial level—are never complete until all appeals have been exhausted." Jopling concluded, "[I]f this case was unduly delayed and awaited all the appeals in the earlier case, evidence might be lost, witnesses might disappear or die, and for those reasons among others, this case has to be brought on for trial, it being an entirely separate and distinct case from the one in Miami."[36]

Blair and I split the burden of questioning the jurors. At the outset, we were both so eager to do something that we had a running argument about who was going to question each juror—"I'll do this juror." "No, I can do it." "You did the last one." "But I'm still fresh." By the end of the two weeks, we were still arguing—"You take the next juror." "No, you take the juror." "I'm worn out, you take him." We worked out our differences without coming to blows. Register took notes, made suggestions, and went back and forth from the courtroom to our office to give Wallace instructions about various things we wanted done.

Jopling ordered Register to stay put, but Blair kept sending him out of the courtroom.

By the beginning of day three, a panel of 15 jurors had survived cause challenges—but each side had 20 peremptory challenges, and we began to exercise them. Jopling had us exercise our peremptories in chambers away from the prying eyes and eavesdropping ears of the media, who were unhappy about being excluded. Peremptory challenges whittled the panel down to 11.[37] The defense burned their peremptories much faster than the prosecution. By the end of day three, Dick Hagood thought we were further along than we were by day three in Live Oak.[38]

On the morning of day four, we did something besides question jurors. The defense filed another motion for change of venue,[39] and Jopling took time out from jury selection to hear evidence on the motion. At the hearing Africano introduced 259 news articles on Bundy and 68 photos of Bundy, all of which had been published in the *Orlando Sentinel*,[40] but the heart and soul of this motion was the testimony of Dr. Phillip Taylor, who had done a survey and written a report entitled "A Descriptive Study of Orange County, Florida Registered Voters' Knowledge and Attitudes about Theodore Bundy and the Kimberly Leach Case."[41] Taylor testified that "as a group . . . the registered voters in Orange County sampled in the present survey know little about the Kimberly Leach Case. By contrast 98 percent of those sampled recognized the name Theodore Bundy."[42] Taylor had to admit, however, that 66 percent of those surveyed had never heard of Kim Leach.[43] Taylor also testified that of those who were aware of Bundy's conviction in the Chi Omega murders, 31 percent thought the conviction was a strong indication of guilt in another murder case.[44] Half of those polled thought Bundy could get a fair trial in Orlando, and half thought that he couldn't.[45] It looked to me as though if you took every word Taylor said as true, then a significant minority of voters knew little about the Leach case and weren't prejudiced against Bundy. I thought we could get a jury out of that sizeable minority of voters—and we did.

Jopling took the motion under advisement, and we went back to jury selection that afternoon. By the end of the day our cumulative total was 59 jurors questioned and 49 excused.[46] We were making progress, but we were making it very slowly. Jury selection would go into another week, and we were left with little to do over the weekend. On Saturday we went shopping and stocked the refrigerator in our war room with drinks and snacks. On Sunday we walked across to First Baptist Church, where we attended a Sunday school class taught by a lawyer friend of Blair's.

By some odd coincidence, the topic of the lesson was "Forgiveness." The teacher held us up as examples of forgiveness, telling the class that although we were prosecuting Bundy we still were able to extend Christian forgiveness to him. I didn't contradict him, but I certainly didn't agree with him. Forgiveness for Bundy was not high on my agenda. I worked hard to make sure my feelings did not cloud my judgment, but I could not dismiss my feelings. As Blair told a reporter who had asked about my attitude toward the case, "When you work on something so hard for so long, I don't see how it could not become somewhat of an obsession."[47]

Court began that next Monday at 9:15 A.M.,[48] and none of the lawyers looked like they had gotten adequate rest. Jopling kept us in court until 6:45 P.M. that Monday evening, prompting Dick Hagood to report that the judge was "obviously growing impatient."[49] None of us were at the top of our game mentally, and we tended to say and do things without thinking them through. Once, while we were outside the hearing of the jury and away from the press exercising peremptory challenges, I referred to the jury selection process as "American Roulette." Africano took offense at my comment, and I got a mini-lecture from Jopling. Africano, on the other hand, put his foot in his mouth before the jury and got quoted in the papers. He told a juror that the death penalty was "the final insult," prompting a vigorous objection. Jopling gave Africano an admonition that went out over the Associated Press wire service.[50] I was responsible for the faux pas that the press found most entertaining. Africano could sometimes ask convoluted questions, and on this occasion he asked one of his most opaque and confusing questions. I knew it was objectionable but couldn't quite put my finger on the legal grounds. Undeterred, I sprang to my feet and cried, "Your honor, I object! That just ain't right!" The comment got reported in several sources[51] and even made it into Michaud's book on Bundy,[52] but no one reported Jopling's ruling—sustained.

The next morning we were back at the grind of questioning jurors, but that afternoon we heard a renewed motion for change of venue.[53] Lynn Thompson reminded the judge that the defense had almost completely run out of challenges, and that many of those jurors tentatively seated had opinions on the case. Blair countered that we had questioned 85 jurors and only 15 had been excused because they had preconceived opinions about Bundy's guilt. Blair went on to say, "Mr. Bundy is a cause célèbre. He'd be a cause célèbre in Two Egg, Pahokee, or Sopchoppy." Thompson told the judge, "There's no place this thing can go where it will meet with an unbiased public."[54] The defense made it clear that they didn't really want a change of venue—they wanted the case "abated" until such time as everyone had forgotten about Bundy. Blair argued that "Abatement in this case will constitute the death of this trial. Abatement would have the net effect of letting the defendant walk free."[55] Jopling said he didn't want the case going "into the next generation," and denied the motion.[56]

We started court the next morning at 8:00 A.M. and Jopling kept us until 9:00 P.M. Peremptory challenges were becoming a problem for the defense. We had exercised very few peremptories, but the defense was down to three. Now that the defense's peremptories were almost gone, we should have been able to pick a jury in short order, but three things happened to prolong the process. First, the defense asked for more peremptory challenges. After much arguing, Jopling gave the defense three additional challenges.[57] Second, Africano changed his questioning style. Instead of interrogative questions, he began to ask coercive questions similar to the type questions you would ask on cross examination of a hostile witness. His objective was to browbeat the jurors into saying they could not be fair so that he could challenge them for cause and not lose any more peremptory challenges. The news media actually noticed the change in Africano's questioning style.[58] Only the lawyers noticed the third thing—Jopling became more liberal in granting the defense's cause challenges. The previous week had been frustrating, the second week became maddening. We adjusted our questioning to be more suggestive in order to try to insulate the jurors from Africano's verbal onslaught, but that didn't stop him from asking the coercive questions. We fought hard on each cause challenge Africano made, but that didn't stop Jopling from granting them. Finally, by Friday the defense was down to one peremptory challenge.[59] And then there were none.

How we got to none is an instructive story. As I recall, it was Friday morning, and Jopling was killing us with his readiness to grant cause challenges against perfectly acceptable jurors. We were near our wits' end when Jopling called a recess. After Jopling recessed us, Africano stood up and made the statement that ended jury selection. I don't recall the exact wording of the statement, but the gist of the statement was that Africano congratulated Jopling for being able to overcome his prejudice and make proper rulings on Africano's cause challenges. I don't think the statement got reported because we were already recessed, but everyone in the courtroom heard it. Africano thought he was flattering Jopling, but we could tell by the judge's body language that he felt insulted by Africano's intimation that he was prejudiced. When court resumed, Jopling had transformed from the liberal granter of cause challenges to the ultra-conservative denier of cause challenges. All close calls went to the prosecution.

I tried many cases before Jopling, and he was always an even-tempered, courteous judge who would let you try your case. Some judges are control freaks who try to micro-manage the actions of trial counsel, but Jopling never was. As long as you behaved ethically and professionally, he would let you do it your way. That day Jopling was not even-tempered and became downright coercive in trying to make the lawyers do things his way, and it was our fault. When the defense burned their last peremptory challenge, we were still loaded with them. We had an acceptable jury, but we didn't have anyone who looked like a natural leader. We thoroughly discussed the situation and decided that we would go on a foreman hunt. Jopling seemed nonplussed when we burned our first peremptory on an acceptable juror, and he got agitated when we burned our second on another acceptable juror. He called us to the bench and wanted to know what we thought we were doing. We told him we were exercising our lawful privilege to excuse jurors we didn't like. He didn't say it in so many words, but his message came through loud and clear—we'd better get our act together and accept the jury. Although Jopling didn't seem to understand what we were doing, Africano fully appreciated our strategy. Richard Larsen quoted him as saying, "All they're doing now is shopping for a foreman."[60]

Jopling wasn't the only one who was getting testy. After the defense exercised its last peremptory, Bundy got up to walk out of the courtroom in protest. "I'm leaving," he announced, "This is a game and I'll not be a party to this Waterloo."[61] As he walked by, Thor grabbed him by the arm. Due to Thor's size and musculature, Bundy came to a screeching halt. He turned around angrily to confront the man who had grabbed him. The look in his eyes was homicidal—so vicious that it shocked Ann Rule, who saw it on television.[62] It impressed another lady also, but we'll get to that later. When Bundy got fully turned around and saw who had him, Bundy's look immediately transformed from homicidal maniac to horrified milquetoast. Being unwilling to take on Thor, Bundy turned his attention to arguing with Jopling, and there was a standoff between the two. Jopling finally had Bundy escorted out of the courtroom and called a recess. During the recess, I went around to each of the bailiffs and reminded them that the next time Bundy got up to walk out, he would be a fleeing felon and they could shoot him. I was just joking. The bailiffs weren't armed. Africano went back to the defense room to try to reason with Bundy, and after about 45 minutes Bundy was back in the courtroom announcing that he was returning voluntarily.[63]

We brought in another juror and after questioning, Jopling called us to the bench to see if we had any challenges. We did. In all the years I knew Jopling, I never heard him use profanity—except that day. "Damn it" is a mild oath that wouldn't garner a PG rating today, but hearing Jopling say that one word was as traumatic as hearing a diatribe from someone who had an extensive vocabulary of earthy language. We went back to counsel table and had a brief strategy session. Should we cave in and accept the jury, or should we continue in the face of Jopling's anger and find our foreman? We decided that we would continue exercising peremptories. Little did we know, our hunt was almost over.

The door swung open and Patrick Wolski walked into the courtroom. Wolski was a big, shambling bear of a man. The way he carried himself was not graceful in the classical sense, but it told you that he was capable, resolute, and decisive. He looked like a foreman. He had not walked halfway across the courtroom before every lawyer on both sides knew that he would be the foreman. Africano had been questioning coercively for some time, but it was nothing compared to the coercive questioning he used on Wolski. He asked open-ended questions hoping to get Wolski to say something that could be spun into a challenge for cause, and he followed up on Wolksi's noncommittal answers trying to push Wolksi into an admission that he couldn't be fair.

Africano got Wolski to admit that he knew of the Chi Omega case, and that his feelings toward Bundy were not warm and cordial. Africano worked these statements toward what he hoped would be a challenge for cause:

> Q: *The feelings that you had about Mr. Bundy after the trial in Miami, which you have described as not being very good, do you still have them?*
> A: Sure.

Q:   *Well, how do you feel about him as he sits there now?*
A:   He is a convicted murderer.

Wolski assured Africano, however, that the Chi Omega case had nothing to do with the Leach case, and he could sit as a fair and impartial juror on the Leach case.

Q:   *The fact that you know he is a convicted murderer doesn't make you feel any less like giving him all the presumptions of innocence that the Court has instructed you about?*
A:   No. The State has to prove that he is guilty in this particular case.[64]

Africano made a cause challenge, and Bundy joined in the legal argumentation. He told Jopling, "This is a prosecution jury. The state's case is predicated upon knowledge outside the courtroom. It's not based on the shoddy case they bring to you. It's based upon the knowledge people bring in. Look at who they struck! Look at the people they struck! People who did not know about this case. People who did not know about this case. That's who they struck. Use your mind, your honor. Look at what they're doing. They want people who will bring that prejudice into the courtroom. And you're playing their game."[65] It was an eloquent argument, probably better than the arguments we lawyers had made. The only false step was to suggest that Jopling wasn't using his mind.

When Bundy finished his impassioned argument, Jopling told Bundy, "You're overruled," and called for the jury. There was surreptitious celebration at the prosecution table, but the reaction was a little different at the defense table. Bundy went off like a bottle rocket. When Africano accepted the jury but noted that he wanted to "reserve the right to challenge the jury at a later time," Bundy said he wasn't accepting it, got up, and started walking out of the courtroom, announcing, "I'm leaving the courtroom." Jopling told him to stop, and he kept going, saying that he was waiving his presence.[66] Three bailiffs headed him off, but they just stood in front of him without touching him. Bundy was prepared for this. As long as things didn't get physical, he could do a little rooster strutting. He took off his coat and began launching verbal onslaughts. Jopling was the first recipient. He told the judge, "I'm not going to be in this room when the jury walks in.

I'm not going through this. And you knew that, your honor. You knew how far you could push me." Africano tried to defuse the problem by requesting that Bundy be allowed to leave. We had a hurried conference at the prosecution table and decided that Bundy really had to be present for the swearing of the jury. Blair got up to put his oar into the water.

"Your honor," he said, "I don't have my rules of criminal procedure with me, but my understanding is that the defendant must be here when the jury is empanelled."[67] It was Blair's turn to be the recipient of Bundy's wrath. "Try to make me stay," Bundy challenged, "You want a circus, I'll make a circus. I'll rain on your parade, Jack. You'll see a thunderstorm. This will not be the pat little drama you've arranged."[68] I could not help but be amused. Blair was as angry as I had ever seen him. Africano eventually coaxed Bundy back to the defense table, and we brought in the jury and swore it. When court recessed, I reminded the bailiffs of the fleeing felon rule, telling them they had missed another golden opportunity to shoot Bundy.

We had a jury but we needed alternates, and Jopling was determined to finish jury selection as quickly as possible. We spent Saturday picking and swearing three alternate jurors, and trial was set to commence the following Monday.[69] By the time we swore the last alternate, we had questioned more than 130 potential jurors.[70] After Jopling swore the last alternate, we went into more motion hearings.

I made an oral motion to unseal the discovery in the court file, and the defense opposed it. I argued that the jury was sequestered, and there was no need to keep the discovery sealed. Africano argued that the files should remain sealed because there was "always the chance" of a mistrial. Jopling denied my motion. The *Lake City Reporter* correctly pointed out that his ruling reversed a previous written order he had entered saying "in no event shall they [the discovery materials] be maintained under seal after empanelment and sequestration of the jury."[71] The discovery remains sealed to this day.

The defense filed a "Motion in Limine Regarding Limitation of Argument by the State."[72] A lot of the things they didn't want us to mention were things that we had no intention of mentioning, but they also wanted to prevent us from mentioning things that we had to discuss in opening statement in order for the jury to be able to make any sense of the case—Bundy's arrest in Pensacola; the theft of the Media Center van and the orange Volkswagen; the theft and fraudulent use of the credit cards; the theft of the 13d-11300 tag; the purchase of the Buck

General hunting knife; and the testimony of the Parmenters. In other words, they didn't want us to be able to say anything at all. I argued, "What the defense is trying to do is tie the State's hands as to what we can say. If we make a statement that we can't prove during the trial, then woe be to the State. The risk is ours. We shoulder that risk."[73] Jopling denied the motion, and we recessed at 3:30 P.M. that Saturday afternoon.[74]

# 16

# The Trial

Sunday was a busy day. Our first batch of witnesses came in, and we spent the afternoon prepping them for testimony on Monday. Blair put the finishing touches on his opening statement, and I kidded him about his theme. The theme, "It was a cold and rainy day," bears a striking resemblance to the worst opening line in all of English literature— "It was a dark and stormy night." The phrase was coined by Edward Bulwer-Lytton, a Victorian-era writer best known as the author of *The Last Days of Pompeii*. Blair had devised a good theme, which proves that good trial advocacy does not necessarily equal good literature. It would have been an excellent theme if not for the testimony of Clinch Edenfield.

When we arrived in court Monday morning, we hit a roadblock. The defense served us with yet another motion for change of venue. We spent the entire morning dealing with that motion, and Jopling finally denied it.[1] Then the trial began in earnest. Blair opened for the State, painting a vivid picture of the storyline we would present over the next two weeks. When Africano made his opening statement, he did little to tip his hand as to any affirmative defense; he basically spent his time highlighting the many weaknesses in our case. Africano did make some helpful admissions. He admitted that Bundy was at the Holiday Inn in Lake City on February 8 using stolen credit cards.[2] Some defense attorneys will never admit anything—one colorful old former prosecutor used to tell me, "I wouldn't admit to swallowing the cat even if they caught me with its tail hanging out of my mouth." A good advocate will sometimes admit facts that can be readily established. Africano's admissions were good advocacy.

It became clear from Africano's opening that the heart of the defense would be the straw man fallacy. In this fallacy you take a weakness in your opponent's case, set it up as a straw man, knock it down, and pretend you have defeated the whole case.[3] Andy Anderson was Africano's straw man. Africano told the jury that the State's evidence was going to be a chain of circumstances, and he warned them that "a chain is only as strong as its weakest link." Anderson, he said, was that weakest link. Africano went on to say, "The State's case will rise and fall on the testimony of one man—Anderson. Mr. Blair did not tell you that Anderson was aware of the notoriety. He did not come forward with what he saw for five months afterward. He was immediately placed under hypnosis by someone who was totally unqualified. Between the hypnotic sessions Anderson was told things and in the second session he could spit out those facts. We will prove it was physically impossible for him to see what he thinks he saw."[4]

We started our presentation with Kim's disappearance from Lake City Junior High, which meant that the first day we introduced no evidence directly incriminating Bundy. Freda Leach testified first, and she described taking Kim to school, going home with a headache, and later receiving the call from the school asking Kim's whereabouts. We asked if she and Kim had any plans for that afternoon, intending to prove that Kim would not have run away on the very day she was going to pick up a formal gown for a ball at which she was to be honored. Africano objected and Jopling sustained the objection. We heatedly argued that the testimony was relevant, but Jopling decided that it would only become relevant if and when the defense offered evidence to the jury suggesting that Kim ran away. This was a false step on the defense's part. Everyone knew they would offer such evidence, and when they did we could recall Mrs. Leach to testify about the plans to purchase the ball gown. One of the very last witnesses the jury would hear before they retired to deliberate would be Kim's mother. The doctrine of primacy and recency teaches that you should start strong and finish strong. The story of the ball gown gave our rebuttal a strong finish.

When we ended our evidence on Kim's disappearance, we still had some time left. This was not good, because we had to go ahead and begin presenting our three eyewitnesses. We wanted another evening to work on that testimony, but we weren't going to get it. Our problem was this: We had two eyewitnesses, Jackie Moore and Anderson, who had said they could not positively identify Bundy. They would only say the man they saw "looked like" Bundy. Clinch Edenfield was our only eyewitness who would positively identify Bundy, and he did not inspire confidence. Not only did he wear glasses with very thick lenses, he also had picked the wrong photo in a photospread shown to him by Joe Uebehler.[5] Was a less-than-positive identification admissible? Register researched and briefed the issue,[6] and the answer was "yes," but it came with qualifications. Uncertainty as to the identification did not render the identification inadmissible, but it certainly affected the weight of the testimony. The cases also repeatedly spoke of the less-than-positive identification as being "corroborative" of other, more certain evidence of identification. We interpreted the cases to mean that before we could call an eyewitness giving a less-than-positive identification, we had to lay a predicate by having at least one eyewitness positively identify the defendant. We planned to call Edenfield first, have him positively identify Bundy, and then call Moore and Anderson. But something happened to change our plans. When Moore arrived in Orlando on Sunday evening, she told us that she was now positive that Bundy was the man she saw in the van. She had seen the news report of Bundy's tantrum during jury selection and his confrontation with Thor. She said the look on Bundy's face when he turned around to confront Thor was identical to the look on the van driver's face. Ann Rule wasn't the only person whose perspective was changed by Bundy's outburst.

We asked for an early recess, but Jopling insisted that we continue. All we had was Moore, so we went with her. It didn't go well. It is possible to be a truthful witness but not a good witness, just as it is possible to be a "good" witness but not a truthful one. Moore told the truth, but she neither told it well nor did we help her tell it well. We began with her describing how she saw the van driving erratically. At this point, I could have just asked her to point out the driver and turned her over for cross examination. Instead I asked her to describe the process by which she became able to identify the driver, and worked through that explanation toward having her point to Bundy. The order of examination was technically correct, because I was laying a predicate for validating the identification. It was not, however, persuasively powerful. I should have asked for her bottom-line conclusion and then asked her to explain. Lawyers sometimes forget that a direct examination need not be chronological. When we got to the verge of having her point to the driver of the van, I had her explain that it was only recently that she became sure of the driver's identity. She said she had seen Bundy snarl at Thor, and that made her sure. Unfortunately for her credibility, she attempted to mimic the snarl as she described it. She looked like she was trying to bite her shoulder. Then I asked her to identify the van's driver, but Thompson immediately objected and we removed the jury to argue the admissibility of her in-court identification.

Thompson made two arguments against Moore's in-court identification. He first argued that we had exposed Moore to a highly suggestive pretrial identification procedure by letting her watch television and see Bundy snarl at Thor. I argued that we had no control over Moore's television viewing habits, and that the identification was admissible. Jopling seemed to agree with me on that point, but Thompson's second argument sank us. In April of 1979, the Florida Supreme Court had allowed cameras in the courtroom on a one-year trial basis. When the Supreme Court made its ruling allowing cameras in the courtroom, it provided that none of the film or pictures were admissible in evidence.[7]

Thompson argued that Moore's identification was inadmissible because it was based on what she saw of an inadmissible televised court proceeding. Jopling bought the argument, held the identification inadmissible, and recessed the trial for the day. As we were leaving the courtroom, I decided to ask one of the bailiffs what he thought of our proof so far. "Alex, how are we doing?" I asked. "You haven't shown me anything," he replied. With those words of discouragement ringing in our ears, we went back to the Harley Hotel to prepare for the next day.

When trial resumed the next morning, we were back to Edenfield being the only eyewitness who could positively identify Bundy. That meant we would have to call him before we continued with Moore's testimony. We called Edenfield as our next witness, but first Jopling told the jury: "Ladies and gentlemen, before this witness takes the stand, I direct you that you will not consider or give any consideration or weight to the statement of the witness Mrs. Jackie Moore, who testified yesterday, relevant to any observation or expression that she saw on television. You will disregard that and that will not take part and be considered by you in arriving at your verdict."[8] If Edenfield muffed the identification of Bundy, we were in trouble.

Edenfield did not instill confidence. He was elderly, had poor eyesight, and looked like a country bumpkin. I ran him through his questions quickly and efficiently and asked him to point out the man he had seen on February 9, 1978. He pointed toward the defense table. The identification got confusing because the defense team was playing musical chairs. Every time I turned around, Bundy had swapped seats with Africano or Thompson. When I stated for the record the chair to which Edenfield pointed, Bundy was sitting in another chair. Jopling finally told Edenfield, "Would you go over there and touch the man you say you identified." Edenfield got up and walked over to the defense table and pointed directly to Bundy.

So far, so good, but cross examination came next. Thompson hammered away at Edenfield, and amazingly, Edenfield withstood the cross examination—up to a point. Edenfield was not sure whether the man had a beard, a moustache, or was clean-shaven. He could not describe the clothing Bundy was wearing. He could not describe Bundy's facial features. He could not describe the van. The only thing he knew for certain was that Bundy drove that van around the junior high the morning Kim Leach disappeared. Thompson questioned Edenfield about the photospread shown him by Joe Uebehler. Edenfield stated that he picked Bundy out of the photospread, and that Uebehler had confirmed the selection by winking at him. Then Thompson asked about the weather. Edenfield testified that "it was pretty good. It was good weather." The examination continued:

Q: *What kind of good weather are you talking about?*
A: Well, the sun was shining and it wasn't raining.

Q: *You said the sun was shining, right?*
A: Yeah.

Q: *Okay. So you don't remember that being cold weather?*
A: No, sir. To the best of my memory, I don't think it was cold weather.

Q: *Do you remember it being in the summertime?*
A: I think it was, yes, sir.[9]

With each answer Edenfield gave, Blair's "cold and rainy day" got warmer and sunnier. It would have been a complete disaster except for one thing. The weight of Edenfield's identification may have been slight, but it was sufficient to render the less-than-positive identifications by Anderson and Moore admissible into evidence. We expected to do better with Anderson and Moore. We didn't.

Anderson was our next witness. He described how, as he drove along Duval Street going home from the fire station, he came upon a line of cars blocked by a white van parked in the middle of the traffic lane. He saw a man leading a girl to the van, putting her into the van, and driving away. The story was so improbable that Stephen Michaud, in *The Only Living Witness,* marveled that Africano did not accuse Anderson of lying.[10] Africano didn't accuse Anderson of lying because he knew Anderson was telling the truth—a liar would have made up a much better lie than that. Anderson's manner of identifying Bundy also spoke volumes in favor of his truthfulness. Although he positively identified Kim Leach as the girl, he would only say that Bundy "closely resembled" the driver of the van.[11]

If Anderson had been lying, he would have positively identified Bundy. The weaknesses in his testimony actually were strengths as to his credibility. Regardless of how silly it might seem, he actually saw a white van parked in the middle of the road blocking traffic, and he actually saw Bundy leading Kim to the van. Completely disregard the fact that Bundy later confessed to kidnapping and killing Kim and answer this question: In the light of all the other evidence placing Bundy in that white van, who else could Anderson have seen that morning?

When it came time for cross examination, I thought that Africano destroyed Anderson. Patrick Wolski, the jury foreman, agreed with me. He was "shocked" that we were leading off with such poor witnesses.[12] We then got away from the eyewitnesses and presented the testimony of Kim's dentist to put in dental records and lay the groundwork for identifying her body. We closed out the day with testimony about the discovery of Kim's body. After the jury left for the day, we proffered Moore's less-than-positive identification of Bundy. Her testimony went so poorly that we decided not to place her back in front of the jury. As we left for the day, I asked Alex, "How are we doing?" He replied, "You still haven't shown me anything."

Up until that day, I had gone back to my hotel room each evening and watched the news accounts of the trial to see what they were saying. That day, when I flipped on the television, I heard the announcer solemnly intone, "The State fired its biggest guns today in the trial of Theodore Robert Bundy." I turned off the television and never watched the news again until after the verdict.

The next day we began with the testimony of Jack Duncan and Dr. Pete Lipkovic. Duncan's testimony did not directly incriminate Bundy, but it laid the predicate for later testimony that would. Because we intended to have both Duncan and Lipkovic refer to photographs of Kim's decomposed body, we proffered the testimony outside the presence of the jury. We had a battle royal over the admission of those photos. Africano contended they were too gruesome to be shown, and we contended that they were necessary for the witnesses to explain their testimony. Because Jopling sometimes had a tendency to saw the baby in half, we offered more photos than we really wanted or needed to get in. Jopling ruled that "Although they are gruesome, they are not so exceptionally gruesome that they would unduly inflame the jury,"[13] but just as we expected, he let us use only two of the photos we offered. We were satisfied with his ruling.

Duncan presented a slide show as he described how he processed the death scene, and also used a large, expertly done diagram of the scene. It reminded me of a poster for a science project. Using the diagram, Duncan described where he found every piece of evidence. Then we had him identify and authenticate each piece of evidence, describe how he preserved it, and describe how the evidence was distributed within the FDLE Crime Lab.[14] Other than the slide show and the diagram it was yawn-inducing, but it was absolutely necessary.

When Lipkovic arrived to testify, he showed us a chart that he had made of the temperatures near the Suwannee River State Park for the months of February through April. He said it would help him to establish Kim's time of death. We told him that we could not use the chart because it had not been disclosed in discovery and because it was based on hearsay reports from weather stations. He said, "Don't worry, I'll get it in."

Lipkovic took the stand and testified that he believed Kim died from homicidal violence to the neck area, and that the violence was accompanied by copious bleeding. He gave the jury the same explanation he had given me at the autopsy. Next he testified to the approximate time of death based on the evidence of the differing stages of maggot development. The temperature chart would have been helpful, because it showed the number of days that the temperature was too cold for maggots to be active. Michaud noted in his book that we didn't ask Lipkovic about the evidence suggestive of sexual battery.[15] The omission was not an oversight. We had opted not to indict Bundy for sexual battery because the evidence was suggestive but not conclusive. We opted not to confuse the issues by offering evidence of the trauma to the groin. Besides, Richard Stephens was going to give us much stronger evidence of sexual assault.

On cross examination Africano tried to use Kim's turtleneck sweater to undermine Lipkovic's opinion as to cause of death. Africano had the serology reports from FDLE, and the reports said nothing about blood on the turtleneck. He took this absence of evidence as evidence of absence and crossed Lipkovic accordingly. Africano led Lipkovic through a series of questions culminating in Lipkovic admitting that if there was no blood on the turtleneck, then he would be absolutely wrong about there being homicidal violence to the neck area. Lipkovic qualified his answer by saying his bottom-line opinion was "not negotiable"—Kim was the victim of a homicide.[16] Africano moved on to time of death thinking he had set up the doctor for a crushing impeachment when the turtleneck came into evidence. Africano did not know that the turtleneck had been so soaked with decayed blood and body fluid that nobody at the lab wanted to fool with it. The only test they did with it was to take a fiber sample for comparison, and then they put it in a shed on the roof of the lab. When he went to the crime lab to inspect the evidence, Africano didn't go onto the roof to look at it as I had done when I inspected the evidence. I thought I knew how to refute the "unstained turtleneck hypothesis."

After setting Lipkovic up for what Africano thought would be a crushing refutation, he moved on to a line of cross suggesting that Lipkovic's calculation of the time of death was faulty. He and Lipkovic launched off into an interminable discussion of flies and maggots. At one point Lipkovic, who spoke with a heavy Eastern European accent, said, "Zee maggot is zee medical examiner's best friend." About that time a fly landed on his shoulder. Africano observed, "There's one of your friends, now." Then Africano began working on time of death in earnest, and Lipkovic answered every question by saying, "I could demonstrate my answer to you with a chart that I have in my briefcase." Africano initially ignored Lipkovic's offers but finally gave in and asked him to produce the chart. Lipkovic pulled a roll of paper out of his briefcase and handed Africano one end of the roll. He then unrolled the paper to a length of approximately six feet and signaled Thompson to come over from the defense table and hold the other end. Then, with the defense team serving as his easel, he pulled a pointer out of his coat pocket and began to explain the chart. Neither defense attorney looked particularly happy. Ellen Burgess, our clerk, was an amateur cartoonist, and she immortalized the moment with a cartoon showing the defense team holding the inadmissible chart while Lipkovic pointed to it saying, "And zees is a high, and zees is a low." She titled the cartoon "Egg on Zee Face."

We finished the day with testimony from employees of the Holiday Inn. They proved that Bundy rented a room at that Holiday Inn the evening before Kim went missing, and they proved it well. It was the strength of this testimony that induced Africano to concede in opening statement that Bundy had been in Lake City on February 8. As we left the courtroom, I again inquired of Alex, who still opined, "You haven't shown me anything yet."

Thursday started out well, as a matter of fact, it went too well. We presented evidence that day of Bundy's thefts of the credit cards, cars, and license tags in Tallahassee and of his confrontation with and escape from Deputy Keith Daws. We also made a full presentation concerning the disappearance of the Media Center van. We expected the testimony to take all day. It didn't. We were through at noon. The next batch of witnesses was a contingent of officers from the FSU Police Department who were not scheduled to arrive in Orlando until after 5:00 P.M. We went to Jopling, explained our dilemma, and asked for a recess until the following day. Jopling let us know in no uncertain terms that we were recessing for lunch and that at 1:00 P.M. the State had better have some witnesses to present. At lunch we discussed what we could do and came up with nothing. Then, as we were walking back to the courthouse, we saw our witnesses. They had arrived early and decided to come down to the courthouse and check out the facilities. I had never been happier to see a group of witnesses than I was that afternoon.

We didn't have time to properly prepare them. We didn't have time to prepare them at all. We simply gathered them up and herded them to the witness room. By the time we had them deposited in the witness room, it was time to begin court. We started calling witnesses and examining them cold turkey, and things went well again. The adrenalin surge induced by the appearance of the witnesses had left me somewhat euphoric. As I called Captain C. S. Hooker to the witness stand, I leaned over to Register and whispered, "I do my best work when I'm flying by the seat of my pants." I began the examination by qualifying Hooker and establishing his credentials. I then turned to the reason we had brought him from Tallahassee.

Q: *During the course of your duties in the month of February, did you have occasion to become involved in the recovery of a white FSU Media Center van?*
A: Yes, I did. . . .

Q:   *All right. Describe for the jury, please, sir, just how you became*
     *involved in the recovery of that van.*

A:   As chief investigator for Florida State University, I hold the
     rank of captain. I was intimately involved with the investiga-
     tion of the Chi Omega murders. I was called in regard to a
     van which had been recovered.

I was not sure how Hooker worked a mention of the Chi Omega
murders into the totally unrelated recovery of the Media Center van. I
was sure, however, that Jopling had solemnly warned us against mentioning the Chi Omega murders, and when we prepped the witnesses
on the evening before their testimony, we passed on that solemn warning. I made the noise of a tire going flat—shhhhhhhh. Everyone else
says they heard me make a scatological reference, but I maintain that I
merely made the sound of a tire going flat.

I stopped the examination and turned to look at Africano, who was
sleeping at the switch. Bundy was elbowing him hard in the side and
loudly whispering, "Object! Object! Object!" Africano tentatively rose
to his feet, not sure of why, and asked to approach the bench. As the
hordes of lawyers assembled around Jopling's bench, Bundy filled
Africano in on the problem. When Africano arrived at the bench, he
moved for a mistrial. I urged that a curative instruction to disregard
the testimony would be sufficient. After a brief argument, Jopling denied the motion and instructed the jury to disregard Hooker's remark.
Needless to say, Ellen Burgess drew a cartoon of that little exchange,
which had completely depleted my supply of hubris. I don't recall
asking Alex how we were doing that afternoon.

Finally Friday came, and we were all looking forward to some rest
over the weekend. We had two packages of proof to present that
day—Bundy's activity in Jacksonville and testimony about our failure
to find Bundy's fingerprints anywhere. One package of proof was very
dramatic; the other was at best soporific and at worst exculpatory. We
opted to put on the dramatic testimony in the morning and the soporific testimony in the afternoon.

Things again began well, but again took a turn for the worse in the
afternoon. John Farhat positively identified Bundy as buying the Buck
General hunting knife with the $26 price tag. Bundy became very agi-
tated and blurted out, "That's a damn lie!" Jopling summoned us to the
bench. Africano assured Jopling that he would counsel with Bundy
about his behavior. Bundy was not helping his cause by acting out

like that in front of the jury. Next came John McCarthy, who testified that John Farhat's label maker could very well have made the $26 price tag found on the floorboard of the Media Center van. We coupled McCarthy's testimony with evidence that no other Green Acres store in Florida had such a label maker, and then put on the Parmenter incident. Danny and Leslie did exceptionally well on direct and weathered cross examination with their credibility intact. We were beginning to make some real progress toward convincing the jury to convict, and then disaster struck. We devoted the afternoon to testimony concerning fingerprints. The testimony was long, drawn out, and painful, and the bottom line was that Bundy's prints could be found nowhere.

I blithely led Doug Barrow through all the places he couldn't find Bundy's fingerprints and had him describe the extreme measures we took to find Bundy's fingerprints. Barrow also testified that the likely places for fingerprints within the van had been wiped—possibly with a rag soaked in Coca Cola. I thought everything was going well until I tendered Barrow for cross examination and went back to sit down. Register tugged on my shoulder and said, "Keep a stiff upper lip. The jurors are looking worried. Don't let them think you are concerned about the lack of fingerprints." Until Register called the matter to my attention, I was completely unconcerned. After what he told me, I was in a state of panic. The panic worsened during Thompson's cross of Barrow.

Although Barrow hadn't found Bundy's prints in the van, he had found a lot of others—87 to be exact. Thompson had Barrow describe the location of every single one of those 87 prints and had him reiterate that none of them matched Bundy. We were shaken when the jury was released. They were going to have all weekend to think about the absence of those prints before we could repair the damage with more inculpatory evidence. As we walked out of the courtroom, however, my spirits were somewhat lifted when Alex told me, "You're doing a little better."

We went back into chambers for a meeting with the judge, and I had to communicate to everyone that we were not harmed by the lack of fingerprints. Laughter signals lack of fear, so I made a joke of it. When they escorted Bundy into chambers, I said, "There's the man who leaves no fingerprints." Thompson responded, "At no time did the fingers leave the hands." Even Bundy got into the act. He said, "There are no holes in these hands."[17] The pool reporter who came back to the meeting in chambers asked a question about rumors of friction among the sequestered jurors. I wasn't through bantering, so I unleashed a verbal barrage at him and deeply offended him. The next Monday I learned the wisdom of Mark Twain's advice to never pick a fight with someone who buys ink by the barrel. The reporter had written a story entitled "'Beauty, Beast' train talents at Bundy." Blair was Beauty and I was the "loose-shouldered and somewhat pear shaped" Beast.[18]

On Monday, our case began to get real traction. That day we called Richard Stephens, David Lee, Norman Chapman, and Don Patchen. But first we had to contend with a motion to exclude Lee's testimony and motions to suppress our shoe track, fiber, and serology evidence. As to the shoe tracks, fiber, and serology, Africano argued that it was inconclusive, and I replied, "It's no secret that we are in the process of weaving a web of circumstances to incriminate the defendant, and this is one more link in the chain of circumstances." Despite my mixed metaphors, Jopling denied the motion, saying that the inconclusive nature of each individual piece of evidence went to the weight of the evidence, rather than its admissibility.[19]

The defense wanted to suppress Lee's testimony because it was evidence of flight by the defendant. Guilty people tend to run away from charges, while the innocent stand their ground and fight it out. I told Jopling that the flight from Lee indicated "a tremendous amount of guilt." Bundy slammed his hand down on the table and began to stand up, but he didn't call me a liar. Jopling told him, "Sit down, I will permit no interruptions."[20] Bundy sat down, and I concluded my argument. Bundy argued the motion himself and made the point that he had a lot of charges to run away from other than the Leach case. He concluded by saying that the evidence put him at a great and grave disadvantage. Of course, that's why we were presenting the evidence. Every particle of evidence we presented at the trial was intended to put him at a great disadvantage, and we were free to do so as long as we observed all the pertinent rules of evidence. Jopling denied the motion.

We finally started presenting witnesses. Most of our witnesses testified to various predicates necessary to paving the way for Stephens and Lynn Henson. Jim Skipper and J.O. Jackson testified about the seizure of Bundy's blue blazer from the Big B Laundry, and Jackson testified that when he presented Bundy with the search warrant for the blazer, Bundy acknowledged the blazer was his.[21] When I offered the coat into evidence, Africano objected because it was not in substantially the same condition as it was when Jackson seized it. When it was taken into evidence, the coat was pressed and on a hanger. When

I offered it into evidence, it was wrinkled and in an evidence bag. Jopling made short work of that objection.[22]

We began Stephens's testimony but were unable to conclude it. As we walked out of the courtroom, I again asked Alex how we were doing. "You're doing a lot better, but you're still not there yet." That would come on Tuesday when, according to Michaud, we administered the "coup de grace."[23]

Stephens had done a superb job analyzing a massive amount of evidence, both relevant and irrelevant. He had written more than a dozen separate lab reports on the case describing the results of testing almost 100 individual items of evidence.[24] His most significant findings were blood staining of Type B on the van carpet and semen staining of Type O on the crotch of Kim's panties. Kim had Type B blood and Bundy had Type O blood. This sort of evidence is merely consistent with guilt. Anyone with Type B blood could have contributed the stain to the carpet. The semen stain was even less persuasive of identity.

For the bloodstains on the carpet, in addition to ABO typing, the lab could test for a number of different enzymes found in the blood and could further narrow their results with the enzyme types. Unfortunately, testing for enzyme types on the bloodstained carpet was inconclusive. Even before Kim's body was found, we already knew her blood type by testing her parents. The father was Type O and the mother was Type B,[25] which meant that Kim was either Type B or Type O. When Kim's body was found, Stephens was able to identify two enzymes in the decomposed tissue sample he collected at the autopsy. They were erythrocyte acid phosphatase type B ($EAP^B$) and esterase D type 1 ($EsD^1$).

When prepping Stephens to testify, I asked him if he had gotten any indication at all as to the enzyme types of the bloodstain on the van carpet. He had. Although the results weren't sufficiently clear for him to swear to, they had indicated enzyme types identical to Kim's. Although I tried, I could not persuade him to testify to those results. I had no choice but to omit any reference to enzyme typing from the direct examination. On cross examination, Thompson asked Stephens about enzymes and got the same answer I got when I prepped him. Thompson also tried to persuade him to share the indications, but he refused. I got very nervous. If Thompson stopped cross examining at that point, it would look as though the State might be hiding exculpatory evidence. Thompson, however, asked Jopling to order Stephens to testify to the indications. Stephens then reluctantly testified that they were $EAP^B$ and $EsD^1$. On redirect, I confirmed that the enzymes matched Kim's enzyme types perfectly. The cross exemplified two time-honored maxims of cross examination: don't ask a question if you don't know the answer, and know when to stop.

Stephens said one thing that I didn't agree with. He characterized the stains on the van carpet as small. I had seen the stains and they looked huge to me. I didn't see this testimony as a problem, though, because I had a way of demonstrating how large the stains were.

We were in high spirits when we called Henson to the stand as our last witness. In addition to her scientific testimony, I wanted to accomplish two other objectives with Henson's testimony. After getting Kim's turtleneck into evidence, I asked Henson to unfurl it and display it to the jury. When she did, you could hear an audible gasp in the courtroom. The neck and chest of the shirt had a large brownish stain, and you didn't need a serologist to identify it as a bloodstain. We heard no more from Africano about the turtleneck being unstained. I had Henson do the same thing with the van carpet. We unrolled it on the floor in front of the jury, and the huge stain was readily apparent.

Henson's findings were complex, and if they weren't presented properly her testimony could fall flat. The first thing to do would be to establish that a fiber comparison is not like a fingerprint—it is never conclusive. You can never prove that a certain fiber found on the victim's clothing definitely came from an article of the defendant's clothing; you can only say that the fiber is consistent with the material in the defendant's clothing. Having established this, if you properly present the findings, the jury will nevertheless be very impressed with the evidence.

Before a microanalyst will call a match between fibers, they must match perfectly in every detail. The analyst looks at color, cross section, size, composition, and in the case of synthetic fibers, the amount of delustrant in the fibers. Henson had to explain that delustrant was placed in shiny synthetic fibers to take the luster off the material. In the case of blue and white cotton fibers, a match is not very significant. Everybody has at least one pair of blue jeans. A match with synthetic fibers, however, can be highly significant. Once all the matches between and among all the fibers are cataloged, the jury is convinced despite the initial disclaimer. If, instead of leading with the disclaimer, you conclude your direct with the disclaimer, the testimony will fall flat.

Henson summarized her findings in a complex chart that graphically demonstrated all the various cross transfers from van carpet to Kim's clothing, from Kim's clothing to van carpet, and from Bundy's clothing to Kim's clothing and the van carpet. We did Henson's shoe track

comparisons first and saved the chart for the grand finale. In the beginning, the chart was completely blank with three boxes signifying the
fiber types in Kim's clothing, the van carpet, and Bundy's clothing. As
she described each fiber in each item, she accented the finding by placing a color-coded sticker in the appropriate box. As she described each
transfer, she placed another color-coded sticker on the chart to signify
the transfer. When she finished, the chart was full of color-coded stick-
ers, and Bundy was finished. Henson summed up by saying, "I have
never seen anything like the combination of fibers which is present in
this particular case in any other case. I have never seen so many fibers
which were similar to the standards in any other case." She concluded
by expressing the opinion that it was "probable" that Bundy's clothes
came in contact with Kim's clothes, "very probable" that Bundy's
clothes came in contact with the van carpet, and "extremely probable"
that Kim's clothes came in contact with the van carpet. Thompson cross
examined for 90 minutes but could not put a dent in her testimony.[26]

We rested at 3:32 P.M. The defense moved for a judgment of acquittal, and we argued the motion until 5:05 P.M. Bundy argued the motion
for the defense, and Blair replied by saying that Bundy had made "an
excellent closing argument."[27] Jopling denied the motion, and court recessed. As I left the courtroom, I asked, "How are we doing, Alex?" He
said, "You're over the top." If I could have asked Wolski how we were
doing, he also would have said, "Over the top."[28]

We may have been over the top, but we were not across the finish
line. As Sherlock Holmes once said, "Circumstantial evidence is a very
tricky thing. It may seem to point very straight to one thing, but if you
shift your own point of view a little, you may find it pointing in an
equally uncompromising manner to something entirely different."[29]
Wolski assessed our case as being good enough for a conviction but
not good enough to survive evidence putting Bundy somewhere other
than Lake City on February 9.[30] When trial resumed the next day, Africano would try to shift the jury's point of view ever so slightly and have
them see something sufficiently different to raise a reasonable doubt.
He attacked on several fronts:

1. He tried to get Bundy out of the Media Center van and into
   another white van.
2. He tried to separate Kim from Bundy by suggesting that she
   ran away from school and died at another time by different
   means than shown in the State's case.
3. He tried to discredit Andy Anderson's testimony.

# FIBER TRANSFER CHART*

| CARPET | JEANS | PURSE | BRA | SOCKS | TAN COAT | BU.JERSEY | TURTLENECK | COAT | TQ. SHIRT |
|---|---|---|---|---|---|---|---|---|---|
| GR.POLYPR | ↓↓↓↓ | ↓↓↓↓ | | ↓↓↓↓ | | | | | |
| BU.POLYPR | ↓↓↓↓ | ↓↓↓↓ | | ↓↓↓↓ | | | | | |
| TQ.POLYPR | ↓↓↓↓ | ↓↓↓↓ | ↓↓↓↓ | ↓↓↓↓ | | ↓↓↓↓ | | | |
| BK.POLYPR | ↓↓↓↓ | ↓↓↓↓ | ↓↓↓↓ | ↓↓↓↓ | | | | | |
| ↑↑↑↑ | BU.COT | BU.COT | | | | | | | |
| ↑↑↑↑ | W.COT | W.COT | | | | | | | |
| ↑↑↑↑ | | RD.COT | | | | | | | |
| ↑↑↑↑ | | GR.COT | | | | | | | |
| ↑↑↑↑ | | YW.COT | | | | | | | |
| ↑↑↑↑ | | OR.COT | | | | | | | |
| ↑↑↑↑ | | | W.POLYES | | | | | | |
| | | | W.ELASTIC | W.ACRYLIC | | | | | |
| | | | | BU.ACRYLIC | W.ACRYLIC | | | | |
| ↑↑↑↑ | | | | | W.MODAC | | | | |
| ↑↑↑↑ | | | | | BU.NYLON | | | | |
| ↑↑↑↑ | | | | | | | W.ACRYLIC | | |
| ↑↑↑↑ | ↑↑↑↑ | | | | ↑↑↑↑ | | | BU.POLYES | |
| ↑↑↑↑ | ↑↑↑↑ | | | | ↑↑↑↑ | | | BU.WOOL | |
| ↑↑↑↑ | | | | | ↑↑↑↑ | | | | |
| ↑↑↑↑ | | | | | ↑↑↑↑ | | | BG.POLYES | |
| | | | | | | | | GR.COT | |

*NON-MATCHING FIBERS OMITTED TO ENHANCE READABILITY.

**FIBERS**

COT= COTTON  
MODAC=MODACRYLIC  
POLYES=POLYESTER  
POLYPR=POLYPROPYLENE  

**COLORS**

BG=BURGUNDY  
BK=BLACK  
BU=BLUE  
GR=GREEN  
OR=ORANGE  
RD=RED  
TQ=TURQUOISE  
W=WHITE  
YW=YELLOW  

Reproduction of Lynn Henson's Fiber Chart. (Courtesy of the author)

Africano had already begun his campaign to put Bundy in another white van during the State's case in chief. On cross examination, he got a number of witnesses who saw Bundy in the Media Center van to testify that Bundy's van had a sticker on its windshield that said "Texas." It was obvious that no such sticker had ever been on the windshield of the Media Center van. I nearly went batty trying to figure out where this testimony came from, but I finally figured it out when I carefully studied the photospread of white vans that had been shown to the witnesses. It appeared that the Media Center van had a Texas sticker in the windshield. What was it doing there? I asked one of the officers who helped compile the photospread. He told me, "Oh, that's not the Media Center van; it's a photo of another van which was the same make, model, year, and color as the Media Center van." So there was a kernel of truth in Kline's testimony about suggestibility, but a witness didn't have to be under hypnosis to fall prey to it. The witnesses who correctly identified the photospread van as looking like the Media Center van made my mistake. They thought it was a picture of the Media Center van. When they saw the Texas sticker on the windshield, they retrojected that image back to their observation of Bundy in the van. To paraphrase Sherlock Holmes, it was a trifle, "but there is nothing so important as trifles."[31] I discussed the matter with Blair and Register, and we all agreed that we would just tangle things up worse by trying to explain what happened. Try as he might, however, Africano couldn't offer any credible proof putting Bundy in another van.

Africano offered the testimony of representatives of Adidas and Bass that the patterns of the shoe tracks in and on the van were common patterns used in the manufacture of tens of thousands of shoes, but he offered no testimony impeaching the fiber evidence. We knew he had employed experts to examine the fiber evidence. I distinctly remember going to the FDLE Crime Lab and watching one of Africano's experts try to examine Henson's fiber slides without taking the lens cap off of the microscope. Africano jettisoned that expert and called in another. The bottom line from that expert was that he had never seen as many fiber matches in a single case.[32]

To suggest that Kim ran away and died by some other means than Bundy, Africano attacked on two fronts. On the first front, he called two witnesses who thought they had seen Kim walking down US 90 a few miles west of the junior high on February 9. These witnesses were William James Truluck and Roy Bedenbaugh. The two had been interviewed early in the investigation, and their information had been discounted without searching inquiry.[33] When they were disclosed as defense witnesses on the eve of the Live Oak trial,[34] we took a closer look at them. Truluck seemed to have some kind of an axe to grind against Tom Leach, but Leach didn't remember ever meeting the man. Bedenbaugh, however, seemed to be simply a concerned citizen reporting what he saw. The difference in attitudes displayed by the two men caused us to take different measures with each of them.

Larry Daugherty told us that another girl had run away from the junior high the same day that Kim had gone missing. This girl looked like Kim but had some behavioral problems. These problems contributed to her untimely death not long after she ran away. We got a picture of the girl, and she certainly did look like Kim. We showed the picture to Bedenbaugh, and he said that this other girl looked more like the girl he saw on US 90 than Kim did. He repeated that statement on cross examination before the jury and we were halfway to discrediting the Kim-ran-away theory. We didn't show Truluck the photograph of the other girl until cross examination, and his bewildered reaction made it obvious that this other girl was the one he saw.[35] We made a mistake, however, by not introducing evidence of the girl's death. Wolski was puzzled that we did not call her in rebuttal.[36]

Africano actually undermined the contention that Kim ran away and walked west on US 90 by calling another witness to testify that on February 9 she saw Kim at the bus station, which was to the east of the junior high. The testimony was patently incredible for a number of reasons, including the fact that the witness testified that Kim was wearing a red dress and high heels as she waited to board the bus.[37] In calling this witness, Africano wasn't trying to prove that Kim was at the bus station. He was trying to prove that the prosecution had misbehaved. When we initially interviewed the witness, I was perfectly satisfied that we could destroy her patently ridiculous story on cross examination, but one of the officers present became irate and threatened her with a perjury prosecution. The remark upset me, but I said nothing. I didn't know what to say. Trying to undo such a statement is like trying to get toothpaste back into the tube. In addition to calling the girl, Africano played the tape recording of the officer threatening her.[38] I was profoundly embarrassed by the situation, but the jury seemed unimpressed. Perhaps they agreed with the officer that she should have been prosecuted for perjury.

Second, Africano called Dr. Joseph Burton, an Atlanta medical examiner, to testify that Lipkovic was dead wrong when he said Kim died from homicidal violence to the neck area. Burton said that Kim's body was so decomposed it was impossible to tell what caused her death or when she died. The cross examination aimed at proving four points:

1. Burton could rule out natural causes as a manner of death for Kim.
2. Burton could rule out accidental death.
3. Burton could rule out suicide.
4. Burton could not rule out homicide.

Burton readily admitted all four points, which led to the inescapable conclusion that Kim had been murdered. Burton did not disagree with Lipkovic about the manner of death; he simply disagreed about the cause of death.

Anticipating that the defense might produce a witness like Burton, we had carefully worded the indictment to allege that Bundy killed Kim "in some manner and by some means to the grand jury unknown." The jury didn't need to believe the killing was by homicidal violence to the neck area. Homicidal violence to any area was good enough. At the next recess I thanked Africano for calling a backup medical examiner to confirm Lipkovic's findings. He was not amused by my attempt at humor.

Africano then called Milton Kline. He planned to use Kline as the sledgehammer to completely flatten Andy Anderson, the straw man. Little did he or anyone else know, Anderson was already flattened in the eyes of the jury foreman,[39] and Kline's testimony was largely superfluous. Because we had no way of knowing how little regard the jury had for Anderson's testimony, we were very concerned about Kline.

Kline's testimony mirrored what he had said at the suppression hearing, but he was even more emphatic before the jury. In summary, he testified that Jack Burnette's hypnotic session was "almost a ludicrous picture of an omnipotent hypnotist dominating a compliant, cooperative, highly suggestible human being."[40] On cross examination Blair asked him about an article he wrote describing how he made a hypnosis subject think that she was a chimpanzee. Kline countered by saying that she was fantasizing that she was a chimpanzee and was in no way dominated. Blair then asked about the article Kline wrote in which he described age regressing a hypnosis subject to age three and frightening her with a toy snake and a decapitated doll. Kline said this was all in the interest of science and she wasn't dominated to the point of helplessness, prompting Blair to ask:

> Q:  *Isn't it a fact that the subject actually urinated in her pants when exposed to a decapitated doll?*
> A:  That's not helplessness, that's a panic reaction.

Kline was especially insistent on the point that only a doctor like him was qualified to perform a forensic hypnosis, but Blair finally got him to admit that someone with a master's degree in psychiatric social work might be able to pull it off.[41] Both our hypnotists had master's degrees in psychiatric social work. It would have been nice to have known about Kline's work in *People v. Lewis*,[42] where he had employed fewer safeguards than Burnette and Keene. We could surely have devised a few questions based on that case. It would have been nice to know another highly relevant fact about Kline, but we didn't learn that particular fact until long after the trial was over.

We didn't think that the defense had hurt us, and Wolski concurred. He would later write an article for the *Orlando Sentinel* saying that "the defense beat the state's evidence around, but didn't do much damage."[43] Our rebuttal was a nightmare. Jopling had highly restrictive ideas about what could be proven in rebuttal, and he held important evidence inadmissible. The most important piece of evidence that he would not allow us to present was evidence that the Media Center van was the only white van stolen in North Florida and South Georgia during the month of February 1978. We couldn't make Jopling understand that the evidence rebutted Africano's two-van theory. In final argument Africano told the jury that Bundy was in another white van, and the jury never heard our evidence to refute the argument. It turned out, however, that we didn't need the evidence. Wolski later had this to say about the two-van theory: "The defense contended that Bundy was driving a white van, but not the one from the Media Center. I asked myself why they did not support that claim with evidence. If Bundy had a white van he had to get it somewhere. He had to get rid of it somewhere. Where did he get it? Where is it now?"[44]

Our biggest problem was created when our hypnosis expert, Dr. Martin Reiser of the Law Enforcement Hypnosis Institute in Los Angeles, could not come to testify in rebuttal to Kline's testimony. We had anticipated a voir dire of only one week and had scheduled Reiser to testify at the end of the second week, but the trial moved too slowly, and the window of opportunity closed. When we were ready for him to come, he had subpoenas to honor in California. He did, however, recommend a replacement, whom we recruited in short order. Dr. Raymond LaScola flew first class from California and took full advantage of the complimentary cocktail service. When he arrived at the Harley Hotel, he looked like an inebriated leprechaun. He wore a ring with a gigantic diamond and a Stetson hat that nearly swallowed his head. The Stetson was purportedly a gift from John Wayne. I don't recall which celebrity supposedly gave him the ring. He scared us to death. We all thought that he was so eccentric he might self-destruct on cross examination. But LaScola was a bona fide M.D., and he was all we had to rebut Kline. Amazingly, he did quite well on the witness stand, and when he was excused, we immediately whisked him away to the airport and put him on a plane back to California.

We rested and then came final arguments. I opened for the State and methodically explained what the evidence showed, referring to an aerial photo of the junior high, a huge map of the FSU campus, Duncan's crime scene diagram, and Henson's fiber chart. It was probably the longest final argument I have ever given, and the jury became restless right about the time that I planned to conclude the argument with the relationship triangle made for us by the graphic designer. When I unfurled the relationship triangle (see page 147), the jurors immediately perked up and leaned forward in their chairs. Along the top of the triangle were the 12 items of evidence that tied Bundy to Kim; along the left leg were the 12 items connecting Bundy to the van; and along the right leg were the 12 items putting Kim in the van. When I began with the triangle, each item of evidence was covered with a white strip of paper. As I made each point, I pulled the strip off the corresponding point on the triangle. The jury listened in rapt attention.

When I concluded, I left the triangle on its easel and went back to counsel table. I could hear Bundy telling Africano, "Get up there and tear that chart up!" Instead of following directions, Africano took the chart off the easel, walked over to the wall, and propped it up with its face toward the wall. He then went back to the lectern and gave the most stirring final argument I ever heard him make. My heart was sinking as Africano worked toward the climax of his argument, but someone completely spoiled its dramatic effect. Bundy jumped up from counsel table, ran over to Africano, and stuck a note in his face. Africano was thrown off his game by this and made a disjointed conclusion. Bundy had torpedoed Africano's final argument.

Blair closed for the State with a rousing speech, and it was time for jury instructions. After instructing the jury, Jopling told them that because there was so much evidence, everyone would leave the courtroom and they could deliberate there. He gave the case to the jury at 7:10 P.M. and they deliberated until 9:30 P.M.[45] When we came back into the courtroom to formally recess for the day, I saw something that made me very happy. The jury had pushed the counsel tables together and spread all the evidence out. At first it looked like a bomb had exploded and thrown evidence all over the courtroom, but closer inspection showed that they were systematically grouping the exhibits by subject matter. The photospreads were fanned out in one corner, the credit card receipts in another, and the rest was laid out in orderly fashion. I told anyone who would listen that if the jurors were studying the evidence that closely, they were going to have to convict, because the only way it all fit together was for Bundy to be guilty.

Sometime between our resting and the jury coming back with its verdict, I had occasion to go to the defense room behind the courtroom looking for Africano. When I stuck my nose in the door, the only person in the room was Bundy. I started to back out, but he asked me to stop. I stopped. As he had once done with Jerry Thompson, Bundy apologized for all the trouble he had caused and hoped that I had no hard feelings. I mumbled something noncommittal and backed out, closing the door. Had he just given me a veiled confession? I think he had. Apparently Bundy had an urge to purge his soul. He also got Blair in a one-on-one situation in the hallway and told him, "Mr. Blair, I'm sorry." Blair replied, "Yeah, Ted, I'm sorry, too," and walked into our office to get away from him.

The second day of jury deliberations began at 9:00 A.M., and the jury had a verdict by 2:00 P.M.—guilty as charged. It took them 7-½ hours, a half hour longer than the Chi Omega jury.[46] Jopling set the penalty phase for February 9, the second anniversary of Kim's murder. When court recessed, Blair, Register, and I shook hands, Blair and I hugged our wives, and then went on a round of shaking the hands of J. O. Jackson and the other law enforcement officers assembled for the verdict. Just 2-½ hours after the jury brought back their verdict, the *Lake City Reporter* ran a special edition announcing the conviction.[47] It sold quite well. I even had some family members back in Lake City buy a few copies for me.

# Death Sentence to
# Death Chamber

At some point or another, death penalty litigation begins to look like a chapter from *Alice in Wonderland.* This is especially true with highly publicized prosecutions of sociopaths. Up until the verdict, the Bundy prosecution had wavered from unusual to very unusual. Beginning with the penalty phase, it became bizarre with occasional flashes of the surreal.

As the trial neared its end, Bundy seemed more concerned with getting a blood test for a marriage license than defending his case. When the sheriff would not allow it, Bundy made a mini-scene in chambers and Jopling ordered the sheriff to allow Bundy to get the test. Jopling probably thought, as did Blair and I, that nothing would come of the blood test.

Because most of the aggravating circumstances had come out during the guilt or innocence phase, we made a minimal presentation during the penalty phase. Mike Fisher, a Colorado detective, came to testify about Bundy's escape in Colorado; Jerry Thompson brought a certified copy of Bundy's kidnapping conviction from Utah; and Larry Simpson did the same for Bundy's conviction in the Chi Omega case.

After our brief presentation, Bundy took the stage to conduct his own defense. Dressed in a grey jacket and wearing a bow tie, he looked every bit the dapper lawyer. Calling Carol Boone to the witness stand, he led her through a dissertation about how wonderful he was and then asked her if she wanted to marry him. She did. He said, "I hereby marry you,"[1] and the farcical nature of the proceedings made it hard to keep from laughing out loud. I said to Blair, "Now watch him tell the jury 'you can't give me the death penalty on my wedding day.'"

Blair didn't do much on cross examination. He didn't need to. Ann Rule would later write that the eyes of the spectators were decidedly dry for Bundy's wedding,[2] which apparently had been Carol Boone's idea.[3] I thought the wedding was a sham until Dick Hagood reported that an Orlando notary public who thought Bundy was innocent had sat on the back row and signed the marriage license.[4] Don Kennedy, who was a notary public, told me neither he nor Africano wanted anything to do with the wedding.

In final argument, Blair used the same Bible verse used by the preacher at Kim's funeral—"But whoso shall offend one of these little ones which believe in me, it were better for him that a millstone were hanged about his neck, and that he were drowned in the depth of the sea."[5] Bundy also made reference to scripture. He told the jury he was no Christ figure, but he urged them to remember how Christ was executed.[6] He also mentioned Barabbas, and Stephen Michaud understood him to be comparing himself to Barabbas.[7] I understood him to be comparing himself to Christ, and I think that is the way the jury took it. I could see their faces harden when Bundy made the reference. Ann Rule said the jury was out 45 minutes;[8] Michaud said 10;[9] I can only say that it didn't take long. Sentencing was set for February 12.

Shortly after the advisory sentence came in, Blair and I were invited to a local news station for an interview on the case. During the interview, I was asked if we would ever know how many people Bundy had killed. I replied, "Once all his appeals are spent and when he is on the verge of execution, he may start confessing in order to stave off the death penalty." I didn't know it at the time, but Thompson and Fisher thought it was more than a possibility. They predicted Bundy would start confessing to delay his execution.[10]

I gave another interview to *Orlando Sentinel* reporter Laura Kavesh, who told me that it was hard to believe someone as normal looking as Bundy could do something as horrible as murder a child. I told her, "Most people think a criminal is a hunchbacked, cross-eyed little monster with warts all over his face slithering through the dark leaving a trail of slime; but they're not. They're human beings." Despite my poor grammar, the comment got some play in the papers at the time. Michaud even used the hunchback metaphor as a theme in his book, *The Only Living Witness*.

At the sentencing hearing, Jopling found that four aggravating factors existed: Bundy was under sentence of imprisonment when he committed the murder; Bundy had numerous prior convictions for violent felonies (the Chi Omega convictions); Bundy committed the murder during the commission of a kidnapping; Bundy's crime was "indeed heinous, atrocious and cruel in that it was extremely wicked, shockingly evil, vile and with utter indifference to human life." Finding no mitigating circumstances, Jopling imposed the death penalty.[11] Bundy went back to death row, and we went back home thinking the craziness was all behind us. Then we received the defense motion for a new trial. Most of the 49 allegations were either boilerplate or easily refuted, but one interesting question was raised. Patrick Wolski had written an article for the *Orlando Sentinel* telling his impressions of the trial. Ground 45 of the motion claimed the jury had disobeyed the court's instructions by shifting the burden of proof to the defense. The motion supported this allegation with a quote from Wolksi's article:

> But I remember that I felt if Bundy had any reasonable witness putting him somewhere else on the morning Kimberly Leach disappeared from school, he would give me reasonable doubt.
>
> More importantly, I felt if he had any evidence that he had another white van, he could blow the State's case. At this point I assumed he would defend against the State with an alibi of being in a different location or of using a different van or car.[12]

Before we could hold a hearing on the motion for new trial, Africano filed a supplement to his motion raising a 50th ground. He buttressed the supplement with a sworn transcribed statement and a sworn affidavit from one of Raymond LaScola's hypnotherapy clients. When LaScola got back to California, he began to boast about his involvement in the Bundy case. He told his client that he had hypnotized an eyewitness in the case and had testified about the hypnosis for eight hours over two days, withstanding a rigorous cross examination. He also told the client that he had bought a ring with a huge fake diamond for $7, had put it on his pinkie finger, and had hypnotized the jury by waving the ring at them while he testified.[13] From what we had seen of LaScola while he was in Orlando, we could easily believe that he would say something like that, but not that he could actually do something like that. We stipulated the transcript and affidavit into evidence at the hearing on the motion for new trial.[14]

Jopling summarily denied the motion for new trial on almost all grounds, but he did write a brief opinion about grounds 45 and 50.

As to ground 45, he cited a long line of Florida cases holding that a jury may not impeach its own verdict on such matters as whether they misunderstood or misapplied the instructions of the court.[15] As to ground 50, Jopling wrote:

> The court finds it beyond belief that this witness was capable of tampering with the fifteen people making up the jury in the presence of Court and Counsel, none of whom made any objection or observation on the record or otherwise as to any improper conduct of said witness during the trial.[16]

With that ruling, we thought we had heard the last of LaScola. We hadn't. Whenever Africano and I were on a case together, he would tease me about what a great expert we had found in LaScola. The teasing escalated when *Time* magazine ran an article entitled "The Doctor and the Moneyed Monk." It seems that LaScola had convinced a rich Buddhist to adopt him and make him the beneficiary of her will. When she died, he signed her death certificate, had her cremated, and started carrying her ashes around in the trunk of the Lincoln he inherited from her. An ex-convict named William Schenley came forward and claimed that LaScola had confessed to murdering the lady with an insulin overdose. LaScola got indicted for first-degree murder,[17] arrested, and put in jail. While LaScola was in jail, his cellmate, a convicted murderer named Conrad Acker, came forward and testified that LaScola had confessed the murder to him.[18] LaScola's arrest naturally caused speculation in the press that Bundy might be able to use it to overturn his conviction.[19] The LaScola melodrama came to an end on March 12, 1981, when the murder charge was dropped and LaScola pleaded guilty to writing fictitious prescriptions. He got three years' probation.[20]

Although LaScola turned out to be a poor excuse for a witness, at least he was actually a doctor. Kline was not. I learned this one afternoon when I received a telephone call from an assistant district attorney in New York City. He told me his name was Allan Sullivan and that Kline was a defense witness in a murder case he was prosecuting. He never mentioned to me that it was the John Lennon murder case. I offered any assistance Sullivan might want, and he asked me to send copies of transcripts of Kline's testimony in the Bundy case. He also wanted me to know that Kline was not a doctor. This revelation reminded me of the photocopied degrees on the walls in Kline's office, and I mentally kicked myself for not being more suspicious at the time.

Kline's claim to have a doctorate from Penn State was false. Africano later told me that Kline had been in a doctoral program there but had gotten expelled for punching one of his professors. Kline testified in numerous high-profile criminal trials in New York without being discovered, but he tripped himself up while testifying in *People v. Lewis*,[21] the case in which he failed to follow his own safeguards. While testifying in the Lewis case, he told the court: "I am a member of the visiting teaching faculty in forensic hypnosis of the Academy of the Federal Bureau of Investigation at Quantico, West Virginia."[22] Almost anyone in law enforcement knows that the FBI Academy is in Quantico, Virginia. This false step got Sullivan to digging, and he discovered Kline had also made false claims to postdoctoral work, psychoanalytic training, and status as faculty at a medical school.[23] Sullivan indicted Kline on five counts of perjury,[24] Kline pled guilty,[25] and the judge fined him $5,000. At sentencing, the judge told him, "It seems you have been in a charade for a number of years."[26]

Blair decided that our office should not prosecute Kline because he and I would be witnesses and asked the governor to appoint a special prosecutor. Robert Eagan, the Orlando State Attorney, was named to the job. He charged Kline on a single count of perjury, alleging a number of false statements, including:

1. That he held a doctoral degree in Clinical Psychology at Penn State University, or
2. That he received post-doctoral training in Clinical Psychology at New York University, or
3. That he had received psychoanalytic training at William Allyson White Institute of Psychiatry and Psychoanalysis.[27]

Africano represented Kline on the charge and moved to dismiss the charge on the grounds that Kline's falsehood was not material. Judge Arthur Lawrence, who heard the case, decided that it was material, despite Jopling's testimony that he would have found Kline to be an expert even if Kline had not claimed to have a doctor's degree. Kline pled nolo contendere to the charge and Lawrence sent him to prison. In his article "Mountebanks among Forensic Scientists," James E. Starrs said it was "quixotic" that Kline would criticize Jack Burnette and Imogene

Keene for their lack of training.[28] That wasn't the most quixotic aspect of the Kline debacle.

While the Bundy appeal was pending, Africano took every opportunity to tell me that he was going to win the appeal, and he was going to win it on the issue of hypnosis. My customary reply was, "We'll see." Eventually the Florida Supreme Court issued its opinion overruling previous case law and holding hypnotically enhanced testimony to be inadmissible. The law of Florida changed on the basis of perjured testimony. The Supreme Court went on to say, however, that it was "harmless error" to admit Anderson's testimony. Based on a comparison of my taped interview with the two taped hypnotic sessions, they said that Anderson's testimony had been refreshed as to only three minor details relating to clothing, and that there was "no reasonable possibility that the tainted evidence complained of might have contributed to the conviction."[29] Africano had won the battle but lost the war.

Years passed as Bundy's two convictions worked their way through the labyrinthine process of appeals and postconviction proceedings. Weird reports kept emanating from Bundy's death row cell—he had apparently impregnated Carol Boone in the death row visiting park; he had been found with escape tools hidden in his cell; he had been the victim of a gang rape by fellow death row inmates. The last allegation never made the news, but I got it through the Department of Corrections rumor mill. Apparently a number of inmates confessed to the crime, but Bundy said it never happened. Finally the time was ripe for Bundy's clemency hearing in the Chi Omega case. It was scheduled and rescheduled three times, and on the eve of the final hearing, Bundy fired his court appointed lawyer. Governor Bob Graham said, "We will not permit our judicial system to be endlessly manipulated," and ordered that the hearing proceed with Bundy unrepresented. Tony Guarisco, who had prosecuted John Spinkelink, argued the case for the State.[30] Unsurprisingly, Bundy was denied clemency, and Graham signed his death warrant.

After the warrant was signed, Bundy gave an exclusive interview to Jon Nordheimer of the *New York Times*. In the interview, which was reprinted in the *Lake City Reporter*, Bundy claimed that he was being rushed to judgment and that Graham was trying to build political capital by signing his death warrant. Nordheimer pointed out that Bundy's warrant was just one of 158 death warrants that Graham had signed, but Bundy modestly asserted that Graham got more political capital out of his death warrant than the 157 others combined.[31] Over the years many journalists and law enforcement officers came to see Bundy on death row, and he obviously enjoyed it. Bundy probably had a twofold agenda for granting the interviews—first to stoke his ego, and second to try to manipulate his way out of the death chamber. Stephen Michaud and Hugh Aynesworth repeatedly interviewed him for their books; Robert Keppel, with the Washington State Attorney General's Office, consulted with him on the Green River killings;[32] Bill Hagmaier and Robert Ressler,[33] both of the FBI Behavioral Sciences Unit, had extensive interviews with him. Ronald Holmes, of the University of Louisville, interviewed Bundy for a book and came away saying that he hated to see Bundy executed because "there's so much to be learned from him." Bundy actually "speculated" on how Kim was abducted for Holmes. He told Holmes that the kidnapper read her name off the back of her jersey and then called to her by name and told her she had to go home with him because of an accident in the family.[34] Bundy never explained how the kidnapper could see through the coat that concealed the name on the back of her jersey.

Lake Citians planned to caravan over to Florida State Prison for Bundy's execution,[35] but it was stayed, and the Guardian Angels came to Lake City to demonstrate against the stay.[36] On the 10th anniversary of Kim's abduction, the *Lake City Reporter* ran interviews with all the local participants in the investigation.[37] Bundy's lawyers petitioned for a writ of habeas corpus before Federal Judge Kendall Sharp in Orlando, claiming that Bundy was incompetent to stand trial when he was convicted of the Leach murder. Sharp summarily denied the petition, and the defense appealed to the Eleventh Circuit Court of Appeals.

The Eleventh Circuit reversed Sharp's ruling and remanded with an order that Sharpe hold an evidentiary hearing on whether Bundy was incompetent at the time of trial. It found that Sharp had "ignored strong indicia of Bundy's incompetence." Among those indicia was Dr. Tanay's report from the Tallahassee trial. It chided Sharp for referring to the fact that Judge Cowart had found Bundy competent, but it placed great stock in the report Cowart rejected. The Court also noted several instances where Bundy ignored the advice of his lawyers, such as when he "reneged" on the plea agreement and when he performed the "mock wedding" with Carol Boone.[38]

The case went back to Orlando, where Sharp held a five-day evidentiary hearing to determine if Bundy was competent to stand trial. Blair and I both testified at the hearing, as did Jopling. Florida's attorney general handles federal habeas corpus matters, and Attorney General

Bob Butterworth was there in person. Apparently neither side invoked the rule of sequestration, which requires witnesses to remain outside the courtroom when they are not testifying. The witnesses were allowed to sit and listen to other witnesses' testimony. I may be a partisan observer, but I thought that the evidence clearly showed Bundy competent. Sharp saw it that way, also. He wrote an opinion that covered 14 pages of small type in the case reports, carefully refuting each claim of the defense, and summarizing the testimony of each witness as to Bundy's behavior at trial and during the pretrial proceedings.[39] His summary for the press was more succinct—"Bullshit."[40]

Finally, on January 17, 1989, Governor Bob Martinez signed Bundy's fourth and final death warrant. It was the first death warrant for the Leach case, and Martinez refused to hold a clemency hearing prior to signing the warrant. This offended me because it was a breach of protocol, but Martinez felt the Chi Omega clemency proceeding was all Bundy needed. He did something else that offended me. Normally, the superintendent of Florida State Prison appoints the witnesses to each execution, but Martinez's office took over assigning seats and I was told I wasn't invited. I felt very strongly that, as a prosecutor who had worked for years to achieve Bundy's execution, I should finish the job by attending it. A week or so later I was told that the governor's office had given the task of assigning seats for witnesses back to the superintendent, and I had a seat. The governor's office apparently decided it was too big a headache to deal with all the applications.

Then Bundy fulfilled the prophecy made by Fisher, Thompson, and me—he started confessing to murder after murder in an effort to stave off his impending execution.[41] Law enforcement officers came from all over the United States to try to talk to Bundy in an effort to solve old homicide cases. Bundy asked Keppel to come back to Florida to hear his confessions, and Keppel complied. Keppel took hours of tape-recorded confessions from Bundy, but Bundy stayed away from confessing to Kim's murder. In the end, Keppel tried to get Bundy to describe his first murder, but Bundy refused. As he left the interview room, Keppel observed that Bundy had bungled the endgame. When Bundy failed to comprehend, he explained, "You just killed yourself, Ted."[42] Keppel was right. Bundy's last-minute confessions had driven the last nail into the lid of his coffin.

The number of officers who came to Florida State Prison was nothing compared with the number of reporters who flocked to Florida in the waning hours of Bundy's life. One reporter tried to get Bundy to verify that he had committed 30 murders. Bundy replied, "Put a zero after that."[43] It is highly unlikely that Bundy killed as many as 300 victims. After his execution, the FBI invited us to join officers and prosecutors from all over the nation for a symposium at the FBI National Academy and share what we knew about Bundy. The final product of that symposium was a multiagency report describing Bundy's modus operandi and giving a timeline of his life, trying to document his every movement from birth to death.[44] Officers all over the nation who had unsolved homicides fitting Bundy's modus operandi could refer to the timeline to determine if Bundy was in the area when their victim died or went missing. If he was in the area, there was a better than even chance he was the killer. The timeline did not solve 300 murders.

Bundy wasn't the only person the reporters wanted to interview. A reporter actually buttonholed me as I was leaving church the Sunday before the execution. He wanted to know how I, as a Christian, could countenance the execution. I told him, "The execution is a political act. As far as religious terms, there is nothing in this book I'm holding that indicates to me in any way, shape, or form that an execution for a heinous murder is spiritually, ethically, or morally improper."[45]

Finally, Bundy played his last card. He gave a videotaped interview to Dr. James Dobson of Focus on the Family, an evangelical Christian organization headquartered in Colorado Springs, Colorado. In the interview, Bundy portrayed himself as having repented of his sins and committed to tread the paths of righteousness all the days of his life. He also tried to portray himself as a victim of that demon, soft-core pornography. Dr. Dobson naturally thought he was talking about nudie magazines, and that's probably what Bundy wanted him to think. When he was captured in Pensacola, he told Patchen, Bodiford, and Chapman that in addition to nudie magazines he was aroused by—cheerleader magazines.[46] I once heard of an arsonist who was aroused by photos of the White House Christmas tree. The problem wasn't pornography, the problem was Bundy. If there were any doubt about whether Bundy was running a con on Dobson, it was removed when Dobson asked Bundy about the Leach murder, and Bundy lowered his face saying he couldn't talk about that. Dobson interjected "Too painful," and Bundy cut his eyes up to look at Dobson. I could not see a soul behind those eyes. It was obvious from the expression on his face that whatever Bundy's reason for not wanting to talk about the Leach case, it wasn't because it was too painful. Bundy's career as an antipornography spokesperson was posthumous; Dobson did not release the interview until after Bundy's execution.[47]

As I recall, it was chilly the morning of January 24, 1989, when Blair and I arrived at Florida State Prison. The sun had not yet risen, but we had light enough to see the horde of people gathered in a vacant field across the road from the Administration Building. The field was usually occupied by death penalty opponents, but that morning they were decidedly outnumbered by death penalty proponents and media vans equipped with satellite dishes. At the Administration Building, they escorted us into a large conference room where we met with other men who had been involved in the investigation—Len Register, Ken Robinson, Jim Sewell, Don Patchen, and others. Not all of the witnesses were law enforcement officers. Wayne Hollingsworth, the state senator from Lake City was there, as were Bundy's lawyer, James Coleman, and a preacher named by Bundy as one of his two witnesses. Those two looked ill at ease and out of place among the other witnesses. There were no high-fives, but we were all happy that this ordeal soon would be over. They fed us breakfast and then loaded us into two vans to be transported to Q Wing and the death chamber.

The death chamber has undergone some remodeling since Florida started using lethal injection for executions. Old Sparky has been removed to accommodate the gurney, and the three-legged oaken electric chair now sits in a small room off to the side of the death chamber. The room, which is divided into two compartments by a glass panel, now looks larger than I remember it being that January morning when I first saw it. On one side of the panel are the seats for the official witnesses, who sit near the glass with reporters crowded behind them. The condemned prisoner and the officers assigned to the execution detail are on the other side. I don't recall the glass panel being curtained when Bundy was executed, but it was curtained when I later witnessed an execution by lethal injection. On that occasion, we filed in and took our seats, and then the curtain was opened to show the condemned man strapped to the gurney.

When we were seated for Bundy's execution, I found myself with Len Register on my right and Wayne Hollingsworth on my left. There, through the glass panel, I could see Old Sparky. I could see the head and shoulders of the black-hooded executioner through a window on the back wall. A telephone hung on another portion of the wall, and an officer stood beside it with the receiver to his ear. The rear door opened and two burly officers escorted Bundy into the room. The officers flanked him, holding his arms securely and giving him little opportunity to resist. He had his head shaved and one of his pants legs was hiked up to accommodate the placement of one of the straps that would deliver the electric charge. He was scared to death. The man who always wanted to be in control now controlled nothing but his own emotions. They sat him in the chair, strapped his arms and legs down, and allowed him to say his final words. He nodded at Blair and spoke to his lawyer and preacher, telling them, "Jim and Fred. I'd like you to send my love to my family and friends."[48] Then they strapped his head to the back of the chair and lowered the skull cap with its black hood onto his head. There was an interminable wait as the officer listened over the phone on the wall. He finally signaled to the executioner, and the executioner threw the switch. Bundy tensed, and continued to tense as the electricity flowed through his body. As his fists tightened, I wondered how many women's throats they had tightened around. Someone later said smoke rose from the strap on his leg, but I didn't see it. My attention was fixed on his clenched fists. When the current was cut off, a doctor came and listened to Bundy's heart. After what seemed like an eternity, the doctor concluded his examination and an officer made a formal announcement that Bundy had been executed. Hollingsworth said to me, "That was too easy. They ought to bring him back and do it thirty more times."

# Epilogue

I trust that the twin mysteries weren't too hard to crack. You should recall that when Mark Safarik responded to my e-mail, he asked me for my evidence supporting the proposition that Bundy was lying and also for my hypothesis as to why he lied. I replied as follows:

Why I believe Bundy lied, and why I think he was motivated to lie, will take some preliminary explanation.

First, my reasons for believing that the murder occurred in the van: The van had a carpet remnant in the cargo area, and the carpet remnant contained a huge bloodstain consistent with Kim's type. The turtleneck sweater Kim was wearing when her body was found had a huge rust colored stain on the chest area front. This stain was never analyzed because the lab techs were averse to handling the highly corrupted piece of clothing (they stored it on the roof of the lab). Myriads of fibers from Kim's and Bundy's clothing were found on the carpet, and myriads of carpet fibers were found on Kim's clothing. All this led us to believe that Kim was assaulted and killed in the van, and that was the way we presented it to the jury.

Second, my reasons for believing that the murder did not occur as Bundy said: Kim's body was partially mummified, with her face relatively intact. Neither I nor Dr. Lipkovic saw any mud or debris in her nostrils or mouth (her throat was missing). Dr. Lipkovic testified in court that the cause of death was homicidal violence to the neck area accompanied by copious bleeding. The defense team built their whole case on refuting this opinion. They believed (and rightly so) if Dr. Lipkovic's opinion were true, Kim's turtleneck would have been covered with blood. They further believed that the absence of a finding of blood on the turtleneck meant that there was no blood on the turtleneck. What it really meant was that nobody wanted to analyze the shirt because it was so soaked with putrefied body fluid. I made a point, when we got to introducing the turtleneck in evidence, to unfurl it so that the stain on the front was accentuated. The courtroom gasped, and the defense abandoned the argument that there was no blood on the turtleneck. Dr. Lipkovic's opinion stood on two legs—the complete absence of the neck and the complete presence of the eyeholes, ears, nostrils, and mouth. The bugs had entered the body through the throat, ignoring the traditional routes. This indicated that the throat provided a more attractive entrance, which led to the conclusion that the throat had been opened. I later learned from Dr. William Maples ("Dead Men Do Tell Tales")[1] that it is a common occurrence for bugs to prefer an open wound for their invasion route instead of the more usual bodily orifices. We believed the murder weapon to have been a huge Buck General hunting knife that Bundy had bought the day before from John Farhat, the owner of a sporting goods store in Jacksonville. The knife was never recovered, but we found its pricetag in the van. Bundy was extremely agitated when Mr. Farhat positively identified him as the purchaser of the knife, to the point of blurting out that Mr. Farhat was lying.

I believe that the foregoing explanation gives a satisfactory refutation of Bundy's version and that it also suggests his reason for telling this particularly useless lie.


Q:   *Why would Bundy lie about the cause of death while telling a horrific story about the manner of death?*
A:   He had to be smarter than the people who brought him to justice. He had to show that Dr. Lipkovic was wrong about the cause of death, that I was wrong about the location of the death, and that John Farhat was wrong about the murder weapon. Bundy's narcissism was so great that he had to tell this lie to show that, although he got convicted, he was really superior to his captors. Although he lost his case, he lost it to

a "falsehood" perpetrated by the prosecution, which wasn't smart enough to figure out what he "really" did.

Safarik responded promptly. He said:

I think your reasoning is sound and the additional information regarding the state of her body is helpful. I have testified a number of times as an expert. And in most of the cases (I just testified for the Los Angeles County DA in a sexual homicide of an 18-year-old) part of my overall analysis is to make sense of both the behavioral and forensic evidence. The story must make sense chronologically, temporally, behaviorally, and forensically. The integration of those attributes must be seamless.

I think that you are most likely right about this. If you only look behaviorally, the van provided a private, clean and controlled environment for Bundy. His activity with Leach would have been visually and audibly hidden from the public. With her in the van he could then transport her body for disposal. When you add in all of the forensics then it becomes clear, at least to me, that Kim was assaulted and murdered in the van as you assert. The story of her murder then makes sense as to location and cause of death.

I have seen a number of cases where those same dynamics were at work. You don't have to look far in terms of serial killers to see others doing the same thing. Bittaker and Norris in LA, Gerald Gallegos in Sacramento, and Robert Yates in Spokane to name a few.

I also agree on the reason for why Bundy would have said that. He was not only a narcissist but a psychopath as well. He loved being in control not only in his murders but of the system, the audience, the courts. He always thought he was smarter than everyone else. That's why the psychopath thinks he won't get caught. Playing mind games like this is one way to demonstrate that you are in control.

Flies attack the eyes, nose, mouth because they are normally the only moist area available in a fresh clothed body but a gaping neck wound would be the deposition site of choice. If she had died from asphyxia due to mud blocking her airway, that certainly would have been revealed at the autopsy especially if her facial features were mostly intact.[2]

All this brings us to a rather neat paradox. Every lie has some truth value, but this particular lie has such a high truth value that, for most purposes, it is the functional equivalent of the truth. Bundy's lie communicated the truth that he killed Kim in brutal, disgusting fashion. The evidence confirms that truth, but the brutal, disgusting fashion was not the one he described. It was, in the final analysis, a pathetic lie told by a pathetic person.

# Notes

### Prologue

1. Robert K. Ressler and Tom Schachtman, *Whoever Fights Monsters: My Twenty Years Tracking Serial Killers for the FBI* (New York: St. Martin's Press, 1992), 72.
2. Personal communication.

### Chapter 1: The Cold and Rainy Day

1. Serial Report #143, FDLE Case File 522–1A-0035 (Hereafter cited as "FDLE Serial [number]").
2. FDLE Serial 179.
3. FDLE Serial 93.
4. FDLE Serial 93, attachment.
5. FDLE Serial 179.
6. FDLE Serial 285.
7. FDLE Serial 122.
8. FDLE Serial 331, exhibit.
9. FDLE Serial 143.

### Chapter 2: On the Road with Ted Bundy

1. George E. Lohr, "Memorandum Opinion and Order," People v. Bundy, No. C-1616 (Pitkin County, Colo., Nov. 4, 1977).
2. George E. Lohr, "Memorandum Opinion," People v. Bundy, No. C-1616 (Pitkin County, Colo., Jan. 9, 1978).
3. Ann Rule, *The Stranger beside Me: The Shocking Inside Story of Serial Killer Ted Bundy,* updated edition (New York: Pocket Books, 2009), 2–3.

4. Prosecution Trial Brief, State v. Bundy, No. 78-169-CF (Columbia County, Fla.), 70.

5. Ibid., 80.

6. Ibid., 78.

7. Barbara Frye, "Ringing phone scared attacker, saved coed's life," *Orlando Sentinel,* January 17, 1978.

8. FDLE Serial 54.

9. FDLE Serial 84, attachment.

10. FDLE Serial 82, attachment.

11. Prosecution Trial Brief, State v. Bundy, No. 78-169-CF (Columbia County, Fla.), 720.

12. Ibid., 71.

13. Ibid., 80.

14. FDLE Serial 71.

15. FDLE Serial 172.

16. FDLE Serial 180.

17. FDLE Serial 59, attachment.

18. FDLE Serial 38, attachment.

19. FDLE Serial 87.

20. Ibid.

21. Ibid.

22. FDLE Serial 192.

23. Prosecution Trial Brief, State v. Bundy, No. 78-169-CF (Columbia County, Fla.), 54, 55.

24. FDLE Serial 77, attachment.

25. FDLE Serial 92.

26. FDLE Serial 168.

27. FDLE Serial 126.

28. FDLE Serial 220.

29. FDLE Serial 126.

30. FDLE Serial 113, attachment.

31. Ibid.

32. Ibid.

33. FDLE Serial 54, attachment.

34. FDLE Serial 113, attachment.

35. FDLE Serial 219.

36. FDLE Serial 113, attachment; Prosecution Trial Brief, State v. Bundy, No. 78-169-CF (Columbia County, Fla.), 115.

37. Prosecution Trial Brief, State v. Bundy, No. 78-169-CF (Columbia County, Fla.), 84.

38. FDLE Serial 54, attachment.

39. Prosecution Trial Brief, State v. Bundy, No. 78-169-CF (Columbia County, Fla.), 85.

40. Ibid., 90, 91.
41. Ibid., 116–120.
42. Ibid.
43. Ibid.
44. Ibid.
45. Ibid.
46. FDLE Serial 84, attachment.

## Chapter 3: A Tale of Two Cities, Part I: Tallahassee

1. Lynn Alan Thompson, "Motion for Change of Venue or in the Alternative to Abate Prosecution," Exhibit 9, State v. Bundy, No. CR79-4650 (Orange County, Fla., Jan. 9, 1979).

2. Michael Goldman, "Intruder kills two FSU coeds," *Orlando Sentinel,* January 16, 1978.

3. Pete Spivey, "FSU coeds mourned by 1,700," *Orlando Sentinel,* January 17, 1978.

4. Larry Simpson, personal communication.

5. Pete Spivey, "FSU coeds mourned by 1,700," *Orlando Sentinel,* January 17, 1978.

6. Pete Spivey, "Coed survivors can give no clues to killer," *Orlando Sentinel,* January 18, 1978.

7. Ibid.

8. UPI, "No new clues after all-out search at FSU," *Orlando Sentinel,* January 19, 1978.

9. UPI, "Mental patient called suspect in coed deaths freed," *Orlando Sentinel,* January 19, 1978.

10. Barbara Frye, "Hypnosis may prompt clues to coed-killer," *Orlando Sentinel,* January 21, 1978.

11. "Coed death film halted in state on Askew plea," *Orlando Sentinel,* January 25, 1978.

12. UPI, "News play could stir killer to repeat," *Orlando Sentinel,* January 27, 1978.

13. UPI, "FSU beating victim to receive state aid," *Orlando Sentinel,* February 13, 1978.

14. AP, "Impostor quizzed in coed killings," *Orlando Sentinel,* February 16, 1978.

15. Prosecution Trial Brief, State v. Bundy, No. 78-169-CF (Columbia County, Fla.), 734.

16. AP, "Impostor quizzed in coed killings," *Orlando Sentinel,* February 16, 1978.

17. AP, "Mystery man tagged as No. 1 mass killer," *Orlando Sentinel,* February 17, 1978.

18. UPI, "Suspect nabbed in 38 sex killings," *Post Standard*, February 18, 1978, http://www.newspaperarchive.com/PdfViewerTags.aspx?img=20050 003&firstvisit=true&src=search&currentResult=7&currentPage=0&fpo=False.

19. Charlie Jean and Pete Spivey, "FSU suspect linked to 35 other murders," *Orlando Sentinel*, February 18, 1978.

20. Christina Evans, "Bundy neighbors horror-stricken," *Orlando Sentinel*, February 18, 1978.

21. "Bundy coed tie sought," *Florida Times Union*, February 18, 1978.

22. Charlie Jean and Pete Spivey, "FSU suspect linked to 35 other murders," *Orlando Sentinel*, February 18, 1978.

23. Jim Leusner, "Bundy once did research on assaults," *Florida Times Union*, February 22, 1978; Charlie Jean and Pete Spivey, "FSU suspect linked to 35 other murders, *Orlando Sentinel*, February 18, 1978.

24. UPI, "Ted Bundy a man of many faces," *Florida Times Union*, February 18, 1978.

25. Pete Spivey, "Bundy taken to Tallahassee to face charges," *Orlando Sentinel*, February 19, 1978.

26. Ibid.

27. Richard W. Larsen, *Bundy: The Deliberate Stranger* (Englewood Cliffs, N.J.: Prentice Hall, 1980).

28. "Bundy moved to capital after refusing to talk," *Florida Times Union*, February 19, 1978.

29. *ABA Standards for Criminal Justice: Fair Trial and Free Press*, 3rd ed. (Washington, D.C.: American Bar Association, 1992), 8–1.1(b)(4), www.abanet.org/crimjust/standards/fairtrial.pdf.

30. Prosecution Trial Brief, State v. Bundy, No. 78-169-CF (Columbia County, Fla.), 507–516.

## Chapter 4: A Tale of Two Cities, Part II: Lake City

1. "Girl reported missing," *Lake City Reporter*, February 10, 1978.

2. Patti Roth, "Police still search for missing girl," *Lake City Reporter*, February 13, 1978.

3. Patti Roth, "FBI called in missing girl search," *Lake City Reporter*, February 14, 1978.

4. Robyn Feldman, "Appeal made for help in girl search," *Lake City Reporter*, February 17, 1978.

5. Robyn Feldman, "But Kimberly isn't there . . .," *Lake City Reporter*, February 16, 1978.

6. Robyn Feldman, "Team plans search for Kimberly," *Lake City Reporter*, February 17, 1978.

7. Thomas E. Slaughter, "Is Bundy linked to 12-year old's disappearance?" *Orlando Sentinel*, February 21, 1978.

8. Paul Henkemeyer, "Bundy identified as would-be abductor here," *Jacksonville Journal*, February 21, 1978.

9. "Bundy linked to Lake City," *Lake City Reporter*, February 21, 1978.

10. Ibid.

11. Ibid.

12. "Police try to link Bundy to lost girl," *Jacksonville Journal*, February 22, 1978.

13. Jim Leusner, "Bundy once did research on assaults," *Florida Times Union*, February 22, 1978.

14. Ibid.

15. AP, "Lake City girl—Bundy tie claimed," *Orlando Sentinel*, February 22, 1978.

16. "Bundy linked to Lake City," *Lake City Reporter*, February 21, 1978.

17. "Local search effort is intensified—FHP mounts wide search for missing girl," *Lake City Reporter*, February 23, 1978.

18. Chuck Dupree, "Kimberly hunt into Suwannee," *Lake City Reporter*, February 23, 1978.

19. AP, "Bundy charged with theft, other crimes," *Orlando Sentinel*, February 23, 1978.

20. "Bundy probe centers in Lake City," *Florida Times Union*, February 23, 1978.

21. AP, "State crime lab checks on Bundy," *Orlando Sentinel*, February 24, 1978.

22. Pete Spivey, "One thing baffles police—no evidence," *Orlando Sentinel*, February 26, 1978.

23. Ibid.

24. Ibid.

25. Jim Leusner, "Landfill sifted for clues to missing girl," *Florida Times Union*, February 25, 1978.

26. "Photoplane ordered to track missing girl," *Florida Times Union*, February 24, 1978.

27. Jim Leusner, "Landfill sifted for clues to missing girl," *Florida Times Union*, February 25, 1978.

28. Patti Roth, "'Task force' heads search for girl here," *Lake City Reporter*, February 27, 1978.

29. UPI, "Criminal law enforcers cleared of power abuse," *Naples Daily News*, July 10, 1975, http://www.newspaperarchive.com/PdfViewerTags.aspx?img=65341649&firstvisit=true&src=search&currentResult=1&currentPage=0&fpo=False.

30. Patti Roth, "Tangible clues in search," *Lake City Reporter*, March 2, 1978.

31. Patti Roth, "Task force takes info to Tally," *Lake City Reporter*, March 3, 1978.

## Chapter 5: Much Ado about Something

1. FHP report in author's possession.
2. 18 U.S.C. § 1385.
3. FDLE Serial 102, attachment.
4. FDLE Serial 51, attachment.
5. FDLE Serial 132.
6. Robyn Feldman, "Team plans search for Kimberly," *Lake City Reporter,* February 17, 1978.
7. Prosecution Trial Brief, State v. Bundy, No. 78-169-CF (Columbia County, Fla.), 669.
8. "Hunt: . . . needle in a haystack . . . ," *Lake City Reporter,* February 24, 1978.
9. FDLE Serial 86.
10. Not her real name.
11. Not her real name.
12. Prosecution Trial Brief, State v. Bundy, No. 78-169-CF (Columbia County, Fla.), 1054–1065.

## Chapter 6: The Searchers

1. FDLE Serial 26, attachment.
2. Rex Stout, *The Final Deduction* (New York: Bantam Books, 1985/1955); *If Death Ever Slept* (New York: Bantam Books, 1992/1957).
3. "River may hide missing girl," *Independent Post,* March 8, 1978.
4. FDLE Serial 76b, attachment.
5. Patti Roth, "'. . . Like you're dreaming . . .'" *Lake City Reporter,* April 10, 1978.
6. FDLE Serial 100.
7. Karl Popper, *Conjectures and Refutations: The Growth of Scientific Knowledge* (New York: Routledge Press, 2003/1963).
8. Michael Mello, *The Wrong Man: A True Story of Innocence on Death Row* (Minneapolis: University of Minnesota Press, 2001), 392–393.
9. Christine Wicker, *Lily Dale: The Town that Talks to the Dead* (New York: HarperCollins, 2003), 197.
10. Cyndie Zahner, "The Paranormal, Missing Persons, and Ted Bundy: An Exclusive Interview with Spiritual Medium Anne Gehman," *Erie Life Magazine,* Vol. 1, No. 10, 2008, 61.
11. Walter F. Rowe, "Psychic Detectives," *National Capital Area Skeptical Eye,* Vol. 5, No. 4, 1991, 7–10, www.ncas.org/eyes/SE-5.4.pdf.
12. Robert Todd Carroll, *The Skeptic's Dictionary—A Collection of Strange Beliefs, Amusing Deceptions, and Dangerous Delusions* (Hoboken, N.J.: John Wiley and Sons, 2003), 78–80.
13. Edgar Allan Poe, "The Mystery of Marie Roget," *Complete Stories and Poems of Edgar Allan Poe* (Garden City, N.Y.: Doubleday, 1966/1842), 27 n.1;

Daniel Stashower, *The Beautiful Cigar Girl: Mary Rogers, Edgar Allan Poe, and the Invention of Murder* (New York: Berkley Books, 2007).

14. Cyndie Zahner, "The Paranormal, Missing Persons, and Ted Bundy: An Exclusive Interview with Spiritual Medium Anne Gehman," *Erie Life Magazine*, Vol. 1, No. 10, 2008, 61.

## Chapter 7: Crime Scene Investigation

1. FDLE Serial 117; Prosecution Trial Brief, State v. Bundy, No. 78-169-CF (Columbia County, Fla.), 39–42.

2. Prosecution Trial Brief, State v. Bundy, No. 78-169-CF (Columbia County, Fla.), 33–35, 420–425.

3. Jim Leusner, "Police confirm girl's body was Kim Leach's," *Florida Times Union*, April 9, 1978.

4. UPI, "Identity of body sought," *Tyrone Daily Herald*, April 8, 1978, http://www.newspaperarchive.com/PdfViewerTags.aspx?img=102971394&firstvisit=true&src=search&currentResult=0&currentPage=0&fpo=False.

5. Jim Leusner, "Police confirm girl's body was Kim Leach's," *Florida Times Union*, April 9, 1978.

6. George R. Dekle, "Affidavit in Support of Motion for Protective Order," State v. Bundy, No. 78-169-CF (Columbia County, Fla., Feb. 21, 1979).

7. "Girl's body found," *Independent Post*, April 12, 1978.

8. The following description of the attempts to interview Bundy comes from FDLE Serials 66 and 272.

9. FDLE Serial 272.

10. "Services set for Kim," *Lake City Reporter*, April 11, 1978.

11. Mendenhall v. State, 71 Fla. 552, 72 So. 202 (1916).

12. G.S. Anderson, "Forensic Entomology," in *Forensic Science: An Introduction to Scientific and Investigative Techniques*, 3rd ed., eds. Stuart H. James and James Nordby (Boca Raton, Fla.: CSC Publishing, 2005).

13. "Funeral for slain girl," *Jacksonville Journal*, April 12, 1978.

14. Ann Knight, ". . . Community says farewell to Kim," *Lake City Reporter*, April 12, 1978; UPI, "Friends, troopers bid farewell to Kimberly," *Jacksonville Journal*, April 13, 1978.

15. Ibid.

16. Ibid.

## Chapter 8: Building a Case

1. Fla.R.Crim.P. 3.130(a).

2. Fla.R.Crim.P. 3.133(a)(1).

3. Fla.R.Crim.P. 3.133(b)(1).

4. Fla.R.Crim.P. 3.191.

5. Fla.R.Crim.P. 3.191(p).

6. Jim Leusner, "Police confirm girl's body was Kim Leach's," *Florida Times Union*, April 9, 1978.

7. FDLE Serial 90.

8. FDLE Serial 273.

9. UPI, "Police state or lawful screening in Louisiana?" *Tyrone Daily Herald*, December 13, 1978, http://www.newspaperarchive.com/PdfViewerTags.aspx?img=102978284&currentResult=4&src=search&firstvisit=true.

10. FDLE Serial 273.

11. UPI, "Clerks identify Bundy in credit card case," *Jacksonville Journal*, April 13, 1978.

12. Nathan M. Adams, "To Catch a Killer: The Search for Ted Bundy," *Reader's Digest*, March 1979, 202–222, 226–230, 235–239.

13. UPI, "Identity of body sought," *Tyrone Daily Herald*, April 8, 1978, http://www.newspaperarchive.com/PdfViewerTags.aspx?img=102971394&firstvisit=true&src=search&currentResult=0&currentPage=0&fpo=False.

14. UPI, "Body found in Florida murder case," *Logansport Pharos-Tribune*, April 9, 1978, http://www.newspaperarchive.com/PdfViewerTags.aspx?img=109302023&firstvisit=true&src=search&currentResult=0&currentPage=0&fpo=False.

15. FDLE Serial 126.

16. FDLE Serial 78.

17. FDLE Serial 78, attachment.

18. FDLE Serial 94.

19. FDLE Serial 113.

20. FDLE Serial 93.

21. FDLE Serial 87.

22. FDLE Serial 89.

23. FDLE Serial 95.

24. FDLE Serial 38, attachment.

25. Prosecution Trial Brief, State v. Bundy, No. 78-169-CF (Columbia County, Fla.), 610.

26. FDLE Serial 38, attachment.

27. Prosecution Trial Brief, State v. Bundy, No. 78-169-CF (Columbia County, Fla.), 610.

28. Ibid., 640–643.

29. Larry Simpson, personal communication.

30. UPI, "State asks court for evidence samples that may link Bundy to missing girl," *Florida Times Union*, March 9, 1978.

31. Roger Bennett and Ken Connaughton, "How did Bundy become a mass-murder suspect?" *Florida Times Union*, April 2, 1978.

32. Roger Bennett and Ken Connaughton, "Ted Bundy: Perverted killer or scapegoat?" *European Stars and Stripes*, April 18, 1978, http://www.newspa

perarchive.com/PdfViewerTags.aspx?img=133507809&firstvisit=true&src=search&currentResult=0&currentPage=0&fpo=False.

33. AP, "Bundy charges total 46 after 2 new theft raps," *Jacksonville Journal,* April 6, 1978.

34. UPI, "Bundy unshackled for court hearing," *Florida Times Union,* April 7, 1978.

35. Patti Roth, "Smith to be quizzed in Kim death," *Lake City Reporter,* May 9, 1978.

36. "Kim Leach case to grand jury?" *Lake City Reporter,* May 31, 1978.

37. "Kim Leach probe has pattern," *Lake City Reporter,* June 16, 1978.

38. FDLE Serial 280.

39. FDLE Serial 285.

40. FDLE Serials 287, 305.

41. FDLE Serial 289.

42. Patti Roth, "Bundy prime suspect in slaying," *Lake City Reporter,* June 29, 1978.

43. Prosecution Trial Brief, State v. Bundy, No. 78-169-CF (Columbia County, Fla.), 925–926.

44. Ibid., 928–929.

45. FDLE Serials 313, 371.

46. FDLE Serial 371, attachment.

47. Prosecution Trial Brief, State v. Bundy, No. 78-169-CF (Columbia County, Fla.), 897–899.

48. Ibid., 946–947.

49. Ibid., 948–949.

50. FDLE Serial 363.

### Chapter 9: The Grand Jury

1. Patti Roth, "Bundy prime suspect in slaying," *Lake City Reporter,* June 29, 1978.

2. Patti Roth, "Leach case probe expected, Grand Jury set for July 17," *Lake City Reporter,* July 7, 1978.

3. Patti Roth, "70 called as witnesses for Columbia Grand Jury," *Lake City Reporter,* July 13, 1978; "Jury will undertake Leach murder probe," *Lake City Reporter,* July 17, 1978.

4. Instruction 9.5, Florida Grand Jury Instructions.

5. Fla.Stat. § 905.27(2) (2009).

6. Robyn Feldman, "Leach murder probe starts, jury calls 12 witnesses today," *Lake City Reporter,* July 18, 1978. The discrepancy between the article's title and the text comes from the fact that the title refers to the number of witnesses subpoenaed for the date of the article. The article reports that 15 witnesses had testified the previous day.

7. Kim Wilson, "Leach jury probe to end Friday?" *Lake City Reporter,* July 19, 1978.

8. Kim Wilson, "Leach jury shifts focus to Bundy," *Lake City Reporter,* July 20, 1978.

9. L. Arthur Lawrence, "Petition," State v. Bundy, No. 78-169-CF (Columbia County, Fla., Aug. 3, 1978).

10. "Grand juries indict Bundy for 3 murders," *Independent Post,* August 2, 1978.

11. "Bundy indicted by jury," *Lake City Reporter,* July 28, 1978; UPI, "Bundy indicted in sorority slayings," *Ironwood Daily Globe,* July 28, 1978, http://www.newspaperarchive.com/PdfViewerTags.aspx?img=84312189&firstvisit=true&src=search&currentResult=0&currentPage=0&fpo=False; AP, "Murder suspect dares accusers to convict him," *Garden City Telegram,* July 28, 1978, http://www.newspaperarchive.com/PdfViewerTags.aspx?img=143786121&firstvisit=true&src=search&currentResult=0&currentPage=0&fpo=False; "Grand juries indict Bundy for 3 murders," *Independent Post,* August 2, 1978; Mark I. Pinsky, "Just an Excitable Boy?" *New Times Magazine,* November 27, 1978, 53–65, 63.

12. FDLE Serial 308.

13. Kim Wilson, "It's official, Bundy indicted again," *Lake City Reporter,* August 1, 1978.

## Chapter 10: Bundy's Dream Team

1. Richard W. Larsen, *Bundy: The Deliberate Stranger* (Englewood Cliffs, N.J.: Prentice Hall, 1980), 229.

2. Ann Rule, *The Stranger beside Me: The Shocking Inside Story of Serial Killer Ted Bundy,* updated edition (New York: Pocket Books, 2009), 408.

3. Fla.R.Crim.P. 3.130(a).

4. Ann Rule, *The Stranger beside Me: The Shocking Inside Story of Serial Killer Ted Bundy,* updated edition (New York: Pocket Books, 2009), 407.

5. Millard Farmer and Theodore Robert Bundy, "Motion to Disqualify Trial Judge," State v. Bundy, No. 78-670-CF (Leon County, Fla., Aug. 2, 1978).

6. John A. Rudd, "Order," State v. Bundy, No. 78-670-CF (Leon County, Fla., Aug. 2, 1978).

7. Mark I. Pinsky, "Just an Excitable Boy?" *New Times Magazine,* November 27, 1978, 53–65, 63; Ann Rule, *The Stranger beside Me: The Shocking Inside Story of Serial Killer Ted Bundy,* updated edition (New York: Pocket Books, 2009), 408.

8. Bundy v. Rudd, 581 F.2d 1126 (1978), cert. denied 441 U.S. 905 (1979).

9. AP, "Civil suit filed by Bundy due to Leon jail conditions," *Ocala Star-Banner,* August 31, 1978, http://news.google.com/newspapers?id=vucTAA

AAIBAJ&sjid=vQUEAAAAIBAJ&pg=5397,9252179&dq=civil+suit+filed+bundy&hl=en.

10. Ann Rule, *The Stranger beside Me: The Shocking Inside Story of Serial Killer Ted Bundy*, updated edition (New York: Pocket Books, 2009), 408; J. Victor Africano and Lynn Alan Thompson, "Motion for Change of Venue or in the Alternative to Abate Prosecution," Exhibit 9, State v. Bundy, No. 78-169-CF (Columbia County, Fla., Sept. 17, 1978); Kim Wilson, "Bundy to be here Monday," *Lake City Reporter*, August 11, 1978.

11. AP, "Civil suit filed by Bundy due to Leon jail conditions," *Ocala Star-Banner*, August 31, 1978, http://news.google.com/newspapers?id=vucTAAAA IBAJ&sjid=vQUEAAAAIBAJ&pg=5397,9252179&dq=civil+suit+filed+bu ndy&hl=en.

12. "Farmer says Bundy should not have to use court for fair prison treatment," *Lake City Reporter*, September 1, 1978.

13. Kim Wilson, "Bundy to be here Monday," *Lake City Reporter*, August 11, 1978.

14. Kim Wilson, "Miami public defender looking at Bundy in Kim Leach case," *Lake City Reporter*, August 9, 1978.

15. Patti Roth, "Bundy pleads not guilty," *Lake City Reporter*, August 14, 1978.

16. Goldie Hudson, "Circuit Court Minutes," State v. Bundy, No. 78-169-CF (Columbia County, Fla., Aug. 14, 1978).

17. L. Arthur Lawrence, "Objection to Appearance Pro Hac Vice and Request for Hearing," State v. Bundy, No. 78-169-CF (Columbia County, Fla., Aug. 14, 1978).

18. Patti Roth, "Bundy pleads not guilty," *Lake City Reporter*, August 14, 1978.

19. Ibid.

20. AP, "Simpson pleads 100% not guilty," *Chicago Daily Herald*, July 23, 1994, http://www.newspaperarchive.com/PdfViewerTags.aspx?img=256222 29&firstvisit=true&src=search&currentResult=1&currentPage=0&fpo=False.

21. Goldie Hudson, "Circuit Court Minutes," State v. Bundy, No. 78-169-CF (Columbia County, Fla., Aug. 14, 1978).

22. Goldie Hudson, "Circuit Court Minutes," State v. Bundy, No. 78-169-CF (Columbia County, Fla., Sept. 14, 1978).

23. Farmer v. Holton, 146 Ga.App. 102, 103, 245 S.E.2d 457, 459 (1978).

24. Farmer v. Holton, 146 Ga.App. 102, 103–105, 245 S.E.2d 457, 459–460 (1978).

25. Ibid.

26. Craig Allsopp, "Bundy lawyer urges contempt charges against Leon sheriff," *Sarasota Herald Tribune*, September 21, 1978, http://news.google.com/ newspapers?id=HJwcAAAAIBAJ&sjid=g2cEAAAAIBAJ&pg=6221,2772477& dq=bundy+lawyer+urges+contempt&hl=en.

27. Patti Roth, "Bundy-Farmer hearing resembles trial," *Lake City Reporter,* September 15, 1978.

28. Goldie Hudson, "Circuit Court Minutes," State v. Bundy, No. 78-169-CF (Columbia County, Fla., Sept. 14, 1978).

29. William Hughes and Jonathan Lavery, *Critical Thinking: An Introduction to the Basic Skills,* 4th ed. (Orchard Park, N.Y.: Broadview Press, 2004), 154.

30. Mark I. Pinsky, "Just an Excitable Boy?" *New Times Magazine,* November 27, 1978, 53–65, 62.

31. Cherie Faircloth, "Farmer hearing determines fitness," *Suwannee Democrat,* September 20, 1978.

32. Patti Roth, "Bundy-Farmer hearing resembles trial," *Lake City Reporter,* September 15, 1978.

33. Ibid.

34. Cherie Faircloth, "Judge says no to Farmer," *Suwannee Democrat,* September 27, 1978.

35. Patti Roth, "Bundy-Farmer decision postponed to Thursday," *Lake City Reporter,* September 18, 1978.

36. Cherie Faircloth, "Judge says no to Farmer," *Suwannee Democrat,* September 27, 1978.

37. Wallace M. Jopling, "Order Denying Motion to Appear Pro Hac Vice," State v. Bundy, No. 78-169-CF (Columbia County, Fla., Sept. 21, 1978).

38. Patti Roth, "Bundy loses Farmer again," *Lake City Reporter,* September 22, 1978; Cherie Faircloth, "Judge says no to Farmer," *Suwannee Democrat,* September 27, 1978.

39. Patti Roth, "Bundy loses Farmer again," *Lake City Reporter,* September 22, 1978.

40. Faretta v. California, 422 U.S. 806 (1975).

41. Patti Roth, "Bundy loses Farmer again," *Lake City Reporter,* September 22, 1978.

42. An *ex parte* communication is a communication with the judge without opposing counsel present.

43. Theodore Robert Bundy, "Motion to Disqualify Trial Judge," State v. Bundy, No. 78-670-CF (Leon County, Fla., Nov. 14, 1978).

44. John A. Rudd, "Order," State v. Bundy, No. 78-670-CF (Leon County, Fla., Nov. 20, 1978).

45. Bundy v. Rudd, 366 So.2d 440 (Fla. 1978).

46. Rule 2.330(f), Florida Rules of Judicial Administration.

47. Bundy v. Rudd, 366 So.2d 440, 442 (Fla. 1978).

48. *In camera* proceedings are held privately in the judge's chambers.

49. *De novo* means "afresh" or "anew." A *de novo* hearing is a full reconsideration of a previously held hearing.

50. David Powell, "Bundy requests Millard Farmer," *Waycross Journal-Herald,* February 21, 1979, http://news.google.com/newspapers?id=HBBaAAAAIB

AJ&sjid=kksNAAAAIBAJ&pg=4218,5580097&dq=bundy+requests+millard+
farmer&hl=en.

51. AP, "Bundy wants Atlanta lawyer," *Tuscaloosa News,* February 21, 1979,
http://news.google.com/newspapers?id=MDAdAAAAIBAJ&sjid=2J4EAA
AAIBAJ&pg=4484,4287683&dq=bundy+wants+atlanta+lawyer&hl=en.

52. AP, "Judge rejects Farmer as lawyer," *Ocala Star-Banner,* February 22,
1979, http://news.google.com/newspapers?id=l-gTAAAAIBAJ&sjid=vAUE
AAAAIBAJ&pg=3246,6104638&dq=judge+rejects+farmer&hl=en.

### Chapter 11: Bundy for the Defense, Part I

1. FDLE Serial 78.

2. AP, "Bundy, left alone in Aspen courtroom, leaps out window, escapes
into hills," *Salt Lake City Tribune,* June 8, 1977, http://www.newspaperarchive.
com/PdfViewerTags.aspx?img=120153485&firstvisit=true&src=search&cur
rentResult=9&currentPage=0&fpo=False.

3. State v. N.B., 360 So.2d 162 (1st DCA, Fla. 1978).

4. See State v. Miller, 437 So.2d 734, 735 (1st DCA, Fla. 1983), which fully
discusses the ramifications of the 1980 amendment to the speedy trial rule.

5. George R. Dekle, "Motion for Extension of Speedy Trial under
Fla.R.Crim.P. 3.191," State v. Bundy, No. 78-169-CF (Columbia County, Fla.,
Sept. 25, 1978).

6. Goldie Hudson, "Circuit Court Minutes," State v. Bundy, No. 78-169-CF
(Columbia County, Fla., Sept. 30, 1978).

7. George R. Dekle, "State's Answer to Defendant's Demand for Discovery," State v. Bundy, No. 78-169-CF (Columbia County, Fla., Oct. 11, 1978).

8. Theodore Robert Bundy, "Motion to Continue Hearing on State's Motion for Extension of Time under Fla.R.Crim.P. 3.191 and State's Motion for
Discovery," State v. Bundy, No. 78-169-CF (Columbia County, Fla., Sept. 30,
1978).

9. Wallace M. Jopling, "Order," State v. Bundy, No. 78-169-CF (Columbia
County, Fla., Oct. 3, 1978).

10. George R. Dekle, "Amended Motion for Discovery," State v. Bundy,
No. 78-169-CF (Columbia County, Fla., Oct. 12, 1978).

11. George R. Dekle, "Motion for Order Sealing Discovery Exhibits," State v.
Bundy, No. 78-169-CF (Columbia County, Fla., Oct. 12, 1978).

12. George R. Dekle, "Memorandum of Law in Support of State's Amended
Motion for Discovery," State v. Bundy, No. 78-169-CF (Columbia County, Fla.,
Oct. 17, 1978).

13. George R. Dekle, "Amended Motion for Discovery," State v. Bundy,
No. 78-169-CF (Columbia County, Fla., Oct. 12, 1978). The modern crime lab
no longer performs this type of analysis because DNA has rendered it superfluous.

14. George R. Dekle, "State's Answer to Defendant's Demand for Discovery," State v. Bundy, No. 78-169-CF (Columbia County, Fla., Oct. 11, 1978).

15. State v. Latimore, 284 So.2d 423 (3rd DCA, 1973), cert.denied 291 So.2d 7 (Fla. 1974).

16. George R. Dekle, "Motion for Extension of Speedy Trial under Fla.R.Crim.P. 3.191," State v. Bundy, No. 78-169-CF (Columbia County, Fla., Sept. 25, 1978).

17. Arthur J. England, Uncaptioned Order, State v. Bundy, No. 78-169-CF (Columbia County, Fla., Oct. 20, 1978).

18. Martha Pogue, "Circuit Court Minutes," State v. Bundy, No. 78-169-CF (Columbia County, Fla., Oct. 23, 1978).

19. George R. Dekle, "Motion for Pretrial Conference," State v. Bundy, No. 78-169-CF (Columbia County, Fla., Oct. 17, 1978).

20. Wallace M. Jopling, "Amended Order," State v. Bundy, No. 78-169-CF (Columbia County, Fla., Nov. 3, 1978).

21. Wallace M. Jopling, "Order Granting State's Amended Motion for Discovery," State v. Bundy, No. 78-169-CF (Columbia County, Fla., Nov. 15, 1978).

22. FDLE Serial 354.

23. Fla.Stat. § 27.04.

24. George R. Dekle, "Motion for Protective Order," State v. Bundy, No. 78-169-CF (Columbia County, Fla., Feb. 15, 1979).

25. Harold B. Wahl, "Answer to Motion for Protective Order and Petition of Florida Publishing Company for Right of Press to Be Present at Depositions," State v. Bundy, No. 78-169-CF (Columbia County, Fla., Feb. 19, 1979).

26. Harold B. Wahl, "Opposition of Miami Herald to State's Motion for Protective Order," State v. Bundy, No. 78-169-CF (Columbia County, Fla., Feb. 19, 1979).

27. George R. Dekle, "Affidavit in Support of Motion for Protective Order," State v. Bundy, No. 78-169-CF (Columbia County, Fla., Feb. 21, 1979.

28. George R. Dekle, "Brief in Support of Motion for Protective Order," State v. Bundy, No. 78-169-CF (Columbia County, Fla., Feb. 21, 1979).

29. Goldie Hudson, "Circuit Court Minutes," State v. Bundy, No. 78-169-CF (Columbia County, Fla., Feb. 23, 1979).

30. Theodore Robert Bundy, "Motion to Prevent Photographing of Defendant in Restraints and for Removal of Restraints in Courtroom," State v. Bundy, No. 78-169-CF (Columbia County, Fla., Feb. 23, 1979).

31. Goldie Hudson, "Circuit Court Minutes," State v. Bundy, No. 78-169-CF (Columbia County, Fla., Feb. 23, 1979).

32. Wallace M. Jopling, "Protective Order," State v. Bundy, No. 78-169-CF (Columbia County, Fla., Feb. 27, 1979).

33. Palm Beach Newspapers, Inc. v. Burk, 504 So.2d 378 (Fla.), cert.denied 484 U.S. 954 (1987).

34. Stephen G. Michaud and Hugh Aynesworth, *The Only Living Witness: A True Account of Homicidal Insanity* (New York: Simon & Schuster, 1983), 269.

35. Theodore Robert Bundy, "Motion for Continuance," State v. Bundy, Nos. 78-169-CF and 78-670-CF (Columbia and Leon Counties, Fla., May 31, 1979).

36. Theodore Robert Bundy, "Defendant's Demand for Discovery," State v. Bundy, No. 78-169-CF (Columbia County, Fla., Sept. 30, 1979).

37. Walker v. State, 284 So.2d 448 (3rd DCA, Fla. 1973).

38. Maxwell v. State, 974 So.2d 505, 509 (5th DCA, Fla. 2008).

39. American Psychiatric Association, *Diagnostic and Statistical Manual of Mental Disorders*, 4th ed., Text Revision (Washington, D.C.: American Psychiatric Publishing, 2000), § 301.7.

40. James E. Coleman, Jr. and Polly Nelson, "Brief of Appellant and Application for a Stay of Execution," Bundy v. State, No. 69,615 (Fla.Sup.Ct., Nov. 17, 1986), 25, 26.

## Chapter 12: Marshaling the Evidence

1. Prosecution Trial Brief, State v. Bundy, No. 78-169-CF (Columbia County, Fla.), 255–264.

2. Robert J. Morton and Mark Hilts, eds., *Serial Murder—Multidisciplinary Perspectives for Investigators* (Quantico, Va.: Behavioral Analysis Unit, National Center for the Analysis of Violent Crime, Federal Bureau of Investigation, 2005), 7.

3. Prosecution Trial Brief, State v. Bundy, No. 78-169-CF (Columbia County, Fla.), 265–281.

4. Ibid., 282–310.

5. Williams v. State, 110 So.2d 654 (Fla. 1959).

6. Williams v. State, 110 So.2d 654, 655 (Fla. 1959).

7. Nickels v. State, 90 Fla. 659, 685, 106 So. 479, 489 (1925).

8. Williams v. State, 110 So.2d 654 (Fla. 1959).

9. Nickels v. State, 90 Fla. 659, 685, 106 So. 479, 489 (1925).

10. A motion in limine is a "threshold" motion, which seeks to resolve objections before trial so that the trial may run more smoothly.

11. Lynn Alan Thompson, "Motion in Limine Regarding the Admissibility of Evidence Purporting to Show Other Crimes," State v. Bundy, No. 78-169-CF (Columbia County, Fla., Sept. 5, 1979).

12. Ibid.

## Chapter 13: Bundy for the Defense, Part II

1. Barbara Frye, "Bundy judge murder trial vet," *Sarasota Herald Tribune*, June 10, 1979, http://news.google.com/newspapers?id=NTEoAAAAIBAJ&

242     Notes

sjid=W78EAAAAIBAJ&pg=6789,4277300&dq=bundy+judge+murder+vet& hl=en.

2. Ibid.

3. "Bundy happy his trial moving to Miami," *Miami News*, June 13, 1979, http://news.google.com/newspapers?id=8pwyAAAAIBAJ&sjid=OukFA AAAIBAJ&pg=2707,1921379&dq=bundy+happy+trial+moving+miami& hl=en.

4. AP, "Bundy's lawyers hunt office space," *Ocala Star-Banner*, June 15, 1979, http://news.google.com/newspapers?id=XYA1AAAAIBAJ&sjid=vQ 4EAAAAIBAJ&pg=5722,5234813&dq=bundy%27s+lawyers+hunt+office& hl=en.

5. Stephen G. Michaud and Hugh Aynesworth, *The Only Living Witness: The True Story of Serial Sex Killer Ted Bundy* (Irving, Tex.: Authorlink Press, 1999), 270.

6. UPI, "Judge orders better lighting for Bundy as trial begins," *Sarasota Herald Tribune*, June 26, 1979, http://news.google.com/newspapers?id=zEk0 AAAAIBAJ&sjid=k2cEAAAAIBAJ&pg=5439,4672263&dq=judge+orders+bett er+lighting&hl=en.

7. UPI, "Bundy trial scheduled to begin in Miami before more than 250 reporters," *St. Petersburg Times*, June 25, 1979, http://news.google.com/ newspapers?id=-4onAAAAIBAJ&sjid=TnwDAAAAIBAJ&pg=2451,2074405& dq=bundy+trial+miami+250&hl=en.

8. Noel Holston, "The Bundy trial—Made for TV courtroom drama," *Orlando Sentinel*, July 10, 1979.

9. Ibid.

10. George L. Thurston, "Bundy prosecutor, staff and files head for Miami," *Deseret News*, June 20, 1979, http://news.google.com/newspapers?id= HIkqAAAAIBAJ&sjid=xVsEAAAAIBAJ&pg=7263,1221826&dq=bundy+pro secutor&hl=en.

11. UPI, "Bundy has final say picking jury," *Chronicle Telegram*, July 1, 1979, http://www.newspaperarchive.com/PdfViewerTags.aspx?img=7717972&first visit=true&src=search&currentResult=0&currentPage=0&fpo=False.

12. AP, "No testimony this week," *Spokane Spokesman Review*, July 2, 1979, http://news.google.com/newspapers?id=h2sjAAAAIBAJ&sjid=HO4DAAA AIBAJ&pg=7202,1364648&dq=spokane+spokesman+july+2&hl=en.

13. Stephen G. Michaud and Hugh Aynesworth, *The Only Living Witness: The True Story of Serial Sex Killer Ted Bundy* (Irving, Tex.: Authorlink Press, 1999), 115.

14. Prosecution Trial Brief, State v. Bundy, No. 78-169-CF (Columbia County, Fla.), 1160.

15. UPI "Coed places Bundy at disco near murder scene," *Logansport Pharos-Tribune*, July 17, 1979, http://www.newspaperarchive.com/PdfViewer Tags.aspx?img=109309530&firstvisit=true&src=search&currentResult=0&cur rentPage=0&fpo=False.

16. Noel Holston, "The Bundy trial—Made for TV courtroom drama," *Orlando Sentinel,* July 10, 1979.

17. UPI, "Bundy guiding defense," *Logansport Pharos-Tribune,* July 11, 1979, http://www.newspaperarchive.com/PdfViewerTags.aspx?img=109309431& firstvisit=true&src=search&currentResult=1&currentPage=0&fpo=False.

18. UPI, "Bundy questions witnesses in own trial," *Chicago Daily Herald,* July 10, 1979, http://www.newspaperarchive.com/PdfViewerTags.aspx? img=15622381&firstvisit=true&src=search&currentResult=2&currentPage= 10&fpo=False.

19. Tex O'Neill, "FSU student may have just missed meeting murderer," *Orlando Sentinel,* July 10, 1979.

20. Ibid.

21. UPI, "Bundy guiding defense," *Logansport Pharos-Tribune,* July 11, 1979, http://www.newspaperarchive.com/PdfViewerTags.aspx?img=109309431& firstvisit=true&src=search&currentResult=1&currentPage=0&fpo=False.

22. AP, "Ted Bundy refuses to appear in court," *Santa Fe New Mexican,* July 17, 1979, http://www.newspaperarchive.com/PdfViewerTags.aspx? img=111392078&firstvisit=true&src=search&currentResult=0&currentPage= 0&fpo=False.

23. Tex O'Neill, "Bundy will take over his defense," *Orlando Sentinel,* July 17, 1979.

24. Ibid.

25. Ibid.

26. Tex O'Neill, "1 Bundy lawyer quits, another tries," *Orlando Sentinel,* July 22, 1979.

27. AP, "Law student Theodore Bundy found guilty of two murders," *Gettysburg Times,* July 25, 1979, http://www.newspaperarchive.com/PdfViewer Tags.aspx?img=431476&firstvisit=true&src=search&currentResult=4&current Page=10&fpo=False.

28. UPI, "Bundy found guilty," *Altoona Mirror,* July 25, 1979, http://www.newspaperarchive.com/PdfViewerTags.aspx?img=69845889&firstvisit=true& src=search&currentResult=0&currentPage=0&fpo=False.

29. AP, "Bundy: I'm not losing any sleep over all this," *Elyria Chronicle Telegram,* July 27, 1979, http://www.newspaperarchive.com/PdfViewerTags.aspx? img=7727634&firstvisit=true&src=search&currentResult=1&currentPage=0& fpo=False.

30. AP, "Bundy discusses verdict, appeal," *Lawrence Daily Journal-World,* July 29, 1979, http://www.newspaperarchive.com/PdfViewerTags.aspx?img= 166156354&firstvisit=true&src=search&currentResult=0&currentPage=0& fpo=False.

31. AP, "Farmer: Florida system of (in)justice," *Daytona Beach Morning Journal,* July 27, 1979, http://news.google.com/newspapers?id=N3ApAAAAIB AJ&sjid=49EEAAAAIBAJ&pg=3160,4199277&dq=farmer+florida+system& hl=en.

32. Patrick McMahon, "Bundy jury gets evidence for its life or death decision," *St. Petersburg Times,* July 29, 1979, http://news.google.com/newspapers?id=yg4OAAAAIBAJ&sjid=UHwDAAAAIBAJ&pg=2633,3478462&dq=bundy+jury+evidence&hl=en.

33. AP, "Farmer: Florida system of (in)justice," *Daytona Beach Morning Journal,* July 27, 1979, http://news.google.com/newspapers?id=N3ApAAAAIBAJ&sjid=49EEAAAAIBAJ&pg=3160,4199277&dq=farmer+florida+system&hl=en.

34. UPI, "Jury urges death in chair for Bundy," *Chicago Daily Herald,* July 31, 1979, http://www.newspaperarchive.com/PdfViewerTags.aspx?img=15626745&firstvisit=true&src=search&currentResult=0&currentPage=0&fpo=False.

35. Dan Sewell, "Bundy psyche remains a puzzle," *Chicago Daily Herald,* July 30, 1979, http://www.newspaperarchive.com/PdfViewerTags.aspx?img=15626622&firstvisit=true&src=search&currentResult=0&currentPage=0&fpo=False.

36. AP, "Sentenced to death," *Marysville Journal-Tribune,* August 1, 1979, http://www.newspaperarchive.com/PdfViewerTags.aspx?img=70543979&firstvisit=true&src=search&currentResult=5&currentPage=10&fpo=False.

37. David Schmid, *Natural Born Celebrities—Serial Killers in American Culture* (Chicago: University of Chicago Press, 2005), 216, 217.

38. James Q. Whitman, *The Origins of Reasonable Doubt: Theological Roots of the Criminal Trial* (New Haven, Conn.: Yale University Press, 2005), 28–49.

### Chapter 14: Motion Sickness

1. Don Kennedy, personal communication.

2. J. Victor Africano, "Motion to File Certain Motions and Supporting Memoranda under Seal and for In Camera Hearings on Said Motions," State v. Bundy, No. 78-169-CF (Columbia County, Fla., Aug. 19, 1979).

3. George R. Dekle, "Joinder of the State in Defendant's Motion to File Certain Motions and Supporting Memoranda under Seal and for In Camera Hearings on Said Motions," State v. Bundy, No. 78-169-CF (Columbia County, Fla., Aug. 20, 1979).

4. William G. Mateer and David L. Evans, "Response to Motion to File Certain Motions and Supporting Memoranda under Seal and for In Camera Hearings on Said Motions," State v. Bundy, No. 78-169-CF (Columbia County, Fla., Aug. 24, 1979).

5. Harold B. Wahl, "Response of Florida Publishing Company to Certain Motions for Closed Proceedings by Defendant Bundy," State v. Bundy, No. 78-169-CF (Columbia County, Fla., Aug. 27, 1979).

6. Dan Paul, "Response of the Lake City Reporter, the Gainesville Sun and the Miami Herald Publishing Company to Joint Motion to File Certain Motions under Seal and for In Camera Hearings on Said Motions," State v. Bundy, No. 78-169-CF (Columbia County, Fla., Aug. 27, 1979).

7. Wallace M. Jopling, "Protective Order," State v. Bundy, No. 78-169-CF (Columbia County, Fla., Aug. 31, 1979).

8. Joseph C. Jacobs and Dean Bunch, "Motion to Permit Inspection of Pre-Trial Motions," State v. Bundy, No. 78-169-CF (Columbia County, Fla., Sept. 12, 1979).

9. Joseph C. Jacobs and Dean Bunch, "Motion to Permit Video Taping of Pre-Trial Hearings," State v. Bundy, No. 78-169-CF (Columbia County, Fla., Sept. 12, 1979).

10. Lynn Alan Thompson, "Motion to Exclude Electronic Media from the Courtroom," State v. Bundy, No. 78-169-CF (Columbia County, Fla., Sept. 6, 1979).

11. Wallace M. Jopling, "Order on Pretrial Motions Heard In Camera," State v. Bundy, No. 78-169-CF (Columbia County, Fla., Sept. 28, 1979).

12. Wallace M. Jopling, "Order Granting in Part and Denying in Part Defendant's Motion in Limine Regarding the Admissibility of Evidence Purporting to Show Other Crimes," State v. Bundy, No. 78-169-CF (Columbia County, Fla., Oct. 24, 1979).

13. J. Victor Africano and Lynn Alan Thompson, "Motion for Change of Venue or in the Alternative to Abate Prosecution," State v. Bundy, No. 78-169-CF (Columbia County, Fla., Sept. 17, 1979).

14. George R. Dekle, "Brief in Opposition to Defendant's Motion to Suppress Testimony of Certain Witnesses Whose Recall Have Been Affected and Altered by Hypnosis," State v. Bundy, No. 78-169-CF (Columbia County, Fla., Sept. 24, 1979).

15. People v. Shirley, 31 Cal.3d 18, 181 Cal.Rptr. 243, 723 P.2d 1354, cert.denied 459 U.S. 860 (1982) (banned); Commonwealth v. Juvenile, 381 Mass. 727, 412 N.E.2d 339 (1980) (restricted); State v. Mack, 292 N.W.2d 764 (Minn. 1980) (banned); State v. Hurd, 173 N.J.Super. 333, 414 A.2d 291 (1980) (restricted).

16. State v. Moore, 188 N.J. 182, 902 A.2d 1212 (2006).

17. Wallace M. Jopling, "Order on Pretrial Motions Heard In Camera," State v. Bundy, No. 78-169-CF (Columbia County, Fla., Sept. 28, 1979).

18. J. Victor Africano, "Defendant's Response to Reciprocal Discovery under Fla.R.Crim.Pr. 3.220 (3) & (4)," State v. Bundy, No. 78-169-CF (Columbia County, Fla., Oct. 2, 1979).

19. Theodore Robert Bundy, "Defendant's Demand for Discovery," State v. Bundy, No. 78-169-CF (Columbia County, Fla., Sept. 30, 1979).

20. George R. Dekle, "Discovery Exhibit XXXVII," State v. Bundy, No. 78-169-CF (Columbia County, Fla., Sept. 27, 1979).

21. Commonwealth v. Juvenile, 381 Mass. 727, 733, 412 N.E.2d 339, 343 n.8 (1980) sets forth Kline's criteria.

22. 103 Misc.2d 881, 427 N.Y.S.2d 177 (New York County Supreme Court, 1980).

23. 103 Misc.2d 881, 883-884, 427 N.Y.S.2d 177, 179 (1980).

24. William Hughes and Jonathan Lavery, *Critical Thinking: An Introduction to the Basic Skills,* 4th ed. (Orchard Park, N.Y.: Broadview Press, 2004), 154; Nigel Warburton, *Thinking from A to Z,* 2nd ed. (New York: Routledge, 2000), 136.

25. Bundy v. State, 471 So.2d 9, 19 (Fla. 1985).

26. Milton V. Kline, Letter to J. Victor Africano, Exhibit 1 to "Defendant's Response to Reciprocal Discovery under Fla.R.Crim.Pr. 3.220 (3) & (4)," State v. Bundy, No. 78-169-CF (Columbia County, Fla., Sept. 27, 1979).

27. Wallace M. Jopling, "Order Denying Motion to Suppress without Prejudice," State v. Bundy, No. 78-169-CF (Columbia County, Fla., Oct. 23, 1979).

28. Milton V. Kline, "A Note of 'Primate-like' Behavior Induced by Hypnosis," *Journal of Genetic Psychology* 81 (1952): 121–131; "The Dynamics of Hypnotically Induced Antisocial Behavior," *Journal of Psychology* 45 (1958): 239–245; "The Production of Antisocial Behavior through Hypnosis: New Clinical Data," *International Journal of Clinical and Experimental Hypnosis* 20 (1972): 89–94.

29. Johnson v. United States, 333 U.S. 10, 14 (1948).

30. Lynn Alan Thompson, "Motion to Exclude Electronic Media from the Courtroom," State v. Bundy, No. 78-169-CF (Columbia County, Fla., Sept. 6, 1979).

31. Lynn Alan Thompson, "Motion in Limine Regarding the Admissibility of Evidence Purporting to Show Other Crimes," State v. Bundy, No. 78-169-CF (Columbia County, Fla., Sept. 5, 1979).

32. J. Victor Africano and Lynn Alan Thompson, "Motion for Change of Venue or in the Alternative to Abate Prosecution," State v. Bundy, No. 78-169-CF (Columbia County, Fla., Sept. 17, 1979).

33. Section 16 has since been amended. The provision is now Section 16(a) of Article I.

34. Wallace M. Jopling, "Order on Motion for Change of Venue," State v. Bundy, No. 78-169-CF (Columbia County, Fla., Oct. 23, 1979).

35. J. Victor Africano, "Notice of Election," State v. Bundy, No. 78-169-CF (Columbia County, Fla., Oct. 26, 1979).

36. Lynn Alan Thompson, "Motion for Change of Venue or in the Alternative to Abate Prosecution," State v. Bundy, No. 78-169-CF (Columbia County, Fla., Nov. 6, 1979).

37. Wallace M. Jopling, "Administrative Order," State v. Bundy, No. 78-169-CF (Columbia County, Fla., Nov. 2, 1979).

38. Dick Hagood and Christine Hammer, "Live Oak quiet on eve of Bundy's 2nd trial," *Florida Times Union,* November 6, 1979.

39. Wallace M. Jopling, "Order at Pretrial Conference," State v. Bundy, No. 78-169-CF (Columbia County, Fla., Nov. 2, 1979).

40. Laura Kavesh, "3 tentatively picked for Bundy jury," *Orlando Sentinel,* November 7, 1979.

41.  Dick Hagood and Christine Hammer, "4 more Bundy jurors given tentative OK," *Florida Times Union,* November 8, 1979.

42.  Laura Kavesh, "Bundy's trial moving to Orlando," *Orlando Sentinel,* November 9, 1979.

43.  Dick Hagood and Christine Hammer, "Bundy trial moved," *Florida Times Union,* November 9, 1979.

### Chapter 15: Try, Try, Again

1.  Ann Rule, *The Stranger beside Me: The Shocking Inside Story of Serial Killer Ted Bundy,* updated edition (New York: Pocket Books, 2009), 494.

2.  Dick Burdette, "Curtain rises on anti-climactic Bundy trial," *Orlando Sentinel,* January 8, 1980.

3.  Patti Roth, "Jopling expects Bundy trial to last at least four weeks," *Lake City Reporter,* January 3, 1980.

4.  Dick Burdette, "Curtain rises on anti-climactic Bundy trial," *Orlando Sentinel,* January 8, 1980.

5.  John S. Gholdston, "Sales of Bundy book reflect trail of convicted murderer's past," *Orlando Sentinel,* January 4, 1980.

6.  Dick Burdette, "Curtain rises on anti-climactic Bundy trial," *Orlando Sentinel,* January 8, 1980.

7.  Laura Kavesh, "Jail, court all set for Bundy trial," *Orlando Sentinel,* January 6, 1980.

8.  Laura Kavesh, "Jail, court all set for Bundy trial," *Orlando Sentinel,* January 6, 1980.

9.  Patti Roth, "Bundy courtroom simple, modern," *Lake City Reporter,* January 10, 1980.

10.  V. Hale Starr and Mark McCormick, *Jury Selection,* 3rd ed. (New York: Aspen Publishing, 2001), 240.

11.  Jeffery Frederick, *Mastering Voir Dire and Jury Selection—Gain an Edge in Questioning and Selecting Your Jury,* 2nd ed. (Chicago: American Bar Association, 2005), 15; Laura Kavesh, "Jury selection in Bundy trial an elaborate, complex affair," *Orlando Sentinel,* January 14, 1980.

12.  Batson v. Kentucky, 476 U.S. 79 (1986) (race); J.E.B. v. Alabama ex rel. T.B., 511 U.S. 127 (1994) (gender); 28 U.S.C.A. § 1862.

13.  Cicero, *De Inventione,* I.xv.20.

14.  Sid Bradley, "Psychology of Jury Selection for Trial of Theodore R. Bundy," (unpublished study in author's possession, 1979), 2.

15.  Ellen Burgess, "Minutes of Trial," State v. Bundy, No. CR79-4650 (Orange County, Fla., Feb. 1, 1980).

16.  Women's Army Corps.

17.  Dick Hagood, "Bundy convicted in school girl's murder," *Florida Times Union,* February 8, 1980.

18. Laura Kavesh, "4 get tentative OK to sit on Bundy," *Orlando Sentinel,* January 8, 1980.

19. Patti Roth, "Bundy courtroom simple, modern," *Lake City Reporter,* January 10, 1980.

20. AP, "Final jurors to be tentatively seated in Bundy murder trial," *Lake City Reporter,* January 9, 1980.

21. Patti Roth, "Bundy courtroom simple, modern," *Lake City Reporter,* January 10, 1980.

22. Paula Schwed, ". . . as woman questions justice," *Orlando Sentinel,* January 10, 1980.

23. Patti Roth, "Bundy plans to write his own book?" *Lake City Reporter,* January 17, 1980.

24. Laura Kavesh, "4 get tentative OK to sit on Bundy," *Orlando Sentinel,* January 8, 1980.

25. Patti Roth, "Bundy plans to write his own book?" *Lake City Reporter,* January 17, 1980.

26. Paula Schwed, ". . . as woman questions justice," *Orlando Sentinel,* January 10, 1980.

27. Patti Roth, "Bundy plans to write his own book?" *Lake City Reporter,* January 17, 1980.

28. Stephen G. Michaud and Hugh Aynesworth, *Ted Bundy: Conversations with a Killer* (Irving, Tex.: Authorlink Press, 2000); *The Only Living Witness: The True Story of Serial Sex Killer Ted Bundy* (Irving, Tex.: Authorlink Press, 1999); *The Only Living Witness: A True Account of Homicidal Insanity* (New York: Simon & Schuster, 1983).

29. Laura Kavesh, "4 get tentative OK to sit on Bundy," *Orlando Sentinel,* January 8, 1980.

30. Dick Hagood, "Another motion made to move Bundy trial," *Florida Times Union,* January 11, 1980.

31. Laura Kavesh, "4 get tentative OK to sit on Bundy," *Orlando Sentinel,* January 8, 1980.

32. AP, "Final jurors to be tentatively seated in Bundy murder trial," *Lake City Reporter,* January 9, 1980.

33. Laura Kavesh, "Possible jurors at 11 . . .," *Orlando Sentinel,* January 10, 1980.

34. Laura Kavesh, "4 get tentative OK to sit on Bundy," *Orlando Sentinel,* January 8, 1980.

35. Patrick Wolski, "A juror reviews the Bundy case," *Orlando Sentinel,* February 17, 1980.

36. Patti Roth, "Jopling: Why the state prosecutes Leach case," *Lake City Reporter,* January 18, 1980.

37. Laura Kavesh, "Possible jurors at 11 . . .," *Orlando Sentinel,* January 10, 1980.

38. Dick Hagood, "Bundy jury list now at 11," *Florida Times Union,* January 10, 1980.

39. Lynn Alan Thompson, "Motion for Change of Venue or in the Alternative to Abate Prosecution," State v. Bundy, No. CR79-4650 (Orange County, Fla., Jan. 9, 1980).

40. AP, "Bundy seeks to change trial site again," *Lake City Reporter,* January 11, 1980.

41. Lynn Alan Thompson, "Motion for Change of Venue or in the Alternative to Abate Prosecution," Exhibit VI, State v. Bundy, No. CR79-4650 (Orange County, Fla., Jan. 9, 1980).

42. Dick Hagood, "Another motion made to move Bundy trial," *Florida Times Union,* January 11, 1980.

43. Dick Hagood, "Selection of Bundy jury set back again," *Florida Times Union,* January 15, 1980; Laura Kavesh, "Decision postponed to move Bundy trial," *Orlando Sentinel,* January 12, 1980; UPI, "Bundy request for trial move major issue in Orlando court," *Florida Times Union,* January 12, 1980.

44. Laura Kavesh, "Bundy seeks venue switch—Poll shows most Orange residents know of him," *Orlando Sentinel,* January 11, 1980.

45. Laura Kavesh, "Decision postponed to move Bundy trial," *Orlando Sentinel,* January 12, 1980.

46. Ibid.

47. Laura Kavesh, "On Opposite Sides—Attorneys in the Bundy case differ in their techniques, backgrounds," *Orlando Sentinel,* February 4, 1980.

48. Ellen Burgess, "Minutes of Trial," State v. Bundy, No. CR79-4650 (Orange County, Fla., Feb. 1, 1980).

49. Dick Hagood, "Selection of Bundy jury set back again," *Florida Times Union,* January 15, 1980.

50. AP, "Final jurors to be tentatively seated in Bundy murder trial," *Lake City Reporter,* January 9, 1980.

51. Neil Chethick, "Bundy became an obsession for prosecutor," *Tallahassee Democrat,* February 9, 1980; Laura Kavesh, "On Opposite Sides—Attorneys in the Bundy case differ in their techniques, backgrounds," *Orlando Sentinel,* February 4, 1980.

52. *The Only Living Witness: The True Story of Serial Sex Killer Ted Bundy* (Irving, Tex.: Authorlink Press, 1999), 302.

53. Ellen Burgess, "Minutes of Trial," State v. Bundy, No. CR79-4650 (Orange County, Fla., Feb. 1, 1980).

54. Dick Hagood, "Selection of Bundy jury set back again," *Florida Times Union,* January 15, 1980.

55. Ibid.

56. AP, "Bundy loses effort to delay, move murder trial," *Lake City Reporter,* January 16, 1980.

57. Dick Hagood, "Judge pushes selection of Bundy jury," *Florida Times Union,* January 17, 1980.

58. Wally Dillon, "Jury still not seated in Bundy murder trial," *Suwannee Democrat,* January 19, 1980.

59. Laura Kavesh, "Bundy jury tentatively reaches 12," *Orlando Sentinel,* January 18, 1980.

60. Richard W. Larsen, *Bundy: The Deliberate Stranger* (Englewood Cliffs, N.J.: Prentice Hall, 1980), 284.

61. Stephen G. Michaud and Hugh Aynesworth, *The Only Living Witness: A True Account of Homicidal Insanity* (New York: Simon & Schuster, 1983), 296.

62. Ann Rule, *The Stranger beside Me: The Shocking Inside Story of Serial Killer Ted Bundy,* updated edition (New York: Pocket Books, 2009), 497.

63. Dick Hagood, "Jury is seated in Bundy trial," *Florida Times Union,* January 18, 1980.

64. Transcript of Trial, 3483–3484, State v. Bundy, No. CR79-4650 (Orange County, Fla., 1980).

65. Patti Roth, "Bundy disrupts into tirade," *Lake City Reporter,* January 21, 1980.

66. Ibid.

67. Ibid.

68. Dick Hagood, "Jury is seated in Bundy trial," *Florida Times Union,* January 18, 1980.

69. Ellen Burgess, "Minutes of Trial," State v. Bundy, No. CR79-4650 (Orange County, Fla., Feb. 1, 1980).

70. Richard W. Larsen, *Bundy: The Deliberate Stranger* (Englewood Cliffs, N.J.: Prentice Hall, 1980), 284.

71. Patti Roth, "Jopling keeps files closed," *Lake City Reporter,* January 21, 1980.

72. Lynn Alan Thompson, "Motion in Limine Regarding Limitation of Argument by the State," State v. Bundy, No. CR79-4650 (Orange County, Fla., Jan. 9, 1980).

73. AP, "Jurors of varied ages, professions, beliefs," *Orlando Sentinel,* January 19, 1980.

74. Ellen Burgess, "Minutes of Trial," State v. Bundy, No. CR79-4650 (Orange County, Fla., Feb. 1, 1980).

### Chapter 16: The Trial

1. Ellen Burgess, "Minutes of Trial," State v. Bundy, No. CR79-4650 (Orange County, Fla., Feb. 1, 1980).

2. Richard W. Larsen, *Bundy: The Deliberate Stranger* (Englewood Cliffs, N.J.: Prentice Hall, 1980), 285; Patti Roth, "Evidence unfolds in Bundy murder trial," *Lake City Reporter,* January 22, 1980.

3. Nigel Warburton, *Thinking from A to Z*, 2nd ed. (New York: Routledge, 2000), 126–127.

4. Patti Roth, "Evidence unfolds in Bundy murder trial," *Lake City Reporter*, January 22, 1980.

5. FDLE Serial 122.

6. Len Register, "State's Brief on Admissibility of Eyewitness Identification That Is Uncertain or Less than Positive," State v. Bundy, No. CR79-4650 (Orange County, Fla., Jan. 21, 1980).

7. In re: Petition of Post-Newsweek Stations, Florida, Inc., for Change in Code of Judicial Conduct, 370 So.2d 764, 784 (1979).

8. Transcript of Trial, State v. Bundy, No. CR79-4650 (Orange County, Fla., 1980), 3962–3985.

9. Transcript of Trial, State v. Bundy, No. CR79-4650 (Orange County, Fla., 1980), 4034–4035.

10. Stephen G. Michaud and Hugh Aynesworth, *The Only Living Witness: A True Account of Homicidal Insanity* (New York: Simon & Schuster, 1983), 298–299.

11. Transcript of Trial, State v. Bundy, No. CR79-4650 (Orange County, Fla., 1980), 4071–4072.

12. Patrick Wolski, "A juror reviews the Bundy case," *Orlando Sentinel*, February 17, 1980.

13. Patti Roth, "Kimberly Leach died during attack, doctor tells Bundy jury," *Lake City Reporter*, January 24, 1980.

14. Transcript of Trial, State v. Bundy, No. CR79-4650 (Orange County, Fla., 1980), 4388–4451.

15. Stephen G. Michaud and Hugh Aynesworth, *The Only Living Witness: A True Account of Homicidal Insanity* (New York: Simon & Schuster, 1983), 300.

16. Transcript of Trial, State v. Bundy, No. CR79-4650 (Orange County, Fla., 1980), 4451–4536.

17. Patti Roth, "Jury to hear about Bundy's arrest," *Lake City Reporter*, January 28, 1980.

18. Gregory Miller, "'Beauty, Beast' train talents at Bundy," *Today*, January 28, 1980.

19. Patti Roth, "Jopling allows chain of evidence," *Lake City Reporter*, January 28, 1980.

20. Laura Kavesh, "Bundy wanted to die, officer testifies," *Orlando Sentinel*, January 29, 1980.

21. Transcript of Trial, State v. Bundy, No. CR79-4650 (Orange County, Fla., 1980), 5249–5269.

22. Transcript of Trial, State v. Bundy, No. CR79-4650 (Orange County, Fla., 1980), 5257–5266.

23. Stephen G. Michaud and Hugh Aynesworth, *The Only Living Witness: A True Account of Homicidal Insanity* (New York: Simon & Schuster, 1983), 300.

24. Prosecution Trial Brief, State v. Bundy, No. 78-169-CF (Columbia County, Fla.), 890–921.

25. Ibid., 911.

26. Patti Roth, "State saves analyst's testimony to end Bundy case," *Lake City Reporter,* January 30, 1980.

27. Laura Kavesh, "State rests its case in Bundy murder trial," *Orlando Sentinel,* January 30, 1980.

28. Patrick Wolski, "A juror reviews the Bundy case," *Orlando Sentinel,* February 17, 1980.

29. Arthur Conan Doyle, *The Complete Sherlock Holmes* (New York: Gramercy Books, 2002), 88.

30. Patrick Wolski, "A juror reviews the Bundy case," *Orlando Sentinel,* February 17, 1980.

31. Arthur Conan Doyle, *The Complete Sherlock Holmes* (New York: Gramercy Books, 2002), 103.

32. Stephen Michaud and Hugh Aynesworth, *The Only Living Witness: A True Account of Homicidal Insanity* (New York: Simon & Schuster, 1983), 302.

33. FDLE Serial 93, attachment.

34. J. Victor Africano, "Defendant's Response to Reciprocal Discovery under Fla.R.Crim.Pr. 3.220 (3) & (4)," State v. Bundy, No. 78-169-CF (Columbia County, Fla., Oct. 2, 1979).

35. Transcript of Trial, State v. Bundy, No. CR79-4650 (Orange County, Fla., 1980), 5717–5760.

36. Patrick Wolski, "A juror reviews the Bundy case," *Orlando Sentinel,* February 17, 1980.

37. Laura Kavesh, "Kim may have hitched a ride with death," *Orlando Sentinel,* February 1, 1980; Patti Roth, "Bundy defense to call hypnotist today," *Lake City Reporter,* February 1, 1980.

38. Patti Roth, "Bundy defense to call hypnotist today," *Lake City Reporter,* February 1, 1980.

39. Patrick Wolski, "A juror reviews the Bundy case," *Orlando Sentinel,* February 17, 1980.

40. Laura Kavesh, "Defense psychologist: Witness' testimony should be thrown out," *Orlando Sentinel,* February 3, 1980.

41. Transcript of Trial, State v. Bundy, No. CR79-4650 (Orange County, Fla., 1980), 6174–6361.

42. 103 Misc.2d 881, 427 N.Y.S.2d 177 (New York County Supreme Court, 1980).

43. Patrick Wolski, "A juror reviews the Bundy case," *Orlando Sentinel,* February 17, 1980. All quotations from Patrick Wolski's article are used with the permission of the *Orlando Sentinel,* copyright 1980.

44. Ibid.

45. Ellen Burgess, "Minutes of Trial," State v. Bundy, No. CR79-4650 (Orange County, Fla., Feb. 1, 1980).

46. Ann Rule, *The Stranger beside Me: The Shocking Inside Story of Serial Killer Ted Bundy*, updated edition (New York: Pocket Books, 2009), 498.

47. Dick Hagood, "Bundy convicted in school girl's murder," *Florida Times Union*, February 8, 1980.

## Chapter 17: Death Sentence to Death Chamber

1. Dick Hagood, "Bundy jury: Death," *Florida Times Union*, February 10, 1980.

2. Ann Rule, *The Stranger beside Me: The Shocking Inside Story of Serial Killer Ted Bundy*, updated edition (New York: Pocket Books, 2009), 498.

3. Stephen G. Michaud and Hugh Aynesworth, *The Only Living Witness: A True Account of Homicidal Insanity* (New York: Simon & Schuster, 1983), 303.

4. Dick Hagood, "Bundy jury: Death," *Florida Times Union*, February 10, 1980.

5. Matthew 18:6 (KJV).

6. Laura Kavesh, "Bundy gives vows, gets death," *Orlando Sentinel*, February 10, 1980.

7. Stephen G. Michaud and Hugh Aynesworth, *The Only Living Witness: A True Account of Homicidal Insanity* (New York: Simon & Schuster, 1983), 302.

8. Ann Rule, *The Stranger beside Me: The Shocking Inside Story of Serial Killer Ted Bundy*, updated edition (New York: Pocket Books, 2009), 501.

9. Stephen G. Michaud and Hugh Aynesworth, *The Only Living Witness: A True Account of Homicidal Insanity* (New York: Simon & Schuster, 1983), 304.

10. Richard W. Larsen, *Bundy: The Deliberate Stranger* (Englewood Cliffs, N.J.: Prentice Hall, 1980), 295, 296.

11. Wallace M. Jopling, Untitled order imposing the death penalty, State v. Bundy, No. CR79-4650 (Orange County, Fla., Feb. 12, 1980).

12. J. Victor Africano, "Motion for New Trial," State v. Bundy, No. 78-169-CF (Columbia County, Fla., Feb. 22, 1980).

13. J. Victor Africano, "Suggestion for Inquiry and Supplemental Motion for New Trial," State v. Bundy, No. 78-169-CF (Columbia County, Fla., Mar. 20, 1980).

14. Jerry M. Blair and J. Victor Africano, "Stipulation," State v. Bundy, No. 78-169-CF (Columbia County, Fla., Mar. 25, 1980).

15. Wallace M. Jopling, "Order Denying Motion for New Trial," State v. Bundy, No. 78-169-CF (Columbia County, Fla., Mar. 25, 1980).

16. Ibid.

17. "Nation: The Doctor and the Moneyed Monk," *Time*, September 15, 1980, http://www.time.com/time/magazine/article/0,9171,924439-1,00.html.

18. AP, "Doctor admits killing victim, cellmate says," *Orange County Register,* November 20, 1980, http://www.newspaperarchive.com/PdfViewerTags. aspx?img=169119173&firstvisit=true&src=search&currentResult=4&current Page=0&fpo=False.

19. Richard Deatley, "Murder case bests films," *Alton Telegraph,* September 12, 1980, http://www.newspaperarchive.com/PdfViewerTags.aspx?img= 117818177&firstvisit=true&src=search&currentResult=7&currentPage=10& fpo=False.

20. "Doctor, once a murder suspect, gets probation," *New York Times,* April 29, 1981, http://www.nytimes.com/1981/04/30/us/doctor-once-a-mur der-suspect-gets-probation-on-drug-charge.html?&pagewanted=print.

21. 103 Misc.2d 881, 427 N.Y.S.2d 177 (New York County Supreme Court, 1980).

22. Mike Fish, "Credentials of defense witness probed," *Syracuse Herald-Journal,* October 8, 1981, http://www.newspaperarchive.com/PdfViewerTags. aspx?img=38959086&firstvisit=true&src=search&currentResult=1&current Page=0&fpo=False.

23. James E. Starrs, "Mountebanks among Forensic Scientists," in *Forensic Science Handbook,* Vol. 2, ed. Richard Saferstein (Englewood Cliffs, N.J.: Prentice-Hall, 1988), 9.

24. Mike Fish, "Credentials of defense witness probed," *Syracuse Herald-Journal,* October 8, 1981, http://www.newspaperarchive.com/PdfViewerTags. aspx?img=38959086&firstvisit=true&src=search&currentResult=1&current Page=0&fpo=False.

25. AP, "Psychologist says he lied in court," *Syracuse Herald-Journal,* December 16, 1981, http://www.newspaperarchive.com/PdfViewerTags.aspx? img=44865089&firstvisit=true&src=search&currentResult=3&currentPage=0& fpo=False.

26. AP, "Psychologist fined for lying," *Gadsden Times,* February 11, 1982, http://news.google.com/newspapers?id=KaUfAAAAIBAJ&sjid=Q9YEAAA AIBAJ&pg=3130,1603463&dq=psychologist+fined&hl=en.

27. Kline v. State, 444 So.2d 1102, 1103 (1st DCA Fla. 1984).

28. James E. Starrs, "Mountebanks among Forensic Scientists," in *Forensic Science Handbook,* Vol. 2, ed. Richard Saferstein (Englewood Cliffs, N.J.: Prentice-Hall, 1988), 8.

29. Bundy v. State, 471 So.2d 9, 19 (Fla. 1984).

30. AP, "Clemency opposed for Bundy," *Ocala Star-Banner,* December 19, 1985, http://news.google.com/newspapers?id=ZiATAAAAIBAJ&sjid=MgY EAAAAIBAJ&pg=4599,1983132&dq=clemency+opposed+bundy&hl=en.

31. Jon Nordheimer, "Talking with Ted Bundy," *Lake City Reporter,* April 1, 1986.

32. Robert Keppel and William J. Birnes, *The Riverman—Ted Bundy and I Hunt the Green River Killer* (New York: Pocket Books, 1995).

33. Robert K. Ressler and Tom Schachtman, *Whoever Fights Monsters: My Twenty Years Tracking Serial Killers for the FBI* (New York: St. Martin's Press, 1992).

34. AP, "Author describes how Kim was lured," *Lake City Reporter*, July 2, 1986.

35. "Execution day car caravan set," *Lake City Reporter*, July 1, 1986.

36. "Bundy's stays are protested," *Lake City Reporter*, November 24, 1986.

37. Margaret LeGuire, "Impact of Bundy's crime was powerful," *Lake City Reporter*, February 19, 1988.

38. Bundy v. Dugger, 816 F.2d 564, 567 (11th Cir. 1987).

39. Bundy v. Dugger, 675 Fed.Supp. 622 (M.D.Fla. 1987).

40. J. Craig Crawford, "Judge's ruling loud and clear—Bundy loses," *Orlando Sentinel*, December 18, 1987, http://articles.orlandosentinel.com/1987-12-18/news/0170040008_1_bundy-death-penalty-sharp.

41. AP, "Bundy details slayings as clock ticks away," *Florida Times Union*, January 22, 1989.

42. Robert Keppel and William J. Birnes, *The Riverman—Ted Bundy and I Hunt the Green River Killer* (New York: Pocket Books, 1995), 365–400.

43. Gary Boynton, "Ted Bundy: The Serial Killer Next Door," in *Famous American Crimes and Trials: Vol. IV: 1960–1980*, ed. Frankie Y. Bailey and Steven Chermak (Westport, Conn.: Praeger Publishers, 2004), 267.

44. FBI, "Ted Bundy Multi-Agency Investigative Team Report" (Quantico, Va.: U.S. Department of Justice, Federal Bureau of Investigation, 1992).

45. Bruce Richie, "The Bible justifies Bundy execution, prosecutor says," *Florida Times Union*, January 23, 1989.

46. FDLE Serial 86.

47. AP, "Complete text of Ted Bundy's last interview," *Lake City Reporter*, January 25, 1989.

48. Ron Word, "Bundy executed," *Lake City Reporter*, January 24, 1989.

## Epilogue

1. William R. Maples and Michael Browning, *Dead Men Do Tell Tales: The Strange and Fascinating Cases of a Forensic Anthropologist* (New York: Doubleday, 1994).

2. Personal communication.

# Index

## About the Author

GEORGE R. (BOB) DEKLE, SR., is a retired prosecutor and a legal skills professor at the University of Florida, Levin College of Law in Gainesville, Florida. During his 30-year career as an assistant state attorney, he investigated and prosecuted hundreds of homicide cases. In 1986, the Florida Prosecuting Attorneys' Association gave Dekle the Gene Barry Memorial Award as the outstanding assistant state attorney in Florida, and upon his retirement in 2005, he received the association's Lifetime Achievement Award for his work in continuing legal education. While serving at the Levin College of Law, Dekle has authored one book, *Prosecution Principles: A Clinical Handbook,* and co-authored another, *Cross Examination Handbook: Persuasion, Strategies, and Technique.*